Imitation and Politics

Imitation and Politics

REDESIGNING MODERN GERMANY

WADE JACOBY

CORNELL UNIVERSITY PRESS

Ithaca and London

First published 2000 by Cornell University Press
First printing, Cornell Paperbacks, 2001

Printed in the United States of America

Library of Congress Cataloging-in-Publication Data

Jacoby, Wade
   Imitation and politics : redesigning modern Germany / Wade Jacoby.
      p. cm.
   Includes bibliographical references and index.
   ISBN 0-8014-3438-6 (cloth: alk. paper)
   ISBN 0-8014-8769-2 (pbk.: alk. paper)
   1. Germany—Politics and government—1990- 2. Germany—Economic
policy—1990- 3. Germany—Social policy. I. Title.
   JN3971.A58 J33 2000
   306.2'0943'09049—dc21   99-054189

Cornell University Press strives to use environmentally responsible suppliers
and materials to the fullest extent possible in the publishing of its books.
Such materials include vegetable-based, low-VOC inks and acid-free papers
that are recycled, totally chlorine-free, or partly composed of nonwood
fibers. Books that bear the logo of the FSC (Forest Stewardship Council)
use paper taken from forests that have been inspected and certified as
meeting the highest standards for environmental and social responsibility.
For further information, visit our website at www.cornellpress.cornell.edu.

Cloth printing   10 9 8 7 6 5 4 3 2 1
Paperback printing   10 9 8 7 6 5 4 3 2 1

For my girls

Contents

Tables and Figures

Preface

In January 1997 the German DE-News Service reported that two eastern German brothers were standing trial for their efforts to extort DM3 million from the supermarket chain Aldi. The prosecutors asked for stiff sentences, but the defense appealed for leniency. Its argument began conventionally enough: milder sentences were warranted because no one had been hurt by the homemade bombs planted in juice containers in Aldi stores in Leipzig, Halle, Braunschweig, and Bergen. But the defense didn't rest there. It also asked for an "East extenuation" for two young men who had been "led astray by the promises of affluent society after the fall of the Berlin Wall." The court didn't buy the argument; it sentenced one brother to nine and the other to four years in prison. But the defense drew on a sense of disappointment with efforts to extend West Germany's "affluent society" to the East. Is such a thing possible? Can an affluent society function as a usable model for change (and not just as an alibi for enterprising attorneys)? This was the German experiment, extreme in its execution but hardly unprecedented in its ambition.

This book is concerned with the question of imitation, and specifically with how policymakers imitate foreign institutions. In everyday usage, "imitation" implies a voluntary choice. I make no such assumption, for policy elites sometimes feel compelled—either by domestic or by external pressures—to use imitation as a way to change institutions. Whatever the motive, this book asks what happens when they do imitate. My inquiry into whether it is possible to "transfer" institutions from abroad uses case studies drawn from the post-1945 Allied occupation of West Germany and from German reunification at the end of the Cold War. In some areas of state and society, but by no means all, the occupation changed German institutions in ways clearly modeled on British or American experiences. Since reunification, West German institutions have been transferred to eastern Germany. How effective have these projects been? Why did some flop? What can we learn about the performance and persistence of these institutions?

The post–Cold War context provides a particularly timely moment to seek answers to these questions. The idea that some modern nations can function as blueprints for change is back with a vengeance. Democracy is widely regarded as something to be "promoted" or "assisted" rather than as an unintended consequence of battles between nineteenth-century socialists and conservatives. Multilateral lending organizations demand institutional or policy change as a condition of lending and often specify precise arrangements that exist in more "liberal" economies. In the young democracies of Eastern Europe, political actors have been conducting a conscious process of institutional transfer. East European governments, often aided by Western academics, have tried to build new institutions based on designs developed in the West, hoping that these institutional changes will call into existence accountable democracy and economic prosperity.

A central claim pursued in this book is that institutional transfer often leads to unexpected outcomes. Most efforts to transfer institutions have unintended consequences for the same reasons that most people miss their targets in a snowball fight. First, if the target is moving, they miss because they aim at the spot where the target was, rather than where it will be when the freshly packed missile arrives. In the jargon of experienced snowball throwers, this falls in the broad category of "windage" problems. Second, on longer throws they may fail to take downward trajectory into account, allowing the snowball to splatter at the feet or (in an overcorrection) sail over the head of the adversary. Among aficionados, this is a problem of "elevation."

Policymakers often miss their targets too. The institutional models that foreign policymakers choose to emulate must be adaptable, capable of changing in response to changing domestic or external conditions. Like targets, models move: by the time foreign leaders study the model, build support, and enact legislation, the original model may, for any number of reasons, have changed significantly in its country of origin. As tricky as this windage problem is, the elevation problem is even more difficult. The model presumably enjoys a certain legitimacy and acceptance in its original political setting, but policymakers may well have to compromise on certain of its formal or informal features in order to build acceptance for it in the new society. Further, indigenous actors may try to steal the new institution and occupy (or create) the strategic high ground that its structure affords certain privileged interests. These twin problems of adaptation and legitimation in the process of institutional creation animate much of what follows.

This study began with a single question—"When can institutions be transferred?"—scratched on a legal pad. In researching and formulating my answers, I incurred debts to many institutions and individuals. For research funding, I thank the Program for the Study of Germany and Europe at the

Harvard Center for European Studies, the MIT Industrial Performance Center, the Jacob Javits Foundation, the Social Science Research Council, the American Council of Learned Societies, and the Alexander von Humboldt Foundation. At Grinnell College, Charlie Duke and James Swartz were committed to the book's success. Harvey Sapolsky and Abby Collins, at different times, put the roofs of the MIT Center for International Studies and the Harvard Center for European Studies over my head. One looks like a warehouse and the other like a villa, but both made profound contributions to my understanding of politics and brought me in contact with stimulating visitors and wily regulars.

For comments on research design or specific chapters, I thank Jens Alber, Günter Albrecht, Chris Allen, Rose Batt, Peter Berg, Volker Berghahn, Robert Boyer, Hans-Joachim Buggenhagen, Angelo Caragiuli, Robert Cox, Roland Czada, Pepper Culpepper, Peter Dombrowski, Joachim Domnick, Klaus Dörre, Burkard Eberlein, Ann Frost, Lily Gardner Feldman, Carola Frege, Eugene Gholz, Robert Grey, John Griffin, Michael Fichter, David Finegold, Christoph Führ, Hal Hansen, Bob Hancké, Fred Henneberger, Rogers Hollingsworth, Marc Howard, Ellen Immergut, Carsten Johnson, Jürgen Kädtler, Roger Karapin, Peter Katzenstein, Berndt Keller, Patrick Kenis, Herbert Kitschelt, Charles Maier, Michael Marks, Wilfried Mausbach, Jörg Mayer, Kent McClelland, Claus Offe, William Patch, T. J. Pempel, Paul Pierson, Lucian Pye, Robert Putnam, Martin Richter, Stephanie Reulen, Richard Samuels, Manfred Schmidt, Rudi Schmidt, Michael Schneider, Karen Schober, Wolfgang Schroeder, Mike Shirer, Stephan Siemer, Steven Silvia, David Soskice, Sven Steinmo, Ira Strauber, Wolfgang Streeck, James Tent, Kathleen Thelen, Ulrich Voskamp, Jim Walsh, Eleanor Westney, Helmut Wiesenthal, Eliza Willis, Klaus-Peter Wittemann, Jason Wittenberg, Volker Wittke, and John Zysman.

I learned an enormous amount from fellow graduate students in a joint MIT-Harvard dissertation seminar run by Peter Hall and Suzanne Berger. I thank Karen Alter, Brian Hanson, Martin Behrens, Jonah Levy, David Hart, and Brian Burgoon—indispensable friends and indefatigable editors. Helen Ray provided counsel, babysitting, and Cheetos. Kevin Crim unsplit infinitives. Karen Groves and Terri Phipps helped with manuscript preparation. Kari Geisler, Bertha Camacho, and Barney Conroy were dependable research assistants. The Frenzel families of Cologne and Wernigerode lent profound insights into Germany, West and East.

Two people at each of four different institutions provided the intellectual support that kept this project moving through its various incarnations. In Germany, Horst Kern and Martin Baethge of the University of Göttingen were early critics and gracious hosts. Much later, Gerhard Lehmbruch and Wolfgang Seibel kindly hosted me for a year as a Humboldt Scholar. Konstanz was a wonderfully stimulating environment in which to write up the first draft of the argument, providing me with helpful colleagues from several disciplines. At the Harvard Center for European Studies, Peter Hall and Andy Markovits provided sound advice, steady encouragement, and good humor; the book benefited enormously from their suggestions. My warmest thanks go to Suzanne Berger and Richard Locke from the MIT Department of Political Science. Since they wore whichever hat was needed, I came to know them as mentors, bosses, research collaborators, and, above all, friends.

I thank my mother and, most of all, my wife and daughters, whose patience made researching and writing this project a joy. The girls chose to see the research travel as an adventure rather than a sacrifice. Kindra interrupted her own career to go to Germany. Taylor and Mackenzie left their friends behind and learned enough German to hold their own, without complaint, in strange schools and strange sandboxes.

WADE JACOBY

Grinnell, Iowa

CHAPTER ONE

Studying Imitation

O imitators, you slavish herd!
—HORACE, *Epistles*

Contemporary culture disparages imitation and prefers innovation. My epigraph from Horace reflects prejudices that ridicule imitators as subservient ("slavish") or developmentally lower than innovators ("herd"). If anything, these prejudices are stronger today, when the public and private sectors chant the mantra of innovation with equal fervor.[1] In politics, however, imitation is suspect also because it is so difficult to copy the success of others. Social scientists, journalists, and policy elites talk incessantly of the Swedish model of this or the Japanese model of that. But much talk of "models" refers to either the misty past or the prescriptive future. Most observers, it turns out, doubt that political elites can really emulate institutions existing elsewhere. Why the skepticism about the imitation of political structures? Commentators often imply that a historical model was once widely imitated by policy elites in other societies—a familiar example is the Bismarckian welfare state—yet the closer one comes to supposed examples of emulation, the harder it gets to pin down the historical transaction. And in the end, *some* purported cases of imitation turn out to be historical mirages: innovation due to indigenous forces was miscategorized after the fact as part of a trend originating in one place and spreading to others through imitation.

A second problem grows out of claims that foreign solutions are the magic bullet to solve pressing domestic problems in the United States. Policy entrepreneurs, journalists, and even social scientists frequently attribute to foreign institutions special efficiency or justice. West German vocational training, for example, widely praised for everything from lowering youth unemployment

---

1. MIT's *Technology Review* (December 1997, 5) has proclaimed that innovation distinguishes contemporary society "just as philosophy distinguished the ancient Greeks and artistic humanism the Italians of the Renaissance."

to easing the restructuring of business firms and promoting general education, is often held up as worthy of imitation by other societies—even as it plunges ever deeper into crisis in Germany. But showing that foreign institutions have problems too (and so deflating grandiose claims about the utility of foreign models) engenders further skepticism about the very possibility of imitation.

Like the thirsty traveler who has seen the oasis turn to sand one too many times and so crawls past the waterhole, we now hold to a skepticism that is dysfunctional. In scholarship on institutional change, imitation has become nearly invisible, relegated to the status of a curiosity mentioned in historical footnotes or superficial prescriptive asides. I believe that imitation should in fact be acknowledged as crucial to many cases of institutional change. Surely, the idea that the fortunes of societies have no influence on choices beyond their own borders is implausible. Our vocabulary constantly invokes foreign models, and psychological theories of learning assign a prominent place to modeling.[2] A widely used text on the policy process argues persuasively that "political reasoning" often takes place through a competition of metaphors.[3] Some of our metaphors are clearly inspired by foreign practices. Under many different conditions, people look eagerly—or feel compelled to look—beyond their own experience for institutional clues in the pursuit of material and moral goods.

This book shows that imitation is not only possible but important in political life—too important to remain invisible. It develops its claims through a study of institutional transfer, a key mode of imitation. Institutional transfer involves three necessary conditions: first, state elites refer explicitly to a model prominent in another place; second, they try to identify the foreign model's legal framework and the actors that help it function; finally, these elites build a replica of all or part of the model (either from scratch or by re-molding indigenous institutions to approximate the foreign model).

Policy elites *attempt* transfer when they use foreign models to change institutions in their own country. But does transfer work? If so, by what process? I pursue these questions in one country, Germany, and its extraordinarily rich experience with institutional transfer during two watershed periods of reconstruction: immediately after World War II, and following reunification. Both periods involved far-reaching efforts to use existing institutional designs in new places. Dramatic examples of transfer attempts involved institutions of industrial relations and of secondary education. Each period and policy area had cases both of effective transfer and of failure—a pattern this book seeks to explain.

There are few sustained theoretical discussions of imitation. Most accounts

---

2. A theory that locates imitation as a central feature of human cognition and behavior is Susan Blackmore, *The Meme Machine* (New York: Oxford University Press, 1999).

3. Deborah Stone, *Policy Paradox*, 2d ed. (New York, Norton, 1997), 373–80.

make one of two stylized claims about institution building: that institutional transfer is *inevitable*, or that it is *impossible*. Neoliberal accounts of institutional change, at least those concerning the economy, suggest that competition will weed out less adaptive structures and drive convergence around optimal designs. By privileging particular design features—and often anointing them "best practices"—such arguments fetishize the institutions by emphasizing convergent form over function. In this view, transfer is simply a mechanism for setting up proper institutions. By contrast, arguments that stress the embeddedness of institutions see in institutional transfer a technocratic naiveté that leads to doomed efforts to produce, for example, "cookbook capitalism." From this perspective, institutions are created by a kind of alchemy—the fortuitous combination of ordinary local elements into something extraordinary—through serendipitous historical processes that are implicitly unrepeatable.

Both arguments are inadequate because each can explain only one kind of outcome: rapid and effective diffusion on the one hand, failed transfer on the other. What we need is a description of a range of transfer outcomes and the conditions under which they occur. In the absence of good theories, sophisticated rumors abound: that strong political authority, or preexisting cultural similarity, or the rapid transfer of a group of institutions together account for the best outcomes. But such hypotheses cannot explain why a poorly funded, piecemeal transfer from alien British and American cultures after World War II contributed to striking changes in German institutions, whereas a well-funded, systematic transfer from one half of the German nation to the other in the 1990s contributed to ongoing dilemmas in eastern Germany.

My core claim is that effective transfer results from the combination of an organized society and a flexible state strategy. Without some prior organization of civil society, institutions that presume the exercise of social power become dependent on state elites and often remain mere words on paper. But flexibility is also important because building a power base often involves alliances between the policymakers who are copying a foreign design and particular organized groups. These partners may have substantial disagreements about key details. Such disagreements are normal and can even be beneficial: clashes over institutional design, even among partners, can lead to innovative hybrid forms endowed with a capacity for further change. The flexibility sown in the transfer process can be reaped later, for the institutions that result not only are congenial to local socioeconomic conditions and ideas about justice and fairness but also have the capacity to change as those conditions and ideas evolve.

What is distinctive about this claim? It focuses on political struggle and choice rather than on the notions of futility and necessity—notions that serve to diminish the importance of imitation. Moreover, my focus on the creation of institutions represents a departure from previous accounts in that it treats institutions as outcomes in themselves rather than as variables to explain other outcomes, such as cross-national economic performance. The book avoids taking institutional context as fixed and static. As it conducts an empirical study of the imitation of institutions, it develops a political model of institutional transfer that builds from three distinct research traditions, each grounded in vivid and familiar images: convergence, diffusion, and borrowing.

Marx's *Communist Manifesto* invoked a now familiar image of economic competition driving an ineluctable process of convergence: "The intellectual creations of individual nations become common property. . . . The bourgeoisie, by the rapid improvement of all instruments of production, by the immensely facilitated means of communication, draws all, even the most barbarian, nations into civilization. . . . It compels all nations, on pain of extinction, to adopt the bourgeois mode of production; it compels them to introduce what it calls civilization into their midst, i.e. to become bourgeois themselves. In one word, it creates a world after its own image." The thrust of Marx's famous claim was that advanced societies reveal to developing societies a vision of their own future. A different way to think about institutional transfer is Max Weber's notion of the spread of rationality. Building on his diagnosis of a "bureaucratization of the world," social theorists studied how diffusion occurs across social systems, and their research soon went beyond bureaucratic structures alone. Finally, Montesquieu wrestled with the links between the cultural inclinations of a society and its institutional structures. In book 14 of *The Spirit of the Laws*, he argued that "good Legislators" are those who struggle to oppose the "vices" of their own climate; in other words, policy elites should search for institutional solutions to overcome social and cultural shortcomings. Montesquieu thus raised the possibility that societies might borrow the institutions most appropriate to their own situation.[4] Subsequent research reproduces the basic structure of these arguments about convergence, diffusion, and rational borrowing. By taking stock of the strengths of these three lines of research on imitation, we can also locate weaknesses which the transfer approach seeks to overcome.

THE CONVERGENCE THESIS AND THE OVERCORRECTION OF COMPARATIVE POLITICAL ECONOMY

Marx's convergence image was greatly elaborated by non-Marxist work on modernization. The resulting convergence thesis was ambiguous about insti-

---

4. Karl Marx and Friedrich Engels, "Manifesto of the Communist Party," in *Marx and Engels: Basic Writings on Politics and Philosophy*, ed. Lewis Feuer (New York: Anchor, 1959), 11; Max Weber, *Economy and Society: An Outline of Interpretive Sociology* (New York: Bedminster Press, 1968): vol. 3, chap. 6; Montesquieu, *The Spirit of the Laws* (Chicago: Encyclopaedia Britannica Books, 1990), esp. chap. 5 of bk. 14.

tutional transfer. On the one hand, the idea that previously divergent societies were developing toward a common endpoint implied that institutions everywhere would become similar. Implicitly, transfer could be one route to this outcome. On the other hand, the few modernization theorists who wrote on institutional transfer were generally pessimistic. Daniel Lerner took issue with the concept because it implied that institutions could be transferred as if "from one surface to another." Suggesting the term "communication of codes" as more appropriate, he went on to list the ways premodern codes obstructed the development of those attitudes necessary for modern institutions. He thus suggested that the practices and norms of premodern societies would block introduction of institutions whose functioning presupposed modern attitudes.[5]

Some twenty years later Lucian Pye offered a related view of institutional transfer. Pye's defense of the modernization approach claimed that Asia fit the paradigm much better than did Africa or Latin America and was indeed "modernizing but in ways . . . different from the Western experience."[6] Given these differences, the prospects for institutional transfer were dim, even within Asia, Pye argued, because Asian and Western conceptions of power were different. Indeed, people in all societies develop distinctive, largely society-specific mechanisms for dealing with superiors, and these behaviors help them to defend themselves and even to manipulate the powerful. Foreign organizational patterns threaten to reshuffle these power relations, undercut these coping strategies, and thus trigger "hostile reactions" from those who would have to adjust.[7] The socially vulnerable are loath to give up their home-court advantage, since even disadvantageous arrangements may allow them some room to manipulate the system *if they know it intimately.*[8] Accordingly, Pye concluded, institutional transfer will founder on its presumption that psychological and cultural routines, those that allow defense against the exercise of power, can be replaced.

Yet resistance is not the only possible response to foreign institutional designs. People savvy enough to have made the best of a bad situation often still imagine they could do better in one less prejudicial to their interests. For example, Eleanor Westney's study of Meiji Japan (1868–1912) demonstrates that, in fact, the regime borrowed from Paris its model for the Tokyo police.[9]

---

5. Daniel Lerner, "The Transfer of Institutions," in *The Transfer of Institutions*, ed. William Hamilton (Durham, N.C.: Duke University Press, 1964), 7.

6. Lucian Pye, *Asian Power and Politics* (Cambridge: Harvard University Press, 1985), 10. For a similar argument on the German Democratic Republic, see Lydia Lange, "Warum so viele Ostdeutsche von der rapräsentativen Demokratie enttäuscht sind," *Die Zeit,* January 10, 1997.

7. Pye, *Asian Power and Politics,* 25.

8. The post-modernizationist version of this argument is James Scott, *Weapons of the Weak* (New Haven: Yale University Press, 1987).

9. Eleanor Westney, *Imitation and Innovation: The Transfer of Western Organizational Patterns to Meiji Japan* (Cambridge: Harvard University Press, 1987).

One is hard pressed to find an institution in which the potential for complicated superior-subordinate relations is greater than that of the police, yet the assumptions built into the Parisian system did not make it unusable for the Japanese. Further, although Meiji officials originally adapted the Parisian model to their understanding of local conditions, subsequent changes were actually *more*, not less, along Parisian lines. In eastern Germany today, as in western Germany after 1945, deep cultural differences do reshape transferred institutions. But far from automatically blocking institutional transfer, the hope of change can also strongly promote it.

Of course, a large body of work has attacked the normative assumptions and empirical findings of modernization theory and, by extension, the implied mechanisms of convergence. Yet these objections have contributed to a curious contemporary neglect of processes of cross-societal imitation and emulation—a trend I call the overcorrection of comparative political economy. That literature uses the comparative history of national cases as the dominant methodology. It is concerned not with charting "progress along a presumed unilinear path of societal development but rather with uncovering, interpreting, and trying to explain distinctive patterns of development."[10] National institutional differences often account for the variance scholars observe in the timing and qualitative features of political and economic development. This focus on *diversity* can be seen as a corrective to the work on the spread of "the one best system," which many associated with modernization theory. But although many of these studies derived their theoretical impetus from flogging the horse of institutional convergence, they collectively generated a methodology of comparative national cases designed to highlight institutional *differences* (and their effects). With this focus on difference, it is small wonder that a study of institutional transfer is such a methodological outlier. Indeed, there remains no more ubiquitous dismissal of the possibility of imitation than the assertion that any transfer will be blocked by "cultural differences" or "different traditions."

THE DIFFUSION LITERATURES: IMITATION WITHOUT POLITICS

Like transfer, diffusion is a metaphor; it refers to a physical process in which particles move from areas of high concentration to areas of lower concentration. Social science interest in the spread of human invention among and between various communities has provided ample evidence that cross-societal institutional transfer is not only possible but ubiquitous. Of course, similarity alone is no proof of diffusion, but studies that relate the copying of

10. Peter Evans and John Stephens, "Development and the World Economy," in *Handbook of Sociology*, ed. Neil Smelser (Newbury Park, Calif.: Sage, 1988), 740, 746.

legislation, down to even the typographical errors, raise confidence that institution building often involves some measure of imitation, not just simultaneous invention. Diffusion studies, however, mask the politics revealed by the institutional transfer approach; thus the two approaches are complements, not substitutes.

To be sure, diffusion literatures have varied across disciplines. Sociologists, on the one hand, developed mathematical techniques to measure patterns of spread.[11] To do so, they tended to blend out variations in the meaning of the innovation across cases and simply focused on the timing of adoption. Anthropologists, on the other hand, often used rates of adoption as a window on the characteristic differences between early and late adopting individuals. And the most important political science writing on diffusion has applied it to the American federal system. These works—which now include close to one hundred studies[12]—generally take a particular phenomenon, often a legislative measure but sometimes a judicial or administrative one, and trace its temporal and geographic spread.

There are three significant problems with the diffusion tradition. First, since the literature begins from the observation that innovations often spread from one place to another, it has, plausibly enough, focused on the structural conditions allowing for such diffusion. In doing so, however, it has often implied that the conditions making diffusion *possible* also make it more. or less *automatic*. The methodology of large-N studies encourages the tautological assumption that where diffusion happened, conditions for it were right. This approach blends out much interesting action deriving from the *uncertainty* of collectivities about what their real problems are and what solutions might be both technically effective and compatible with existing interests and cultural frames.

Second, diffusion research has focused on the spread of innovation but has neglected the issues of institutional *performance* or subsequent *modifications*.[13] We need to know more than which state passed what law and when. Many diffusion researchers are poorly situated to judge whether policy innovations actually produce the expected outcomes.[14] William Landes and Lewis Solomon's important study of compulsory school attendance showed, for example, that those U.S. states *already* having the highest levels of schooling

---

11. See, e.g., Stuart Dodd, "Diffusion Is Predictable," *American Sociological Review* 20 (1965): 392–402.

12. The first of these was Jack Walker's seminal article, "The Diffusion of Innovations among the American States," *American Political Science Review* 63 (1969): 880–99. See also Robert Savage, "Diffusion Research Traditions and the Spread of Policy Innovations in the Federal System," *Publius* 15 (1985): 1–27.

13. There are exceptions: Peter Eisinger, *The Rise of the Entrepreneurial State* (Madison: University of Wisconsin Press, 1988); Scott Hayes, "Re-Invention and the Diffusion of Policy Innovations among the American States" (Ph.D. diss., Florida State University, 1991).

14. Savage, "Diffusion Research Traditions," 17.

were also first to adopt compulsory schooling laws, while those with more unschooled children were the last to do so.[15] In this case, then, the diffusion of compulsory schooling laws seems not to have "caused" more compulsory schooling in and of itself. Unfortunately, few diffusion studies are designed to treat historically the links between indigenous and outside sources of institutional change, as the desire for large data sets has led to highly stylized history.

Third, with the methodologically induced neglect of history and social context has gone a striking neglect of power politics. Diffusion research generally focuses on changes in individual laws, which are easy to measure.[16] But the political science literature on diffusion lacks systematic attention to the most important institutions. Many studies treat areas where the "innovation" in question concerns a very small number of elites and where there is scant evidence of political mobilization beyond the actions of concentrated interests seeking to make sure that, for example, advantageous regulatory arrangements existing in other states are extended to them. Such an adoption process will exhibit little need for adaptation. By contrast, my focus is on institutions that are major sources of state-society intersection: the design of schools, the constitution of actors of industrial relations, and the laws that regulate work.

The failure of the diffusion traditions to solve these three problems, a failure anchored in the methodology of large-N comparisons, suggests that the diffusion and transfer approaches are not substitutes for each other. Rather, they ask fundamentally different questions. This book's challenge is precisely to unravel the complicated process of societal imitation under conditions of real uncertainty, time pressure, and abiding conflicts about institutional design. Methodologies designed to track the spread of tort reform from Connecticut to California are bound to be unsuitable for this analysis.

POLICY BORROWING: "FIT," FABRICATION, AND FOREIGN MODELS

If Montesquieu's "good Legislator" seeks to change her society, perhaps she will look abroad for inspiration: this is the premise of the policy-borrowing approach.[17] Governments, argues Jerold Waltman, are "like any other human organization. . . . national governments, behaving like business

---

15. William Landes and Lewis Solomon, "Compulsory Schooling Legislation," *Journal of Economic History* 32 (1972): 54–91.

16. And in many cases they fit an implicit social theory that only "technical" things such as regulations *can* be transferred.

17. Variously known as policy borrowing, policy convergence, policy transfer, policy migration, policy imitation, or cross-national lesson drawing, the approaches I have grouped under this heading focus on elite decision making more than on structural factors in the study of how states imitate policies that exist elsewhere.

firms, schools, hospitals, labor unions, and so forth, frequently copy the policies of other nations."[18] The instrumental, interest-driven core of this perspective (as opposed to the cultural and structural approaches just reviewed) suggests that policy elites may act as "rational shoppers" to locate and emulate advantageous foreign models.[19] Two valuable findings arise from the policy-borrowing literature: policymakers manipulate evidence, and they struggle to "fit" borrowed institutions to new social contexts.

Policy-borrowing studies have usefully documented policy elites' sloppy or selective gathering of evidence about foreign models and those elites' strategic uses of that information.[20] Policymakers often intentionally shape foreign evidence to suit their purposes. Colin Bennett has argued that "elites and activists have a number of interests in using policy evidence from another country: to put an issue to a systemic or institutional agenda, mollify political pressure, provide an exemplar, indicate the range of options or reinforce conclusions already reached. The interests of the importer dictate the nature, timing and origins of the evidence injected into policy debate." Using this framework, Bennett shows that the U.S. Freedom of Information Act was used as a positive example in Canada and a negative example in Britain.[21] Further, since a foreign "model" may actually be a *range* of institutional forms that differ geographically, the borrowing elites may seek to emulate an ideal type, the median form, or some particular variant. Policy-borrowing studies have documented the resulting confusion and showed the short-term significance of such attempts at borrowing.

Policy-borrowing approaches have also suggested that since institutions exist inside larger social and political contexts, borrowed policies may not "fit" the new society.[22] Similar to the "cultural resistance" claim reviewed earlier, for example, David Phillips's work on educational policy borrowing stresses the complexity of interactions between institutions and the social setting that "keeps policies in place and that provides resistance to the implanting of ideas from other systems."[23] Although it is likely true that the short term ra-

18. Jerold Waltman, *Copying Other Nation's Policies* (Cambridge, Mass.: Schenkman, 1980). Colin Bennett suggests that such borrowing can have five kinds of objectives: policy goals, content, instruments, outcomes, and styles; see his "Review Article: What Is Policy Convergence and What Causes It?," *British Journal of Political Science* 21 (1991): 218.

19. For more on rational shopping, see the section under that heading in Chapter 2.

20. Colin Bennett, "How States Utilize Foreign Evidence," *Journal of Public Policy* 11 (1991): 31–54.

21. Ibid., 31, 35–40. Particularly rich on these questions is Harold Wolman, "Understanding Cross National Policy Transfers," *Governance* 5 (1992): 27–45.

22. A fascinating study along these lines is Mark Beissinger, *Scientific Management, Socialist Discipline, and Soviet Power* (Cambridge: Harvard University Press, 1988), which investigates Soviet borrowing of Western management techniques.

23. David Phillips, "Borrowing Educational Policy," *Oxford Studies in Comparative Education* 2 (1992): 45. See also David Phillips, "Neither a Borrower nor a Lender Be? The Problems of Cross-National Attraction in Education," *Comparative Education* 25 (1989): 267–74; Dennis Muniak, "Policies That Don't Fit," *Policy Studies Journal* 14 (1985): 1–19.

tionality of policy elites may conflict with broader social demands, an exclusive reliance on a purported "fit" misses Montesquieu's call for good legislators to struggle against their nation's shortcomings. Thus, despite such warnings, policymakers do persist in trying transfer, and the experience of eastern Germany since 1990 is that even in the area of education this can be a route to very substantial change.

Overreliance on the "fit" idea also obscures the diversity of institutional possibilities *already* present inside different nations at any one time. The political explanation I offer assumes that different pieces of national institutions are often assembled in ramshackle ways, not in coherent "subsystems." Different institutional solutions to fundamental social tasks compete for prominence even as they interact to face the problems of the moment.[24] Taking the societal context seriously, then, leads not to the conclusion that foreign institutional designs are inherently unworkable but to a recognition that policymakers occasionally do come to believe they have something to learn from others. When they do, depending on the flexibility of the adaptation process and the qualities of their domestic allies, both social norms and the connections between institutions can change. In other words, culture can shift through the working of politics even though the shift may not be easily orchestrated. Albert Hirschman's classic article on the "hiding hand" suggests that many useful development projects would never have been undertaken had the original proponents known in advance the difficulties of their realization.[25]

The focus on "fit" thus takes the constitution of actors for granted and leaves unexamined the questions of the malleability of institutions and the plasticity of the borrowing society.[26] Yet the concept of borrowing or transfer, used more broadly, can shed light on the processes of constructing and re-creating institutions. At minimum, one wants to know if the policy fits the aims of important social actors as well as it fits the agenda of opportunistic or threatened bureaucrats. The transfer approach assumes that the boundaries of competence of state and social actors are not fixed and at certain times are open to contestation, and it inquires into the conditions under which power and authority may shift in the process of institutional transfer. This negotiation of institutional designs is itself constitutive not only of new coalitions but

24. For similar arguments about economic policy and cultural traditions, see, respectively, Judith Goldstein, *Ideas, Interests, and American Trade Policy* (Ithaca: Cornell University Press, 1993); and Martha Nussbaum, *Cultivating Humanity* (Cambridge: Harvard University Press, 1996).

25. Albert Hirschman, "The Principle of the Hiding Hand," *Public Interest* 6 (1967): 10–23. For a well-known illustration that locates some roots of French indicative economic planning in a misperception of British institutions, see Andrew Shonfield, *Modern Capitalism* (London: Oxford University Press, 1965), 88.

26. An exception is Richard Rose, *Lesson-Drawing in Public Policy* (Chatham, Mass.: Chatham House, 1993), 143–57.

of new agents of politics. In order to show this, one often needs to look beyond the *state* and beyond *policy*.

THE INSTITUTIONAL TRANSFER APPROACH

Sophisticated rumors too thin to serve as alternative explanations and bodies of theory that acknowledge the phenomenon of imitation but neglect to unravel the workings of the process reveal a clear need for a new approach. This book, unlike the convergence literature, studies imitation directly rather than as an epiphenomenon of modernization processes. Contrary to the diffusion literature, it emphasizes political choices along with structural variables. And unlike the policy-borrowing approach, it analyzes borrowing by social as well as bureaucratic actors, without taking the constitution of those actors as fixed and stable; it thus subsumes the phenomenon of policy borrowing by moving beyond the policies themselves to understand imitation among the actors and within the institutions that generate, implement, or codify the policies.

But what can the institutional transfer approach explain? Broadly, two outcomes are of potential interest. Most obviously, perhaps, one could investigate how well the actors attempting imitation accomplished their aims. When has imitation been "successful," with success defined relative to the objectives of the original advocates? The answers could speak directly to policymakers, perhaps even helping them avoid costly mistakes. A sustained research agenda using this metric might even improve the quality of governance *if* policymakers could be engaged in a dialogue. Yet two serious problems disqualify this approach for my project. First, with German reunification only a decade old, final judgments about success and failure are premature, unless one yields to a temptation to compress transfer into the short-term process of setting up institutions. Second, measuring success against policymakers' aims raises the questions of which policymakers, which aims, and at which times. In both of the historical periods considered here, such aims changed significantly over time.

Since the actors provide no clear and stable standards against which to measure outcomes, analysis cannot center on the question of success.[27] Instead, motivated by an appreciation of the complexity of social change and the frequency of unintended consequences, I choose to focus on the *performance* and *persistence* of transferred institutions. My judgments about performance do capture benefits to the proponents of transfer (as in a "success" ap-

27. It is clearly useful to speak of "failure," however, since some transfer attempts are simply given up without provoking much change at all. In other cases, failures can have significant long-term consequences; see Chapter 4.

proach) but also encompass unforeseen outcomes and effects on other actors and institutions in the new setting. Judgments about persistence encompass issues of the rooting of institutions and their reproduction over time, and also of the ways they gain legitimacy in the new society. Effectiveness occurs when the transferred institution acquires a legal framework, when it performs in the new society in ways broadly consistent with the aims (promoting efficiency or justice) that led to the transfer attempt, and when it persists by being reproduced over time (though presumably not without some subsequent changes). In short, my measure of institutional transfer encompasses the tripartite outcomes of legality, performance, and persistence.

Two Blueprints for Democratic Capitalism

All fruitful comparisons require noting both similarities and differences between cases, and the premise of this book is that one can learn about imitation by comparing institutional transfer in two very different historical periods: the post–World War II Anglo-American occupation of what became West Germany, and the post-1990 reunification of Germany. The central justification for comparison is simple and broad: in each period there was an explicit attempt, by the policymakers who had formal authority, to construct variants of democratic capitalism by reshaping domestic institutions.[28] The Allied military governments in the first period and the West German government in the second saw the previous systems as unacceptable and recognized a need for thorough institutional changes, even if there was no consensus in either case on what those changes should be.[29] In both cases, there was a pervasive, if far from universal, sense of an end to national abnormality enforced by dictatorship. This sense led to the hope of returning to a more "normal" place among a larger community of Western societies. And there were widespread economic problems in both periods, compounded by fears of further deindustrialization.

In each period, key policymakers also believed that the experience of dictatorship had literally changed individual psychology, raising an immediate need for new ideas to be imparted in new settings and in new ways. Most important to this book, policymakers in both periods saw in their own societies

28. That both democracy and capitalism have varied forms, each of which allows spheres of authoritarianism and state ownership of production, need not detain us here.

29. This book treats the U.S. and British governments (post–World War II period) and West German federal and state governments (post-reunification) as the policymakers. In the occupation period, wartime negotiations left the four Allied powers with formal authority over the defeated Germany. The East German regime, in a remarkable act, negotiated its own sovereignty out of existence in 1990. Caveats (e.g., *Land* (state) governments after 1946–47) are noted in the text.

useful models for redesigning the part of Germany they had come to control. Although all were aware of at least some potential pitfalls, the U.S. and British occupation governments and the West German government sought to use their own institutional models to help reform the failed structures of the immediate authoritarian past. In short, despite very large differences in contexts, both periods saw ambitious efforts at institutional transfer.

The policy areas I use to illuminate the politics of institutional transfer are industrial relations and secondary education. Under industrial relations I include the constitution of trade unions and business organizations as legal actors with institutionalized prerogatives in firm-level codetermination, collective bargaining, and industrial policy. Secondary—including vocational—education involves decisions about the length, content, and form of schooling to follow primary education.[30] These areas mark the intersection of normative struggles about democracy and the economy, yet they also provide broad variation along key dimensions: industrial relations were organized along sectoral, regional, and national lines; education was the prerogative of state-level politics. Further, each policy area provides examples of both effective and failed transfer in ways that reflect differences in the central explanatory variables. Hence, factors idiosyncratic to a given policy area can be minimized.[31]

Using the threshold of legal adoption and the metrics of institutional performance and persistence, one can ask, when has transfer been effective, and when has it failed? Table 1 summarizes the main short-term and long-term outcomes in the four cases to be explained in Chapters 3–6.

The effective transfer of industrial relations institutions in the postwar era was marked by both an active civil society and a self-consciously flexible strategy—the two key factors highlighted here. The Allies promoted the piecemeal use of American and British models in dismantling Nazi-era industrial relations, curtailing union ambitions for radical postwar reforms and reformulating the old Weimar system—which ultimately formed the other key pillar of the postwar order. The Allies used their models to justify significant restrictions on the prerogatives of both labor and capital and to shape the forms of the associations that emerged. Since reunification, however, industrial relations institutions have been transferred from western Germany with minimal built-in flexibility and without the benefit of indigenous social support in eastern Germany. Established West German actors have struggled mightily to reproduce familiar patterns of institutionalized economic deci-

---

30. Since vocational training lies at the intersection of the two institutional domains I deal with, its inclusion also helps signal phenomena that are idiosyncratic to particular policy areas and hence have been of less interest in building more general theories of imitation.

31. Theodore Lowi, "American Business, Public Policy, Case Studies, and Political Theory," *World Politics* 16 (1964): 677–715.

Table 1. Summary of results of attempted transfer in the four cases

Case	Short-term outcomes	Long-term outcomes
Post-1945 industrial relations (Chapter 3)	Grassroots unionism stifled; employer association power restricted	Politicized but decentralized industrial relations instead of economic democracy or economic autocracy
Post-1945 school reform (Chapter 4)	Failure	Discredit of common school movement
Post-1990 industrial relations (Chapter 5)	Major defection from core bargaining system; huge increase in industrial policy efforts	Weakening of patterned wage bargaining
Post-1990 school reform (Chapter 6)	Major defection from private financing of vocational training; impressive effort to organize new schooling systems	Competence shifts from private to public sphere; tensions within federalist aggregation mechanisms

sion making. But these transfers have not yet been effective; there have been major defections from the core system of patterned wage bargaining and sharp drops in both official and de facto union and employer association membership rates. On the other hand, in an effort to compensate for the economic misery that has been partly of their own making, the social partners—labor and the employers—in eastern Germany have engaged in very significant experimentation in industrial policy. Yet the more successful these experiments, the more they challenge the larger ambitions of exactly reproducing western German practices.

The transfer of American educational institutions to West Germany after World War II faltered and failed because the Americans did not mobilize the support of a social coalition demonstrably friendly to the aims of the occupation force. Not only was the effort to promote common secondary schools—roughly along the lines of U.S. high schools—a failure, but it also set back subsequent German efforts to reduce the influence of social class in public schools. In eastern Germany since reunification, although educational institutions are still in flux, transfer has been more effective than in the contemporary industrial relations case. Employers have resisted assuming their expected roles in vocational training, but institutional transfer has provided a fairly stable order for the public schools. There is, however, little organized civil society to exploit whatever flexibility does exist. As a result, state officials in eastern Germany have to deal with highly politicized western German actors in their ongoing struggles to finance training and stabilize rules that are both fair and practically sustainable.

THE ARGUMENT IN BRIEF

What explains this pattern of effective and failed transfer attempts? The core of the claim developed in subsequent chapters is that for effective institutional change to persist and perform, it must be "pulled in" by social actors rather than decreed by policymakers alone. Even if initiated by policy elites, the new institutional design must be embraced by domestic actors. Whether innovations are pulled in from abroad is, in turn, a function of two central factors. First, the possibility of flexible adaptation must be built into the legal-administrative transfer process; that is, the mechanism or political strategy employed must not so fetishize the institutional form that its boundaries cannot be adapted in the new society. This "strategy" variable is linked directly to a second, "structural" one: preexisting social groups, motivated by ideology or material gain, must sponsor the new institution. In exchange for the (often incomplete) incorporation of their aims, these groups support the institution with local knowledge, information-gathering capacity, political legitimacy, and material resources.[32]

The focus on these two particular factors represents a choice for parsimony over completeness in explaining the dynamics of transfer. But good theories presuppose analytical priorities, and mine follow from two observations. First, effective institutional change may require more than an improved design for more "efficiency"; it often requires a shift in power and resources— a shift sometimes encoded in the foreign model's design. This shift may create losers as well as winners, so such changes are bound to be politically complicated. Flexibility built into the transfer process gives room to resolve such disputes without obstructing the transfer. Second, there must also be social actors who can support and implement transfer. Foreign models can sometimes legitimate new directions, but they cannot anticipate many specific features of the borrowing society. In other words, the necessary capacity for adaptation lies outside the blueprint itself, because although policymakers using foreign institutional models can radically transform existing social actors, they can rarely create them out of whole cloth. In sum, then, the pervasiveness of unforeseen effects and the need for organizational and political resources that do not simply fall out of the redesign process ground the focus on flexibility and civil society.

How do these concerns relate to the two periods in question? As will become clear, variation in flexibility and in civil society exists even *within* the cases of occupation and reunification, but the argument begins with striking differences *between* the two periods—differences that are central to the re-

32. The analytical distinction between actor and institution is developed in many places: e.g., Douglass North, *Institutions, Institutional Change, and Economic Performance* (New York: Cambridge University Press, 1990), 4–5.

search design. First, there was much greater potential for "pulling in" during the immediate post–World War II period than in eastern Germany after 1990. The East German Communist Party (SED) had been more effective than the National Socialist German Workers' Party (NSDAP) in eliminating non-Party organizations, in part because it ruled for over forty years compared with only twelve for the Nazis.[33] Whereas in the postwar zones of occupation there were many individuals with recent memory of democratic rule in the Weimar period, virtually all personnel young enough to assume leadership roles in eastern Germany after reunification had known no form of government but authoritarian socialism.[34] As a result, indigenous elites emerged from the GDR experience in 1990 with much less understanding of how to formulate democratic policy or run a capitalist society than had been the case after 1945.

A second difference relates to the kinds of opposition directed at the NSDAP and SED regimes, for the East German opposition simply was not as committed to fundamental institutional change as was the opposition to Hitler. On the one hand, even though the *magnitude* of opposition to the Hitler regime was small, historians have shown the breadth of passive and active resistance, segments of which harbored plans for significant changes in institutions.[35] On the other hand, an increasing body of research into GDR opposition movements has stressed their essentially reformist objectives.[36] Thus, though it would be absurd to claim that all opponents of Nazism wanted radical change or that no East German dissidents did, opposition groups in the first era did have a significantly more developed agenda for institutional change than did those of the second era. The implication is that the very idea of radical institutional change came more readily to the leaders of civil society in the first era but that they also had stronger preconceived ideas about the substance of those changes.

If there was cross-period variation in civil society, there was also variation in the flexibility of state strategies. The occupation forces, using what I call the *functional equivalent* approach, pushed institutional transfer with relatively loose reference to their own societies, whereas the post-1990 Federal

33. Christoph Kleßmann, "Opposition und Resistenz in zwei Diktaturen in Deutschland," *Historische Zeitschrift* 262 (1996): 453–79.

34. In one sphere, former GDR *party* organizations have been reshaped to become themselves important parts of civil society: the nonprofit sector (Red Cross and other charities). See Wolfgang Seibel, "Institutional Elasticity in Changing Political Order," Working Paper 7.1 (Berkeley, Calif.: Center for German and European Studies, 1996).

35. Historians of National Socialism have yet to agree on how to differentiate between "opposition" and "resistance" or even whether two different concepts are needed. Surveys include Peter Hoffmann, *The History of the German Resistance, 1933–1945* (Cambridge: MIT Press, 1977); Hans Rothfels, *Die deutsche Opposition gegen Hitler* (Frankfurt: Fischer, 1969).

36. John Torpey, *Intellectuals, Socialism, and Dissent: The East German Opposition and Its Legacy* (Minneapolis: University of Minnesota Press, 1995); Detlev Pollock, "Was ist aus den Bürgerbewegungen und Oppositionsgruppen der DDR geworden?" *Aus Politik und Zeitgeschichte* B40–41 (1995): 34–45.

Republic of Germany (FRG) has relied mostly on what I call *exact transfer* in its construction of institutions for eastern Germany. The causes and meaning of this difference between functional equivalent transfer and exact transfer are discussed later, but its effect vis-á-vis actors can be noted now. Policymakers using the functional equivalent approach, including those in the Anglo-American occupation, thought first in terms of the functions or *tasks* that a model institution performs; they then tried to find indigenous state or social actors who could use an institutional framework to perform these tasks. In contrast, those planning exact transfer extension of West German institutions to eastern Germany after 1990 anticipated very few deviations from West German practices.[37] The exact transfer approach is design oriented in its focus on and commitment to the faithful replication of institutional structures. The functional equivalent approach is more actor oriented than design oriented because adaptations to functionally inspired institutional changes can grow out of the interests and capacity of the indigenous actors.

This argument about the politics of institutional transfer and the logic of pulling in has two crucial implications. The first, pitched at the level of *mass* politics, is that indigenous actors affect whether foreign structures become accepted widely in the new setting, not just to a handful of elites. Between the promises of new efficiency and the taint of foreignness, the work of building mass legitimacy for transferred institutions often falls to domestic actors. The second implication, pitched at the *group* level, is that clashing political values and strategies mean that unintended consequences often flow from acts of political imitation. Familiar institutions can produce unfamiliar results in a new setting. Local knowledge is often indispensable in searching out adaptations to stabilize the new structures, yet the bearers of such knowledge can also steal the revolution and subvert the aims of the original proponents by capturing the new design for their own strategic advantage.

Legitimation

How might institutional transfer conducted in one context endure through others? One answer is that the transferred institutions gain legitimacy of their own.[38] Recent work in organizational sociology emphasizes that institutional structures may be acceptable as much for their relation to dom-

---

37. The GDR government generally did *not* use exact transfer between late 1989 and spring 1990 as it tried to stay in power. The reforming Communists and the opposition's Round Table activists worried that exact transfer from the FRG would undercut their efforts for an independent "third way."

38. Analogously, European elites found that institutional "state building" required concomitant "nation building" or securing loyalty—often through expanded participation; see Charles Tilly, "Reflections on the History of European State-Making," in *The Formation of National States*, ed. Tilly (Princeton: Princeton University Press, 1975), 79–80.

17

inant cultural patterns as for their efficiency.[39] Whereas classic studies of legitimacy focused on "diffuse support" for the democratic system, recent research distinguishes between the legitimation of democracy as a form of governance and the legitimation of its constituent institutions.[40] The legitimacy of a democratic system can remain high even through long periods of poor institutional performance. Constituent institutions, however, appear to acquire and sustain legitimacy only when the system remains unpolarized *and* the institutional performance is strong. This finding is important because it invites a consideration of whether transferred institutions depend on more than just performance to gain acceptance.

One can say with confidence that West German institutions have gained legitimacy since 1945 (though it is too early to gauge its durability in a non–Cold War setting). Polls show that both the democratic system and the constituent institutions of West Germany gained acceptance over time: a composite "trust index" more than doubled from 21% in 1950 to 44% in 1984, and a "support for democracy index" increased from 35% in 1950 to 86% in 1987. Although data on performance do not go so far back, the percentage of respondents who said German democracy "works well" rose from 60% in 1973 to 75% in 1987.[41] Even Daniel Goldhagen's controversial denunciation of the historical pathologies of German culture suggests that antidemocratic sentiment has been almost entirely overcome in the FRG.[42]

Gauging the legitimation of new institutions in eastern Germany since 1990 is trickier. There is ample evidence that dissatisfaction is high, especially with the deep economic slump. In 1997 almost 25% of eastern Germans said the GDR system was better than the FRG system, indicating a strikingly high level of general discontent. Possible explanations for such widespread disgruntlement include, first, the idea that economic disappointments have been generalized to a range of other questions (though eastern Germans seem eminently willing to make precise distinctions and are not given to blanket appraisals). A second idea is that the cultural values of eastern Germans are simply different from those of western Germans (the Berlin newspaper *TAZ* recently reported that only 16% of eastern German respondents thought reunification had brought increased freedom of opinion). Third, eastern Germans may simply be deceiving opinion pollsters; still it seems hard to write off the high vote totals—around 25%—of the reform Communist Party of Democratic Socialism (PDS) as merely strategic dissatisfaction.

39. See the essays in Walter Powell and Paul DiMaggio, eds., *The New Institutionalism in Organizational Analysis* (Chicago: University of Chicago Press, 1991).

40. Frederick Weil, "The Sources and Structure of Legitimation in Western Democracies," *American Sociological Review* 54 (1989): 682–706.

41. Ibid., 691.

42. Daniel Goldhagen, *Hitler's Willing Executioners: Ordinary Germans and The Holocaust* (New York: Knopf, 1996).

Though all three explanations have some plausibility, they are based only on the subjective judgments of individuals responding to opinion pollsters or standing in voting booths. More important, the effort to extend existing western institutions into eastern Germany has forced those western institutions and actors to be agents of their own legitimation; that is, they can call on few preexisting organizations to promote their acceptance. Consider three potential routes to the legitimation of institutions: success (the institution is legitimate because it is *effective*), ideology (it is *just*), and practice (it is *familiar*). A brief look at eastern Germany suggests that transferred institutions are struggling on all three fronts and that the weakness of indigenous civil society is telling in each case.

The first proposition is that if new institutions are effective, they will also rapidly gain legitimacy. Many institutions have indeed done yeoman's work in eastern Germany. Given many outstanding problems, however, even institutions that are working well may succumb to difficulties beyond their control. Like the manager promoted to his level of incompetence, some actors are burdened with more and more new tasks until they fail. And since the magnitude of the problems puts them well beyond the reach of any one actor, the original civil society vacuum in eastern Germany seems to have led to a kind of hypercorporatism. That is, since there were no indigenous actors to lean on, the West German actors who operated there fell back on close consultations with one another. Such "networks" do ensure that everyone can plausibly take some credit for the successes while passing the buck on failures, but it is less clear they can actually solve problems.[43]

A second method of legitimation is to match new institutions to existing values. This proposition suggests that only societies with similar values should borrow from each other. Absent indigenous actors who can perform a kind of moral mediation, individual citizens may focus on the unfamiliarity of the new institutions and come to unwarranted black-and-white judgments about them. For example, a common claim of eastern Germans is that western German structures cannot accommodate their values of solidarity. The result is a kind of exaggerated we/they thinking, an artificial value polarization suggesting that eastern and western Germans are fundamentally different moral creatures and that the institutions appropriate for one cannot, by definition, work for the other.

A third method of legitimation is to come to know the new institutions through experience in working with them: legitimation through participation. At least at the elite level, however, Wilhelm Bürklin and Hilke Rebenstorf and their collaborators have shown how seldom eastern Germans have found their way into these institutions: only 11.6% of people in elite positions

43. I explore this issue in Chapters 5 and 6.

in their sample were originally from eastern Germany![44] The older generation especially has been forcibly removed or has voluntarily withdrawn from activity in many institutional domains. In three areas—local politics, clubs and associations, and workplace affairs— there is a huge gap between those aged forty-four and under, who judge their personal influence since reunification to be *up*, and those aged forty-five and over, who see their influence as very substantially *less* than before 1990.[45] In consequence, there is a kind of skewed socialization, which, when added to hypercorporatism and artificial value polarization, leaves the legitimacy of transferred institutions in doubt.

All of this points to a fourth way of promoting acceptance: the lack of alternatives. The reality in eastern Germany is that West German institutions are faits accomplis. But if there has been a provisional acceptance of them in the aftermath of reunification, more and more eastern Germans are willing to consider other solutions.

The Price of Partnership

This book's central point is that effective transfer depends upon policymakers' finding organized groups in civil society who are willing to sponsor or pull in the foreign design. Both the sociological and power aspects of this claim accord with significant findings from domains as different as social protest and international trade negotiations. Anthony Oberschall showed long ago that most "social movements" and "conflict groups" were actually built upon prior networks of social organization. Using examples ranging from U.S. and Canadian Populist Parties and French Jacobins to the American civil rights movement, the Berkeley free speech movement, West African nationalism, and Indian caste movements, Oberschall argued that "new" protest movements find it beneficial to engage in "block recruitment" of preexisting groups.[46] Similarly, Leonard Schoppa's study of trade negotiations reveals that American pressure on Japan has worked best when teamed with pressure groups inside Japan.[47] My argument conforms closely to this general line of thought: policy elites—whether indigenous elites or foreign occupying powers—find effective institutional transfer much easier when they can

44. Wilhelm Bürklin and Hilke Rebenstorf, *Eliten in Deutschland: Rekruitierung und Integration* (Leverkusen: Leske + Budrich, 1997).

45. Empirish-Methodische Arbeitsgruppe am Sozialwissenschaftlichen Forschungszentrum Berlin-Brandenburg (SFZ), *Leben in Deutschland* (Berlin: SFZ, 1996), questions 10, 11, 26a.

46. Anthony Oberschall, *Social Conflict and Social Movement* (Englewood Cliffs, N.J.: Prentice-Hall, 1973), 124–33; Sidney Tarrow, *Power in Movement: Social Movements, Collective Action, and Politics* (New York: Cambridge University Press, 1994), 135–50.

47. Leonard Schoppa, *Bargaining with Japan: What American Pressure Can and Cannot Do* (New York: Columbia University Press, 1997); see also Peter Evans, *Embedded Autonomy: States and Industrial Transformation* (Princeton: Princeton University Press, 1995).

recruit preexisting organizations and interest groups to their institutional agenda. I make the additional claim, substantiated in the empirical chapters, that indigenous groups are crucial to the process of adapting foreign models to local conditions.

But what if the short-run interests of policy elites who control the legal mechanisms of institutional transfer later diverge from the interests of the groups that sponsored the changes? This potential divergence helps drive the unforseeable long-run consequences of institutional transfer. Thus, although sponsoring groups are crucial, they may try to twist the foreign model to their own ideological or material specifications. Whether or not this happens depends, in part, on certain qualitative features of the groups likely to act as sponsors. For example, Oberschall emphasized that "segmented" groups—those not tightly linked to the channels of power—were most likely to be recruitable for protest. The bonus for protest movements was that because segmented groups' leaders had little opportunity to escape to more prestigious mainstream organizations, those groups carried with them an especially rich talent pool.[48]

Segmented groups are analogous to what I call minority traditions. Minority traditions are institutional ideas that have some organizational foundation but, like segmented groups, have not become part of the society's *dominant* institutional tradition. Examples abound: parochial schools in the United States, the provision of venture capital in most European nations, and civilian control of the military in many African countries. Minority traditions that have an organizational basis can act as self-interested sponsors of alternative institutional schemes. Further, and again like their protest analogues, such sponsor groups can be radically transformed as a consequence of rapid growth. Thus, beyond their mere presence or absence in civil society, it is necessary to be aware of their qualitative features and to recognize the paradox that any group strong enough to help policy elites effectively pull in and implement a foreign design is likely well situated to turn that design to its own purposes. This paradox grounds my focus on political choice and struggle.

Three points important to a theory of imitation have emerged so far. First, for an understanding of how foreign-inspired structures can be effectively pulled in to a new setting, a narrow focus on institutional functionality will not suffice; attention must be paid also to the task of legitimating new structures. Second, because foreign models may be poorly understood before they are imitated, the new structures may provide unexpected opportunities for self-interested actors to reshape the design to their own material or moral ends. This uncertainty suggests that the ideals and interests of such actors may themselves be changed in the process of sponsoring the new institutions. These two points speak to the nexus of "interests, institutions, and ideas"

---

48. Oberschall, *Social Conflict and Social Movement*, 159–60.

more broadly and suggest that for imitation to be effective, policymakers must focus on more than simply "fit" and "design."[49]

Finally, a theory of imitation should not presume a slavish adherence to foreign models, nor should it claim that institutional change emanates *exclusively* from foreign factors. A concept of institutional transfer that admitted only slavish reproduction driven entirely by outside forces would generate a very small universe of cases. In fact, not even the cases from German reunification can meet this standard. Instead, in exploring the dynamics of institution building through transfer, I presume that imitation can go hand in hand with experimentation and that foreign-domestic coalitions can boost the chances of effective transfer. This presumption facilitates the inclusion of imitation in many more cases of institutional change—even those in which imitation is neither the central mode (as it was in the occupation cases) nor an overwhelmingly dominant one (as in the reunification cases). Chapter 2 provides examples where imitation has been an important component of institutional change but where a number of other factors have mattered as well.

49. See Peter Hall, "The Role of Interests, Institutions, and Ideas in the Comparative Political Economy of Industrialized Nations," in *Comparative Politics: Rationality, Culture, and Structure*, ed. Mark Irving Lichbach and Alan Zuckerman (New York: Cambridge University Press, 1997), 188–98.

CHAPTER TWO

Embedded Imitation: The Importance of Context

> With the exception of the instinct of self-preservation, the propensity
> for emulation is probably the strongest and most alert and persistent of
> the economic motives proper.
>
> —THORSTEIN VEBLEN, *Theory of the Leisure Class*

Policy elites have often turned to foreign designs in the hope not only of meeting demands from their own citizens but also of meeting external threats to the integrity of their state. Citizens may regard the imitation of foreign structures as an admission of domestic failure, and so policy elites seldom take lightly the open adoption of foreign institutional models. Yet geopolitical rivalry, military occupation, integration into international regimes, and the conditionality of international financial institutions have all prompted elites to use imitation.

Brief examples will illustrate each of these four contexts. For geopolitical competition, I review material from the modernization of Meiji Japan. For military occupation, I draw on the French and Soviet occupations in postwar Germany. On regime integration, I review the accession of Eastern and Central European states to the European Union (EU). And for the institutional conditionality context, I look at the experiences of the World Bank and the International Monetary Fund (IMF). My purpose is to suggest the range of uses of imitation and to emphasize that imitation is, in each case, embedded in a broader foreign and domestic political context; it occurs alongside other (nonimitative) forces that act on institutions. Separately, each sketch generates questions of general importance. Together, these examples provide compelling evidence that imitation has been significant in episodes of major institutional reconstruction.

MEIJI JAPAN: RATIONAL SHOPPING AND NATIONAL INTEGRITY

Elites in Meiji Japan used institutional transfer to strengthen their society against the threat of foreign penetration and the reduction of national sovereignty.[1] If elites attempt to protect their own traditions by becoming more like those they fear, perhaps imitation is highly strategic. Certainly, one key image flowing out of the Meiji case has been the notion of "rational shoppers"—policy elites who carefully search the globe for institutions "appropriate" enough to their cultural character to allow adoption yet capable of promoting a desirable modernization of some institutional domain.

Meiji has functioned as a rich, if inconclusive, data source on rational shopping. Tomihide Kashioka used Meiji's famous study-abroad program as a window into the empire's strategies for institutional emulation. His finding was that "in terms both of the fields of study and countries of sojourn, the Monbusho study-abroad program was governed by shrewd considerations for practicality and utilization vis-à-vis the nation's developmental strategies." Engineering, industry, law, and education were the most important areas of influence, and the most prominent sources of inspiration—in order of descending importance—were Germany, Britain, France, and the United States. Kashioka argued that Meiji judiciously avoided both borrowing haphazardly from a series of states and relying exclusively on one national model (as he found that former colonies tended to do). His argument thus endorsed the rational-shopper model proposed by the Meiji elites themselves.[2]

A stiff challenge to his image of the rational shopper comes from Eleanor Westney's study of Meiji borrowings from Western Europe of models for police organization, the postal system, and daily newspapers. Although she does not discuss Kashioka's study, she provides evidence that the rational-shopper concept was a tool of the state to promote acceptance of what might otherwise have appeared as "mere imitation." National pride led Meiji leaders to give the process a veneer of rationality. In actuality, however, Japanese state and society made very substantial adaptations in order to incorporate the European models.[3]

For this book, broadening the questions seems more useful than adjudicating the fight. Rather than assessing how "rational" particular acts of imitation actually were, I suggest that researchers regard rational shopping as one of several elite techniques designed to promote the legitimacy of transferred institutions. This raises an important question to which I return at several points: how can scholars move beyond a focus on the "supply" of ideas through networks of bureaucratic elites to issues of "demand" for institutional changes which link policymakers to their own domestic clientele?

1. Allan Mitchell's three-volume history shows that in the same period Germany functioned for France as intimidator, competitor, and object of emulation (especially for socialist and liberal Republicans); see *The German Influence in France after 1870* (1979), *Victors and Vanquished* (1984), and *The Divided Path* (1991), all from Chapel Hill: University of North Carolina Press.

2. Tomihide Kashioka, "Meiji Japan's Study Abroad Program" (Ph.D. diss., Duke University, 1982), esp. 11–14.

3. Eleanor Westney, *Imitation and Innovation* (Cambridge: Harvard University Press, 1987), 21–24.

THE FRENCH ANTI-MODEL AND THE HEAVY SOVIET HAND

Under military occupation, external pressures change from threat to coercion. The U.S. and British occupations form a central pillar of this study, but postwar Germany was powerfully shaped by two other victorious powers as well: the French and the Soviets. Quickly realizing that, contrary to wartime planning assumptions, four-power government would not exist, each nation moved to shape developments in its own zone of occupation. Along a crude spectrum of the extent to which each occupying power tried to reshape its zone in its own institutional image, the Americans and the British fall between the (maximalist) Soviets and the (minimalist) French.

Alone among the Allies, the French showed little sustained interest in institutional transfer. They were determined to prevent the reemergence of any kind of unified national German state and also tried to block the centralization of social actors such as trade unions.[4] In their attempts to promote localization of German political life and to force on Germany a weak state, French elites sought the polar opposite of their aspirations for their own nation. Their hope of building a stronger French state made decentralization appear as an obvious anti-model for keeping Germany from reasserting itself politically. This fiercely asserted preference for decentralized solutions in Germany was eminently clear in the French policies both for administrative structures of the state and for social organizations. The defeated Germans did not deserve French institutions.

By contrast, the Soviet zone of occupation saw intensive efforts at institutional transfer both before and, especially, after the proclamation of the German Democratic Republic in 1949.[5] Although the 1949 GDR constitution had a decidedly bourgeois democratic look on paper, this document was rapidly superseded by an aggressive effort to implant Soviet-style socialism in East Germany; a popular propaganda slogan was "To learn from the Soviet Union means to learn victory!" This effort reached a high point with the 1952 Communist Party Congress, which called for the "building of socialism." The Party used state organs, especially the secret police and the Ministry of Justice, to try to remake institutions in the image of those existing in the USSR. As always, the institutional transfer project was embedded in a larger set of interstate politics. But whereas the zones of western Germany quickly became embedded in a set of *complementary* economic arrangements that halted reparations and allowed them relatively open trading relations under a weak currency, the GDR paid very large reparations and adopted an economic system

---

4. Claus Scharf and Hans Jürgen Schröder, eds., *Die Deutschlandpolitik Frankreichs und die französische Zone, 1945–49* (Wiesbaden: F. Steiner, 1983).

5. See Norman Naimark, *The Russians in Germany* (Cambridge, Mass.: Belknap Press, 1995), 251–352; Hermann Weber, *DDR: Grundriß der Geschichte, 1945–1990* (Hanover: Fackelträger, 1991), esp. 40–46.

geared toward producing *self-sufficiency* in heavy industry in each country in which it was implanted by the Soviets.[6]

A distinctive feature of Soviet institutional transfer was a strict system of personnel control—*nomenklatura*. The Soviet occupation force not only dominated many questions of institutional design but also carefully controlled who would be allowed to populate the institutions. Personnel control helped guarantee that these institutions were embraced by Party chief Walther Ulbricht and other top leaders and implemented with more or less enthusiasm by thousands of committed Communists of the Socialist Unity Party (SED). This extreme case offers a glimpse at the broader point that redesigning institutions in accordance with foreign models may open up competitive advantages for one group over others. Knowing that institutional changes motivated by efficiency or equity concerns can have important distributive effects, one must ask whether these effects might not be exacerbated by the process of imitation, during which the conception of change is often unclear and its real effects uncertain.

THE FIELD OF DREAMS IN EASTERN AND CENTRAL EUROPE

The fall of Communist regimes in Eastern and Central Europe in 1990 precipitated a rush to determine the pathways to market economies and political democracies. Although social science shared in the general triumphalism of that moment, it was not long before cautionary voices warned of the likely difficulties of establishing particular Western institutional forms in these "transitional" societies.[7] Part of the broader debate about institutional change in Eastern Europe has focused on the appropriateness of Western-style institutions and has featured charges of institutional fetishism and cultural insensitivity.[8] For some critics Western "help" is simply a chimera. For example, Stanley Katz—invoking significant formal and interpretive changes in the U.S. constitution over time and also his impression that Western "legal consultants" in Eastern Europe were offering superficial answers to serious constitutional questions—argues that outsiders can offer little help to East Europeans in their constitution writing. In his view, true constitutionalism is not an institutional model at all but a style of politics that respects law and codifies local traditions. He urges East European states to sift through their

---

6. Naimark, *Russians in Germany*, 448. Specialization *among* the Council for Mutual Economic Assistance (COMECON) economies came later; it was not a goal that accompanied the efforts at institutional transfer of the 1940s and 1950s.

7. See Claus Offe, "Designing Institutions in East European Transitions," in *The Theory of Institutional Design*, ed. Robert Godwin (Cambridge: Cambridge University Press, 1995), 199–226.

8. David Stark and László Bruszt, *Postsocialist Pathways: Transforming Politics and Property in East Central Europe* (New York: Cambridge University Press, 1998).

own traditions for solutions.[9] Thomas Carothers's excellent study of U.S. democracy-assistance programs in Romania also criticizes efforts to promote particular institutional designs, suggesting "openness" as a more appropriate goal.[10]

As correctives to the superficial and short-term institutional hucksterism of many visiting experts, these cautionary views have much to recommend them. Yet to put Katz's own point in a different light, emphasizing the value of respect for law presupposes laws worthy of respect. Particular positive values indigenous to the region need institutional homes if they are to prevail in the long run over other indigenous values to which they are opposed. It is obvious that there is no reason such institutional schemes *must* come from outside the society yet clear enough that they *might*. But seeing imitation as a struggle blurs the line between historical traditions, imitation, and subsequent innovation. Privileging political actors allows one to assess the problem-solving capacity of those actors, who exist separate from institutions. Thus, building institutions through imitation also presupposes strengthening those actors who work through them.

Yet there are still more questions than answers on the link between imitation and the development of interests. Previously weak actors may become stronger and richer as a consequence of sponsoring new institutional designs, but can institutional transfer actually create actors where none existed previously? This question is asked with increasing frequency in the new democracies and half-democracies of Eastern and Central Europe. Can institutional designs, some of which are clearly modeled on West European or even American structures, call into existence the kind of organized groups that have helped make such institutions effective in their country of origin? For example, to what extent can a series of new consumer protection laws spark the generation of specialized private organizations whose pupose is to promote that awareness of consumer rights and that articulation of consumer interests whose existence the laws presume? To paraphrase a Hollywood film, if state elites build the structures, will civil society come? This question is profoundly important because new actors are needed for the new democracies to fulfill the conditions of the so-called Europe Agreements, the goal of which is to prepare the countries for EU membership.

The question of imitation is thus bound up with two other crucial issues: the development of civil society and state administrative capacity and the pursuit of these states' most important foreign policy goal. The EU's Phare Program, a commission instrument for promoting the eventual accession of East-

9. Stanley Katz, *Constitutional Democracy in Central Europe Today*, German Historical Institute lecture (Washington, D.C.: GHI, 1993). See also András Sajó, "Universal Rights, Missionaries, Converts, and 'Local Savages,'" in *East European Constitutional Review* 6 (Winter 1997): 44–49.

10. Thomas Carothers, *Assessing Democracy Assistance: The Case of Romania* (Washington, D.C.: Carnegie Endowment, 1996), 129–32.

ern countries, encourages these governments to engage in acts of "legislative approximation." Such approximation will give them institutional and policy structures compatible with those of the EU in policy areas from agriculture to value added taxes (VAT). Phare's task is to "concentrate on building state and non-state institutions and organizations critical for the functioning of a democratic, market-oriented system."[11] More informally, Phare officials describe the process as "fitting the prospective members for the European straitjacket," although it is a straitjacket prospective members clearly wish to wear.[12] The Commission White Paper in which this "pre-accession strategy" is laid out contains many references to the need not only to pass new laws but also to develop competent implementation.[13] The problem is that Phare's exhortations to build actors capable of enforcing new laws are buried in laundry lists of institutional designs that would be consistent with EU membership. Disconcertingly, these EU documents often cast the creation of actors to enforce compliance with the new rules as another in a long series of essentially *technical* tasks.[14] This complicated interplay between foreign designs and the building of indigenous actors matters increasingly as institutional thresholds for EU membership are articulated by the commission in its 1998 comments on the Polish, Czech, Hungarian, Slovenian, and Estonian membership applications and in the ongoing "screening" of these countries' laws in 31 different domains.[15]

MULTILATERAL LENDING AND INSTITUTIONAL CONDITIONALITY

Conditionality refers to demands made on borrowers by lenders—here, the World Bank and the IMF—which go beyond the payment of interest and fees on loan principal. The aims of conditionality-based lending have been quite varied, including regulatory "liberalization," poverty reduction, democratization, reduced military spending, and protection of the environment.

11. Phare, *Jahresbericht 1994* (Brussels: Phare, 1994), 9.

12. Interviews: Brussels, 1996, 1998. Since many of my interview respondents spoke on the condition of confidentiality, I have chosen to identify all interviews only by city and year. For a discussion of the institutional implications of potential EU membership in a non-post-Communist case, see Anton Pelinka, "Österreich: EU-Mitgliedschaft als Katalysator," *Aus Politik und Zeitgeschichte* B10 (1996): 10–17.

13. EU Commission, "White Paper on the Preparation of the Associated Countries of Central and Eastern Europe for Integration into the Internal Market of the Union," COM (95) 163 final (May 3, 1995). Also available on the Internet at http://europa.eu.int/comm/off/white/index_en.htm.

14. Only recently have EU publications begun to stress the magnitude of the challenges that still lie ahead in building capacity to implement these reforms. For an example, see the Czech National Training Fund study, *Proposals for a Strategy of Public Administration Reform in the Czech Republic* (Brussels: Phare, 1998).

15. Wade Jacoby, "The EU as a Force in the Domestic Politics of Eastern Europe," *East European Constitutional Review* 8 (1/2) (1999): 62–67.

The means to pursue these ends are also potentially broad, ranging from persuasion to technical or material support to pressure in the form of promised rewards or threats of the loss of future funding.[16] Some conditions for loans are couched in institutional terms (a classic demand is for more central bank independence), but they may also be in terms of policy content—say, spending less on a subsidy or lowering a tariff. Thus, only some conditionality projects involve imitation of institutions that exist elsewhere; others spring from an ideal-typical "Washington consensus" on economic policy or simply ask the borrowers to cut back some ongoing practice.[17] Even within the context of conditionality, institutional imitation is rarely the sole modality for institutional change, since it is so fraught with symbolic and practical risks.

Like many other cases of imitation, conditionality has a political context that mixes coercion and choice. As the financial and debt crises of the late 1970s and early 1980s accelerated, the two major multilateral institutions turned toward a new kind of lending often described as "policy-based." In contrast to the traditional "project-based lending," the new loans could be disbursed quickly to head off balance-of-payments crises and were given to government officials without the requirement of strictly defined "projects." Such nonproject support had grown to over 25% of the World Bank's portfolio by the end of the 1980s. In the early 1990s, with an environment marked by significant private capital flows, the end of the Cold War, and increased democracy, some scholars saw the era of conditionality as on the decline.[18] But recent financial crises in Asia, Russia, and Brazil soon led to a new wave of conditions.[19]

Does conditionality work? It appears that the changes achieved have been modest, relative to the aspirations of the multilateral lenders.[20] Loans to address immediate balance-of-payments problems seem especially ill suited to generate incentives for institutional changes over the long term.[21] Yet according to one large study, despite many variations in different national

16. On ends and means, see Joan Nelson and Stephanie Eglinton, *Global Goals, Contentious Means* (Washington, D.C.: Overseas Development Council, 1993), 28–31, 52–55.

17. The World Bank has made stopping the practice of female circumcision a condition of recent loans to some African countries (interview: Washington, 1996). Note that conditionality can also be used to remove institutions of "market distortion," such as marketing boards.

18. See Joan Nelson, "Is the Era of Conditionality Past?" (Working Paper 1995/72, Juan March Institute, Madrid), 1–2.

19. The relationship between lender and borrower, however, rather than the actual severity of the borrower's economic problems, seems to determine most the terms of these conditionality packages. See Paul Mosley, Jane Harrigan, and John Toye, *Power and Aid: The World Bank and Policy-Based Lending*, 2 vols. (London: Routledge, 1990), 1:90, 116–29. Nelson and Eglinton (*Global Goals*, 64–67) do show that economically weak countries with heavy dependence on the World Bank are subjected to much more conditionality than those with higher levels of gross domestic product (GDP) or lower levels of dependence on Bank finance.

20. Mosley, Harrigan, and Toye, *Power and Aid*, 1:6.

21. Nelson and Eglinton, *Global Goals*, 17.

settings "one factor remains constant: where there is articulate opposition to policy reform, as there usually is, that opposition must be overcome somehow if implementation is to take place."[22] How then is conditionality blocked? Many line ministries have been unwilling to implement conditionality agreements struck between the lending agencies and the finance or economics ministries, which typically negotiate the packages. Overcoming that opposition may often entail a more aggressive policy to structure loans in ways that build up the competence and authority of line ministries: for example, agricultural loans disbursed by the agricultural ministry in the form of fertilizer.[23] Tensions between the ministry that signs conditionality agreements and those that must implement them reveal the analytical weakness of the assumption that the elites in the imitating state can be treated as unitary actors—a defect this book tries to overcome.

These foregoing examples show that imitation occurs in a politicized context in which policy elites face both pressures from domestic constituents and pressure or coercion from external actors. Although there is some evidence that societies undergoing major transformative processes may more aggressively imitate others, many other cases of imitation occur against fairly stable social and political backgrounds.[24] Thus, imitation can be geared either to exploit opportunity or to respond to a crisis, and it is clear that the kinds of structures involved are often absolutely central to security, democracy, and prosperity in a given nation. Embedding imitation in such political contexts breaks down a simple distinction between purely "voluntary" and purely "coerced" ideal types, raising in its stead a series of more sophisticated and interesting questions. Framing these as research questions is the next step.

INSTITUTIONAL TRANSFER AS A PROXY FOR IMITATION

Institutional transfer and imitation are not synonyms. Rather, transfer is one way—perhaps even the most important—in which imitation can occur. Since I use institutional transfer here as a proxy for imitation, it is useful to consider that process in more detail. Rather than attempting to specify "laws of imitation," I provide a "heuristic of imitation" that suggests ways to unravel this complex and fragmented phenomenon.[25] Four blocks of issues emerge as crucial, and in each block I specify possible lines of analysis of "imitative

22. Mosley, Harrigan, and Toye, *Power and Aid*, 2:301.
23. Ibid., 306.
24. For the former, see John Ikenberry, "Explaining the Diffusion of State Norms" (International Studies Association paper, London, 1989); on the latter, see the policy-borrowing literature reviewed in Chapter 1.
25. Gabriel Tarde, *The Laws of Imitation*, trans. Elsie Clews Parsons (New York: Henry Holt, 1903).

processes": that is, situations where actors use imitation as part of some broader political context. The four blocks run in rough order from the *motivations, agents,* and *processes* of imitation to its *results*: *why* do elites attempt imitation? *who* pushes imitation? *which* kinds of social, political, or commercial phenomena are seen as worthy of imitation? *how* does that process proceed?

Why Imitation?

The most common justifications for imitation are that it may promote either efficiency or justice, and most other motives can ultimately be seen as derivatives of these basic themes. Each motive can result in the emulation of institutional designs either within or across national boundaries.

Clearly, much imitation is motivated by the desire for efficiency, the hope of performing some task better. For example, German vocational training has so often been identified as a source of increased productivity that many nations have sought to imitate either its principles or its institutions—so much so that the Ministry of Education and Science has a special office to field inquiries. Moreover, even within the German system the constant search for improvement has generated an elaborate process of model experiments, accompanied by pedagogical assessment, for possible diffusion throughout the national system.[26] One can expect policy elites to pursue efficiency gains through imitation as long as scholars of comparative government (and the business press) continue to identify and publicize variations in institutional effectiveness.

Other imitations purport to increase fairness or justice. Progressive taxation of income and child labor laws may spread from state to state. At the international level the widespread inclusion of declarations of individual rights in written constitutions has occasionally been inspired by the U.S. Bill of Rights or the French Declaration of the Rights of Man.

Of course, conceptions of efficiency and justice can also motivate resistance to imitation.[27] For every claim that imitation will increase efficiency, justice, or control, there are often counterclaims that it would bring waste, exploitation, and chaos. Whether the motivation is efficiency or equity, authorities may find imitation an attractive mechanism for change precisely because it can obscure the difficulties of change. Paradoxically, the sharpness of "models" as analytical constructs may help boost consensus by drawing attention away from contentious issues and toward the positive outcomes for

26. Notice here that imitation occurs *inside* national borders (through the diffusion of successful experiments) at the same time that internal diversity is blended out to explain the "basic system" to prospective foreign borrowers.

27. See Ronald Dore, "Convergence in Whose Interest?" in *Convergence or Diversity?* ed. Suzanne Berger and Ronald Dore (Ithaca: Cornell University Press, 1996).

which the model is celebrated. Some uncertain situations may privilege small cliques of decision makers who can parlay that uncertainty into brief influence or even enduring power.[28] In other words, descriptions of foreign practices can be *stylized* by political actors to help simplify and channel political discussion. None of this is meant to denigrate the search for efficiency or justice. My premise is simply that translating principles of either one into institutional structures is as difficult and contestable as it is vital for a democracy.

Who Drives Imitation?

Individual citizens may admire foreign institutions and private interest groups may promote policy borrowing, but under this book's definition all attempts at formal institutional transfer must pass through state officials. For two reasons this definition is broad enough to cover both voluntaristic "borrowing" and transfer under duress. First, since all policymakers face pressures, typologizing those pressures is, at this early stage of research on imitation, analytically much less useful than pursuing regularities across the great variety of situations where imitation is used. Second, the distinction between voluntarist imitation by a sovereign actor and imitation forced upon a subordinate actor is vulnerable to the objection that overlapping authority often makes the sovereign-subordinate distinction unconvincing.

More fruitful are simple judgments about whether motives for imitation come primarily from external pressure or from within a society.[29] As a first step it is important to distinguish between imitation under occupation—where foreign soldiers influence or indeed make political choices—and that conducted by indigenous state officials (who may still feel enormous pressure from foreign armies, IMF officials, interest groups, or voters). The reason that external-internal pressures deserve analytical priority lies in the hypothesis introduced earlier: state policy elites may well depend upon existing actors in civil society to make transfer effective. If this hypothesis proves fruitful, there are good theoretical reasons to expect that those linkages to civil society are of a qualitatively different (and more problematic) order for occupying armies.

But although the formal authority to launch imitation is important, many institution-building processes are so complex that mere orders can hardly secure the intended results. For example, in both the periods studied in this book, shifts in sovereignty led to shifts in processes of imitation. The U.S. and British occupation forces were often unable or unwilling to bluntly impose

28. John Ikenberry, "A World Economy Restored," *International Organization* 46 (1992): 289–321.

29. Of course, this distinction can also be taken too literally, since domestic and international factors can be difficult to disentangle; see Peter Gourevitch, "The Second Image Reversed," *International Organization* 32 (1978): 881–912.

their own institutional designs on the Germans. As the Allied forces—which began the occupation with absolute formal powers—slowly relinquished authority into German hands, calculations about the limited duration of foreign control played an important role in stiffening German resistance to Allied reforms. After 1989, imitation was also bound up with control. Institutional transfer was initially undertaken by East Germany's reforming Communist government in a failed attempt to circumvent West German encroachment and preserve GDR sovereignty; later, of course, in the aftermath of reunification, imitation was used to promote (not prevent) the extension of the FRG's territory.

So formal authority is contested, and not only in the imitation of public institutions. The legal constitution of social actors too can be important in structuring the outcomes of institutional transfer. For example, a foreign model may play as influential a role in defining whom a trade union represents as it does in establishing specific parameters of, say, labor market regulation. It is in this sense that actors can be built even as formal institutions are built. Commercial actors also engage in struggles over what formal authority to imitate. For example, managers might disagree with shareholders or with workers over *which* practices to imitate and over whether their contests should be resolved through recourse to property rights or to some form of mediation. In all these arenas, processes of imitation are bound up with issues of contestation and control.

Which Phenomena Appear Worth Imitating?

Objects of imitation can be located in the realm of the state, society, or commerce and at both formal and informal levels. As the simplest way to unpack this range, I limit the cases in this book to focus on institutions having a legal basis. This means that I attempt no systematic analysis of the *informal* norms present in all "organizational cultures," beyond making every effort to note informal practices that directly shape the functioning of transferred institutions.[30] Moreover, I include only formal institutions of the state (school structures) and society (industrial relations laws), thus excluding the commercial level of firm-to-firm imitation of business practices or technologies.[31] The benefit of using the concept of institutional transfer to explore periods of large-scale societal transformation carries the price of limiting the focus to

30. Richard Scott, "Unpacking Institutional Arguments," in *The New Institutionalism in Organizational Analysis*, ed. Walter Powell and Paul DiMaggio (Chicago: University of Chicago Press, 1991).

31. The definitive work on technology transfer remains Everett Rogers, *The Diffusion of Innovations*, 3d ed. (New York: Free Press, 1983). Work on the imitation of firm-based organizations has increased rapidly in recent years; see, e.g., Martin Kenney and Richard Florida, *Beyond Mass Production: The Japanese System and Its Transfer to the U.S.* (London: Oxford University Press, 1992).

formal institutions. But this limitation is strictly practical and not theoretical; imitation of informal institutions cries out for further analysis, as does more theoretically informed investigation of firm-level imitation.[32]

I also focus on the constitution of actors by looking at rules for defining the acceptable forms of social organization and the boundaries for their spheres of action. Put simply, just as institutions help structure politics, actors help structure the institutions, and this process in turn shapes actors in profound ways. Perhaps two brief examples (covered in detail later) can suggest what I mean. In post–World War II Germany, Allied-German reform struggles in industrial relations not only turned on issues of what unions could do but also turned into a dispute about what unions were: agents of economic bargaining, or agents of political democratization. And in eastern Germany today, when works councilors make handshake deals with the managers of their firms to disregard supposedly binding wage contracts, the practice weakens not only formal collective bargaining agreements as such but also the collective actors who pursue them. Actors can change themselves even as they structure institutions, and since transfer so compresses processes of institutional change, it is an excellent vantage point from which to study this interaction.

How Does Transfer Proceed?

Within the concept of institutional transfer, three final distinctions are needed, corresponding roughly to breadth, depth, and intensity of imitation. The first distinction is between wholesale and piecemeal transfer; the second, between exact transfer and the functional equivalent approach; the third, between continuous interaction and single-moment transfer. Each pair forms a spectrum of logical possibilities, and an attempt at transfer may lie anywhere along each spectrum, making logically possible many permutations of the three. Some combinations seem much more likely than others; for example, a wholesale, functional equivalent, and single-moment transfer would seem quite implausible, since it would require that a vast institutional redesign be done all at once.

The continuum between wholesale and piecemeal transfer conveys the difference between isolated institutional changes and the adoption of a bundle of purportedly interlocking and mutually reinforcing institutions.[33] Both modalities are fraught with practical problems. Piecemeal transfer may leave

---

32. A good summary of developments in this literature is Richard Nelson, "Recent Evolutionary Theorizing about Economic Change," *Journal of Economic Literature*, 33 (1995): 48–90.

33. For example, an important study of European industrial relations emphasizes the historical and cultural embeddedness of institutions and suggests that they cannot be uprooted from their original environment: Christel Lane, *Management and Labour in Europe: The Industrial Enterprise in Germany, France, and Britain* (Aldershot, Eng.: Edward Elgar, 1989), 292–97.

the institution without its normal support network; the wholesale transfer approach wrongly presumes that it is possible to tell where institutions—especially those that work well—begin and end. Take the revealing case of Intel. This company, the global leader in computer chip production, has long attempted to "lock in" the design of the fabrication plant for each new generation of its pentium chips through a corporate policy called "COPY EXACTLY!" The program sounds simple: in each new factory, copy everything exactly from the designated model factory unless the board approves a deviation. Gaining such approval is a slow and difficult process, however, for closer inspection shows that even in this case no one knows (or they disagree about) what must be copied and what can be safely left out.[34] Here one sees clearly the uncertainty of institutional boundaries: one of America's most successful firms, in a business it understands possibly better than anyone else, still reveals substantial uncertainty over how to conduct this kind of transfer program. In short, the question of how much to transfer is always likely to be contestable.

The notions of exact transfer and functional equivalence, introduced briefly in Chapter 1, are abstractions that bound a range of interesting possibilities by excluding some less interesting ones. Policymakers can use either strategy at the level of constituting an actor, designing an institution, or creating a policy. But neither strategy is suitable for creating democracy, capitalism, or socialism (although democratization may involve many cases of institutional transfer at, for example, the level of the legal basis of interest groups, the design of parliamentary committees, or the promulgation of specific laws concerning freedom of the press). Also excluded are cases of imitation that do not lead to formal institutional changes based *meaningfully* on foreign models—such as a domestically driven change about which some *ex post* rhetoric refers to the virtues of similar foreign designs. That is public relations, not politics, and it is up to scholars to look past rhetoric and understand the difference.

Exact transfer is the *attempt* to reproduce exactly certain laws that either constitute social and state actors in the first place or regulate their interactions. Notice that "exact" refers to the *ambition* of policymakers and not to their *achievement*. An institution transferred exactly may fail to perform its anticipated function in the new society; alternatively, it may perform that function to a much *greater* extent than did its original. For example, following German reunification, exact transfer was tried in many institutional domains including the "employment and training companies" developed by West German unions for economic crisis regions. A minor institutional practice in

---

34. See the study of "COPY EXACTLY!" by Eric Fears, "An Analysis of the Effect of Technology Transfer Methodology on Manufacturability and Sustainability" (thesis, Sloan School of Management, MIT, 1994), 32–33.

West Germany, the formation of such companies has, in the context of massive job losses, become a major pillar of the eastern German labor market.[35] Thus the concept of exact transfer is suggestive of the *aims* of policymakers as they attempt institutional transfer, but it does not rule out the isomorphism in function or scope which may occur in the process.

The functional equivalent approach does not try for exact reproduction of institutional forms. Rather, policymakers, on their own or influenced by academic writing or political propaganda, abstract from a foreign institution a functional task which is, in their view, incompletely or poorly fulfilled in their own society. Functional analysis, out of favor as a tool of social science, certainly lives on as a technique for imagining institutional redesign from the point of view of *policymakers*. I characterize most Allied efforts at institutional transfer as following the functional equivalent approach.

The final dimension, that of intensity, distinguishes between a single decision to transfer and a process of imitation that occurs over an extended period. Of course, even in an ideal-typical case of single-moment transfer, the foreign model will presumably have attracted potential imitators for some time.[36] The distinction calls attention, however, to differences between cases in which a single legislative act encompasses all the interchange between the two societies and those in which either personnel, aid, or political influence continues to lubricate the flow of ideas about institutional designs. Continuous processes often involve such tools as benchmarking, formal partnerships, and personnel transfer. In the first of these—benchmarking—firms, social actors, and state organizations can all monitor international developments and look to pull in the best innovations from elsewhere.[37] Given this approach, some relationships develop over time, so that imitation can be sequential. Kashioka's and Westney's studies of Meiji Japan show both how the Japanese emulated multiple institutions from the same European societies and also how, within a single institutional area, they returned to ask questions or emulate modifications. Second, formal partnerships often exist which can serve as channels of communication. Of interest since German reunification,

35. Gerhard Bosch and Matthias Knuth, "Beschäftigungsgesellschaften in den alten und neuen Bundesländern," *WSI-Mitteilungen* 7 (1992): 431–39.

36. Since transfer is often attempted in policy domains that have a legacy of failure, short-term failure does not preclude the institution's becoming meaningful under unforeseen future circumstances. Nations can borrow "possibilities" as well as institutions by injecting new designs into their national discussions, even if those designs remain weak or unimplemented for some time. Here is yet another reason for scholars to take a long-term perspective on institutional transfer and pay attention to minority traditions.

37. Benchmarking receives its fullest theoretical exposition to date in Michael Dorf and Charles Sabel, "A Constitution of Democratic Experimentalism," in *Columbia Law Review* 98 (2), (1998): 267–473. For its application to the German policy debate, see the report on the Alliance for Jobs "Benchmarking Working Group" by Wolfgang Streeck and Rolf Heinze, "An Arbeit fehlt es nicht," in *Der Spiegel* 19 (1999): 38–45.

state- and city-level partnerships between western and eastern German local governments have promoted institutional transfer. Third, and related to formal partnerships, personnel transfer can be important in the continual exchange of institutional information. All these issues are explored below in the discussion of how transfer *strategy* shapes transfer outcomes.

METHODS AND COMPARISONS

This book uses case studies to generate and explore hypotheses about imitation. Since institutional transfer is neither inevitable nor impossible, only the detailed exploration of individual cases can reveal the contingent links between competing conceptions of institutional design. What is more, case studies allow one to judge the outcomes of institutional transfer against the qualitative standards of institutional performance and persistence, rather than merely checking to see if the institution is "on the books," as in diffusion studies.

These cases are not intended as freestanding accounts of either the Anglo-American occupation or of German reunification; rather, they work to explore claims about the politics of imitation. Growing secondary literatures (documented in the footnotes) have chronicled the broad processes of social, political, and economic change in each period. The method here, however, is to compare different institutional domains within two broader efforts in which policymakers with vast formal authority attempted transfer. The classic comparative approach to case studies, which calls for maximum similarity in all factors taken as external to the study and for differences only along the dimensions hypothesized to "explain" outcomes, can obviously not be maintained here.[38] Western Germany after 1945 and eastern Germany after 1989 faced any number of unique challenges, and although reunification has been called a "natural experiment," it is hardly a controlled one. It is necessary, therefore, to take a brief look at the dimensions along which these broad cases are and are not comparable.

Two crucial differences between the periods, political exposure and economic background, further illuminate the importance of state strategies of institutional transfer and thus do not require inclusion as additional explanatory variables. The first difference concerns the degree to which the sovereign powers were exposed to the results of their handiwork: the Anglo-American occupation powers knew they would ultimately leave Germany for good, whereas the problem since reunification has been that of one society absorbing another and therefore having something different at stake. Has

---

38. Arend Lijphart, "Comparative Politics and the Comparative Method," *American Political Science Review* 65 (1971): 682–93.

this greater exposure had an independent effect on institutional transfer? The question is very important. But the answer is not that the Bonn government after 1990 "cared" more than the Anglo-Americans after 1945, for indeed the success of institutional transfer was deemed crucial in both periods.[39] Rather, the implication is that Bonn's interest in reproducing familiar and proven institutions helped drive the *particular* strategy of exact transfer in the first place. For the Anglo-American occupiers, fewer concerns about unwanted "feedback effects" from German institutions made the functional equivalent strategy much less risky than it would have been for Bonn.[40] Exposure thus affected strategy, leading to a more ambitious form of transfer after 1990. This important difference between the periods can thus be channeled through the investigation of the flexibility of transfer strategy. The analytical task at hand then becomes that of determining the *consequences* of the differences in strategy between the two periods.

The question of adding an economic variable is more complicated, as it would not so much shape the choice of transfer strategies as either support or undercut them. One might imagine that the outcomes of transfer, especially in industrial relations, would be driven largely by exogenous developments in the economy: could transfer in postwar industrial relations have been effective not because of the character of cross-societal alliances established around institutional redesign, as I emphasize, but simply because the economy performed well?

Two important objections undercut this view. First, some of the policies promoting the economic boom around export-led growth were themselves linked directly to the Anglo-American strategy of functional equivalent institutional transfer. It is clear that the rapid growth of the 1950s was not an inevitable result of the global economic structure of the postwar period.[41] Rather, German exports of capital goods to Europe and North America depended on policy choices made in Washington, D.C., and in European capitals. Rebuilding European production and infrastructure and supplying Fordist America with capital goods meant that German production (re)gained an important position in world markets. The absence of noteworthy trade disputes in this period, despite remarkably high exports as a percentage of gross domestic product (GDP), suggests that the German economy filled a complementary niche in the international division of labor.

---

39. It is easy to forget how much seemed to ride on the success of the Anglo-American occupation of post–World War II Germany. Beyond the horrible cost in civilian and military deaths, the United States had spent more than 45% of its GDP on the war effort, and Britain an even greater proportion.

40. Chapter 3 shows that some U.S. officials did worry about the "feedback" effect to the United States of German cartel policy and especially about codetermination, and they took concrete steps to try to prevent such developments in Germany.

41. Fred Block, *The Origins of International Economic Disorder* (Berkeley: University of California Press, 1977).

In this way, the Anglo-American strategy of institutional transfer was embedded in a larger strategy of economic reconstruction, a strategy that the British and Americans, more than any others, actively shaped.

Second, reference to economic recovery strategies alone is too blunt to explain many specific institutional changes of interest. For example, it is simply not true that the economic miracle gave the Americans and British wide scope for easy institutional transfer, even with regard to the economy. From decartelization to antitrust policy, the occupation forces struggled constantly to forge alliances for grafting their institutional designs onto Germany in ways that appeared to them effective and sustainable. But in 1956, at the *height of the economic miracle*, the West Germans rejected the U.S.-mandated shift from quasi-public chambers of industry and commerce to private ones with strictly voluntary membership. In short, it seems much more plausible that positive economic outcomes reinforced some parts of the provisional and highly contested institutional reequilibration without legitimating them all, and surely without specifying what changes were "required" by the new international economy.

Since reunification, these linkages between strategies of transfer and broader strategies of economic change also underscore the fact that imitation rarely stands in isolation from other crucial policies. In eastern Germany since 1990 the dominant means of promoting economic change has been privatization. Yet the strategy of exact transfer actually fits poorly with efforts to reintegrate the two German economies through privatization. It has proved difficult to construct similar instruments of economic regulation without simultaneously reproducing the structural patterns of the West German economy.

Whence the tension? Because of existing economic capacity in the West, the eastern German economy generally represented an (inferior) competitor rather than a complement to West German business. The western German system of economic regulation has never been particularly good at promoting new markets, relying instead on successive improvements in traditional markets such as automobiles, machine tools, and chemicals. Thus, the only real chances for a complementary role for major portions of the eastern German economy would have been through their connections to markets in Eastern Europe, or as sites of either low-wage or high-tech production of a kind not possible in western Germany. Currency union foreclosed the first possibility; other political choices attenuated the potential for widespread use of the other two. Subsequently, every effort to make eastern Germany different has run into difficulty with regulatory institutions, which tend to minimize regional and sectoral differences within Germany. At this point the only complementarities available are those *inside* company boundaries, as when western German corporations augment existing capacities with acquisitions in eastern Germany.

In short, the tensions between institutional reconstruction and commercial competition powerfully shaped the dynamics of transfer in both the occupation and reunification periods. But since these forces are mediated through strategies of transfer already identified, they do not require *separate* treatment as factors explaining institutional transfer outcomes.

CONCLUSION

The complexity of disentangling foreign and indigenous influences mandates small numbers of cases, and a small number of cases demands limits to the number of variables. Dividing postwar occupation and reunification into a series of attempts to constitute actors and to reform institutions along the lines of existing foreign models allows key factors to be held constant as the number of cases is increased. Even then, however, social phenomena as complex as imitation are unlikely to be fully explained through just a few variables. For that reason I focus primarily on hypothesis generation, using different cases to explore different aspects of imitation, while providing a broad political argument with significant implications for theories of institutional change.

The empirical chapters (3 to 6) develop several claims. The postwar industrial relations case reveals the irony that effective transfer may appear in retrospect as internally generated; in this case, the fuller flowering of antecedent Weimar traditions obscures the hybrid roots of the postwar plant. The postwar education case illustrates the limitations of using cultural factors only to explain resistance to institutional transfer. The Americans actually had many potential allies in their mission to reform German education, but opponents of common schools used German culture as a political tool to block American aims. The systematic transfer of industrial relations after reunification reveals unexpected institutional interactions—especially in wage bargaining—even when institutions were transferred in packages, and it also helps demonstrate the importance of power relationships in holding together institutionalized forms of cooperation. The reunification education case, among other things, leads to a better understanding of the processes whereby transferred institutions are legitimated, and it also helps reveal that civil society matters for reasons not captured only by its "density."

In short, these four cases cover a significant number of the issues raised by the study of imitation and sketched earlier in this chapter. The question "why imitate?" revealed a focus on efficiency, justice, and autonomy as central motivations; each of these motivations plays a central role in one or more of the cases. The second issue concerned the authority to conduct imitation. In both industrial relations cases the formal authority lay with outsiders (the Allies and the West German government); in both education cases the formal authority was soon vested in state government insiders. Third, the cases cover the construction of formal state and social institutions, although they largely exclude commercial institutions such as business practices. Finally, the "exact transfer" and "functional equivalent transfer" heuristics allow me to cover issues of breadth, depth, and intensity in addressing the question of how policymakers use imitation.

Chapter Three

Economic Governance: Models of Industrial Relations after 1945

> We are the sum of all the people who've invaded us.
>
> —David Edgar, *Pentecost*

Until 1945 the development of German economic institutions was dominated not by invading powers but by struggles among German workers, managers, owners, and states. Could foreign models have an appreciable impact on structures as long established as those of German industrial relations in the mid-twentieth century? They could indeed.[1] Occupation forces staffed by American and British union officials used their own traditions of economic organization to check the ambitions of German unionists for "economic democracy" and also to challenge the autocratic structures and practices of German employers. Some allied efforts merely reinforced "lessons of Weimar" already widely held by German elites (see the *Deutsche Arbeitsfront* and *Richtungsgewerkschaften* cases below). Elsewhere, however, crucial, effective Allied interventions did shape the resulting structures and practices (the choice for strong industrial unions and the matter of codetermination), though in some domains, strenuous Allied interventions either had only modest results (antitrust policy) or failed (chambers of commerce).

Yet even where intervention was effective, German industrial relations re-

---

1. And not only in industrial relations. Recent works in German historical scholarship emphasizing Allied efforts to reshape Germany and German emulation of foreign practices are Axel Schildt and Arnold Sywottek, eds., *Modernisierung im Wiederaufbau: Die westdeutsche Gesellschaft der 50er Jahre* (Bonn: J. H. W. Dietz, 1993); Alf Lüdtke, Inge Marssolek, and Adelheid von Saldern, *Amerikanisierung: Traum und Alptraum im Deutschland des 20. Jahrhunderts* (Stuttgart: Steiner, 1996); Konrad Jarausch and Hannes Siegrist, eds., *Amerikanisierung und Sowjetisierung in Deutschland, 1945–1970* (Frankfurt: Campus, 1997); Rolf Winter, *Little America: Die Amerikanisierung der Deutschen Republik* (Hamburg: Rasch und Rohring, 1995).

mained obviously distinct from the British and U.S. versions.[2] The question is to what extent Anglo-American models of capitalism were used in pursuit of these outcomes. Effective institutional transfer, by definition, results in organizations that become part of the fabric of society; hence, later efforts to disentangle their sources are bound to be difficult. The postwar reforms were built on a framework of Weimar institutions and upon German minority traditions that looked attractive as elites considered the lessons of Weimar. The merits and shortcomings of Weimar institutions were, however, deeply controversial within German labor and between labor and capital. This disagreement allowed Allied institutional designs to become central in the choice of new arrangements. Abstract institutional models blend spatial and temporal variation; they suggest ideal types, and occupation officials used such abstract models to narrow the initially wide range of organizational forms considered by the Germans and to promote some initially unlikely winners.[3]

In establishing policies for their respective zones and, after 1947, for the combined U.S.-British zone, the Allies often used functional equivalence models. They did not insist that Germans adopt an entire foreign industrial relations system or even copy exactly any one piece. But they constantly invoked the broad outlines of their own national practices in ways that bore directly on the choices of German actors. For example, the Allies' preferences for the fundamental form (decentralized) and function (collective bargaining) of trade unions profoundly affected the outcomes of intra-German struggles. Further, their experience with corporatist regulation during wartime led both Allies to try to convince German employers of the benefits of accepting labor as an equal but *informal* partner in broad tasks of economic regulation.

This chapter launches the empirical exploration of effective transfer, which I link to social organization and political flexibility. It is clear that the Allies could build on a civil society trying to become more active in the wake of Nazi persecution and in the face of occupation restrictions. But if society was resurgent after twelve years of dictatorship and war, it was also divided; hence, the Allies made clear choices about *which* German actors they would support. On the side of capital, they initially sought to overcome the distinction between employer and business associations by promoting the latter while restricting the former. On the side of labor, they favored unions while

---

2. In the 1950s, U.S. observers emphasized inadequacies of German industrial relations in comparison with those in the United States; see Clark Kerr, "The Trade Union Movement and the Redistribution of Power in Postwar Germany," *Quarterly Journal of Economics* 68 (1954): 535–64.

3. The diversity of organizational forms and practices in the first months after war's end belies any notion that either German labor or German employers were unified in their approaches to postwar organizational reconstruction. There was no "German model" in either practice or conception.

tightly controlling the "antifascist committees" that sprang up all over Germany in the spring of 1945 but generally did not survive the summer. Both the Americans and the British channeled individual "antifa" members into parties or public administration. They used the functional equivalence approach to walk a nebulous line, allowing the Germans to develop their own traditions in more democratic ways but forbidding developments the Allies deemed unacceptable.[4]

The second key factor, flexibility, affected means rather than ends. The Allies were often inflexible when it came to designing institutional *ends*. For example, U.S. dogmatism on chamber of commerce reform became legendary among German employers, to whom the proposed private chambers with voluntary membership seemed both alien and dysfunctional. Once the Allies had drawn certain lines, they were often willing to use their authority to veto all German efforts to cross them—even the efforts of democratically elected German governments.[5] Yet the Allies augmented their functional equivalence techniques with a willingness to listen to the institutional visions of German actors when it came to implementing these functions. Thus, the *means* of pursuing certain institutional ends were regarded by both occupation forces as relatively open.

Both Allies were also aware of the possibility that institutional functions could be circumvented at the implementation stage, and both monitored implementation carefully. Yet for the occupation forces, vigilance in oversight had always to be balanced by concern for supporting the efforts of German democrats, around whom at least part of the new Germany could be built. From the Allied perspective the dilemma was that the "good Germans" often wanted bad institutions. And the occupation governments rarely gave ground on the broad functional ends they desired. Sometimes (as in industrial unionism) they prevailed; in other cases (such as antitrust policy) they fought mostly in vain until well after the founding of the Federal Republic. Nevertheless, flexibility marked the Allies' attitude toward means if they could find German partners with whom they could agree on the pursuit of certain institutional ends. This issue matters more generally because to the extent that policymakers' designs for institutional transfer are not self-implementing, they run the risk that social actors powerful enough to build upon can also steal the design for their own purposes.

I treat the military governments (MGs) of the United States and Britain as prisms through which to view and understand occupation policies.[6] Their

4. The Americans often used polls to gauge how much change they could push the Germans to accept. See Richard Merritt, *Democracy Imposed: U.S. Occupation Policy and the German Public, 1945–1949* (New Haven: Yale University Press, 1995).

5. For example, when the state of Hessen tried to socialize parts of heavy industry, the U.S. military governor set aside that section of the constitution calling for socialization.

6. The military governments' superior organizations—Supreme Headquarters Allied Expeditionary Force (SHAEF) and its replacement, the Allied Control Authority (ACA)—rarely exercised direct influence over trade union development. By the time control officers of the occu-

officers were the policy elites who attempted institutional transfer. Of course, many MG decisions about the organization of industrial relations were taken on instructions from their home governments, and U.S. policy toward Germany was the object of struggle among various American factions.[7] By now familiar, the key fault lines lay between advocates of a harsh peace designed to punish Germany and prevent any economic, political, or military reconstruction, and advocates of reconstructing Germany both to prevent the rise of German Communism based on material despair and, later, to create a bulwark against Soviet Communism.[8] The former position, associated primarily with Secretary of the Treasury Henry Morgenthau but also attributed to Franklin Roosevelt himself, reached its high point in the autumn of 1944. But this "harsh peace" view was gradually eclipsed by the "reconstructionist" view, held by the majority of the State Department and articulated by George Kennan and especially by Secretary of State James Byrnes. During the occupation the rhetoric of the Truman administration perceptibly shifted from discussion of the "German problem" as diagnosed by the first school to that of the "Soviet threat," emphasized by the second.

In industrial relations, actual policy choices did not always follow wartime planning, which focused mainly on denazification and the support of traditional union leaders.[9] The Manpower Divisions of the two MGs were left to react to ever changing shifts of policy directions and unforeseen German initiatives. In this context the functional equivalent approach was more a tool used to respond to the developing facts than a prescriptive vision. In both Manpower Divisions many key officials were on loan from the American Federation of Labor (AFL), the Congress of Industrial Organizations (CIO), the U.S. National Labor Relations Board (NLRB), and the British Trades Union Congress (TUC) and their affiliates. This meant that pragmatic judgments about the acceptability of German ambitions were made by those who knew a great deal about their own labor traditions but relatively little about German ones.

The Allies struggled to explain how their own industrial relations traditions might be useful in Germany. Both MGs tried to minimize the public relations problem of seeming to impose foreign institutions, aware as they were of Ger-

---

pying armies were actually in place in the summer of 1945, SHAEF had been dissolved. By virtue of the need for unanimity among the four Allies, the ACA, though the de jure government of Germany, was effectively blocked for long stretches of time; see Gunther Mai, *Der allierte Kontrollrat in Deutschland* (Munich: P. Oldenbourg Verlag, 1995).

7. A summary is Laura Reed, "The Roads Not Taken: The U.S. Security Debate over Germany, 1944 – 49" (Ph.D. diss., MIT, 1995).

8. British divides were less consequential; see Ian Turner, "Cold-War Diplomacy: British Policy towards Germany's Role in Europe, 1945 – 49," in *Reconstruction in Post-War Germany*, ed. Turner (Oxford: Berg, 1989).

9. Michael Fichter, *Besatzungsmacht und Gewerkschaften: Zur Entwicklung und Anwendung der US-Gewerkschaftspolitik in Deutschland, 1944 – 48* (Opladen, Germany: Westdeutscher Verlag, 1982), 96 – 99.

man fears flowing from the experience with the Versailles Treaty. Instead, with "Americanization" generally used by Germans as a pejorative, the occupation forces usually justified what I am calling institutional transfer with reference to supposedly universalistic processes such as economic modernization or democratization.[10] General Lucius Clay, the acting U.S. military governor of Germany, was particularly cautious about pushing American practices on the Germans, and he often said that he was unwilling to force Germans to do things not yet achieved in the United States.[11] But this principle could be used not just to tame what Clay saw as his own overeager MG personnel but also to disallow popular German initiatives such as codetermination because, as he said, "American unions seem to survive very well without it."[12] In most domains, including industrial relations, the Americans clearly did prefer to see the Germans reform themselves; the British Military Government, headed by General Brian Robertson, shared this basic orientation. Only where reform was not happening did they intervene.

INSTITUTIONAL TRANSFER IN POLITICAL CONTEXT

If transfer was not a centrally steered grand design, how did it work? I argued in Chapter 2 that the complications of political context make institutional imitation hard to conceptualize. In explaining Germany's post–World War II institutional outcomes, most analysts rely on some combination of the four broad categories of causal forces outlined in Figure 1. The first two boxes refer to factors essentially internal to Germany: the range of traditional interests and the structures created over time, combined with the various lessons learned by those who had lived through the dissolution of Weimar and the disillusion of the Third Reich. The second two boxes refer to factors basically external to Germany: specific Allied policies toward the conquered state and the influence of postwar stabilization, but also more dynamic factors such as growing trade openness, monetary stabilization, Cold War tensions, and rearmament. These "forces" are ideal types, and sophisticated analysts have always drawn on more than one. Even by combining only internal or only external factors, one can easily construct an account—coherent if incomplete—either of continuity or of change. Of course, analysts have assigned widely different weights to the categories, and Figure 1 merely recog-

10. U.S. officials often assumed that the American model had universal applicability if only particularistic interests could be overcome.

11. On Clay's approach, see Barbara Fait, *Demokratische Erneuerung unter dem Sternenbanner: Amerikanische Kontrolle und Verfassunggebung in Bayern 1946* (Düsseldorf: Droste, 1998).

12. Quoted in Carolyn Eisenberg, "The Limits of Democracy: US Policy and the Rights of German Labor, 1945–49," in *America and the Shaping of German Society, 1945–55*, ed. Michael Ermath (Oxford: Berg, 1993), 77.

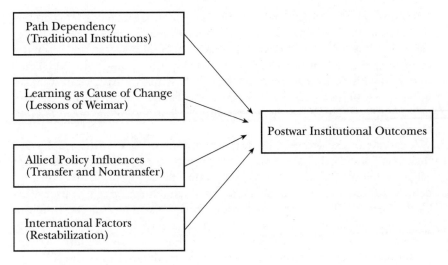

Figure 1. Origins of postwar institutions

nizes the heuristic utility of each factor in all comprehensive discussions of postwar institutional outcomes.

The Allied occupation case enlightens because each of the four categories implies a different story about institutional transfer. Rather than focusing directly on the process of transfer, scholars have usually made one of three other claims about how to characterize institutional change. All are based on important insights, but as the postwar German case reveals, oversimplifying transfer often leads scholars to take these insights to theoretically and empirically unsatisfying conclusions. The three claims revolve around the images of indigenous tradition, blocked transfer, and irrelevant transfer.

The first claim, that of path dependency, is that a cultural or institutional tradition for the arrangement supposedly transferred had *already* existed in the imitating country. Some scholars cite the long history of German federalism to dismiss the U.S. efforts to construct federalism in occupied Germany.[13] Thus, the argument runs, postwar German federalism owes little to outside models. But such arguments work far better in some areas than others.[14] They are most problematic when they imply that existing traditions were retained unchanged or when they can provide only ad hoc explanations for why they were changed.[15] Large and complex modern nations are littered

13. Carl Friedrich, "The Legacies of the Occupation in Germany," *Public Policy* 17 (1968): 7.

14. Indeed, Friedrich restricts his use of the legacies argument to the federalism case and, to a certain extent, judicial review.

15. For example, Germans had had disastrous experiences with both independent *and* state-dominated central banks, but America's apparent success with and clear enthusiasm for the former were crucial in the actual drafting of the *Bundesbank* statutes.

with proposals for institutional redesign. The analytic challenge is to connect these intellectual legacies with explanations of their public or private power bases, legal status, and popular legitimacy. Institutional transfer is often a means for turning minority traditions into majority ones—a crucial change frequently missed by the "legacies" approach. Thus, in many cases it makes sense to see these antecedents as prerequisites that make effective transfer possible rather than as ready-made solutions that obviate any need for imitating foreign practices.

A variant of the indigenous tradition argument is one that emphasizes "learning." If the original claim is that the new was not new at all, the variant suggests that the old was made to work better. By this account, outcomes appearing to result from institutional transfer actually spring from purely German efforts to reform traditional institutions.[16] Nazism was a perversion of German tradition or a monstrous aberration from it which, by the end of the war, had lost its hold on the Germans. Discredited by its own failure, Nazi institutional change was reversed by the Germans themselves (or would have been, had not naive democratization programs been forced upon them), and the economy flourished once it was freed from Allied controls.

What can we make of this line of argument?[17] Certainly, "indigenous" reform is an apt description of *some* policy areas of the occupation, including school reform. There seems little doubt that Weimar elites from most policy areas engaged in both soul searching and lesson drawing. Yet the problems of diversity and voluntarism make indigenous learning a most incomplete explanation for postwar institutional change. For one thing, different German actors drew different lessons from the Weimar and Nazi experiences, and these conflicting visions had to be adjudicated, justified, and implemented. Some lessons had to be forgotten: in the case of trade unions, where there were a number of important institutional continuities from Weimar, one task of this chapter is to show that the Allies prevented some *discontinuities* (based on "learning") which labor leaders expected to achieve. Moreover, since there was no German government for much of the occupation period, the Allies set themselves the task of integrating the lessons learned by diverse groups of German elites into a larger set of domestic and foreign policy priorities. I argue that functional equivalent transfer allowed the Allies to push their own designs, promote some German reform ideals over others, and link individual reforms to broader policies in ways that "voluntaristic" learning could not.

The second of the three claims focuses on the apparent political obstacles to institutional transfer. Some, acknowledging that transfer was tried, argue

---

16. A leading example from the occupation literature is Edward Peterson, *The American Occupation of Germany: Retreat to Victory* (Detroit: Wayne State University Press, 1977).

17. To be fair, research into the occupation was long hampered by the lack of access to MG documents, and this contributed to an inordinate focus on "lessons" learned by German actors.

that it was rejected. They point to instances of Allied failure to persuade the Germans to adopt a particular institutional solution—for example, the short-lived effort to introduce a presidential system of government—or to transfers that were carried out against the combined will of the Germans and reversed after the occupation ended.[18] Here, the process of institutional transfer is treated as an impossibility, so no attempt is made to explain the conditions under which transfer, effective or ineffective, is likely to occur. Further, the focus on the continuity of traditional German institutions after 1945 has often obscured the impact of the Allies or made them appear complicit in a simple "restoration."[19]

The third claim bypasses institutional transfer by maintaining that Germany's political and economic recovery was driven by conditions of macroeconomic expansion and not by particular domestic institutions. Whether the institutions of industrial relations drove economic development or rode on its coattails is an important issue.[20] It cannot be resolved here, but there seems to be little doubt that growth helped legitimate contested institutional changes. As Mary Fulbrook sardonically puts it, the number of Germans who supported democratic views in opinion polls in the 1950s and 1960s "grew in close correlation with the increase in the average weights of ever more satiated Germans."[21] But the intense debates about institutional design took place long *before* that process occurred. Participants certainly acted as if domestic institutions mattered, and differences in cross-national economic performance under the same international conditions give some indirect evidence that they did. And it is simply not the case that any institution could have been transferred to Germany because of the "economic miracle." Local government reforms were changed after the British left; the determined American effort to make chambers of commerce into strictly private bodies was also reversed. Thus, legitimation of transferred institutions is at least partly separate from more general economic conditions (see Chapter 6). More broadly, the fact that international factors clearly mattered hardly implies that domestic institutions did not.

I develop an empirically differentiated picture of the actual process of institutional transfer in post–World War II occupied Germany; doing so rescues from all these arguments key insights that can ultimately help explain the *variation* in transfer outcomes. The process resulted in some true fiascoes but also in some adaptive and legitimate institutions different in important ways from their Weimar antecedents *and* from British and American influences.

---

18. Friedrich, "Legacies," 18.

19. Eberhard Schmidt, *Die Verhinderte Neuordnung, 1945–1952* (Mannheim, Germany: Europäische Verlags-Anstalt, 1970).

20. This debate was sparked by Werner Abelshauser, *Wirtschaft in Westdeutschland, 1945–48: Rekonstruktion und Wachstumsbedingungen in der amerikanischen und britischen Zonen* (Stuttgart: Deutsche Verlags-Anstalt, 1975).

21. See Mary Fulbrook, *The Fontana History of Germany, 1918–1990* (New York: Fontana, 1993).

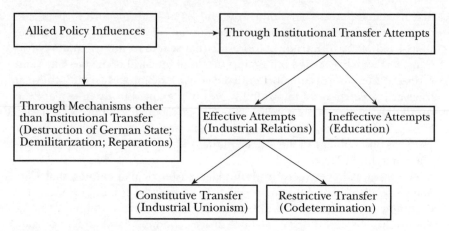

Figure 2. Transfer as a subset of Allied influence

My focus on disagreements among and between Allied and German actors over institution building shows that the Allies' understanding of capitalism and democracy was linked in fundamental ways to their own institutions. Through a combination of power and persuasion they were sometimes able to effect remarkable changes in the goals of German actors and in the form and function of "traditional" German institutions. In this process the ability to recruit German actors who would put their efforts and their credibility behind Allied designs was crucial. The occupation case is further illuminating because it illustrates how institutional conflict and compromise led to social organizations and to institutions that had the capacity for *change* over time. Because they were forged in periods of conflict, these actors and institutions emerged as adaptive.

The claim that U.S. and British occupation forces sometimes relied explicitly on their own models of industrial relations does not mean that *all* the occupation forces' actions were informed by these models. Clearly, they were not. As Figure 2 suggests, institutional transfer was only one tool, although it was an important one, since the military governments could use it to operationalize strategies such as democratization. My task, therefore, is to situate transfer strategies in the context of the lessons of Weimar, traditional structures and interests, and changed international conditions after 1945. To do so, I first describe the reconstruction of institutions representing the interests of labor in the American and British occupied zones.[22] I follow in detail

22. The French had a much less enduring influence on institutional reforms. Their zone was smaller and less economically important than either the British or American zone, and their refusal to accept the Potsdam Agreement's intention to treat Germany as an economic whole meant that they were often absent from discussion of bizonal or all-German institutions.

(1) the debate about the degree of centralization and politicization allowed German labor, and (2) the scope and legal status of codetermination. Thereafter I analyze the reconstruction of business organizations during this period, especially with regard to Allied efforts to promote collective bargaining, to secure "freedom of vocation," and to limit cartels.

LABOR ORGANIZATIONS: WHICH LESSONS, WHICH TRADITIONS?

In both formulating and implementing labor policies, the Allies relied heavily on their understanding of the role of unions in their own societies. Specifically, the British and the Americans urged German unionists to build labor organizations that would be functional equivalents of those of each zone's occupying power.[23] Two key organizational outcomes underpin this claim. First, although the allies were committed to rebuilding unions as a pillar of their democratization efforts, they had a particular type of union in mind: they sought to restrict unions to the pursuit of wages, benefits, and working conditions and to constrain their pursuit of a political program of "economic democracy." Most German union leaders chafed at these restrictions. Some admired British unionism, but few knew much about American unions, and the Allies' persistent bias toward collective bargaining appeared to them a conspiracy against union prerogatives on a host of other issues. Second, German unionists were determined to achieve a more authoritative institutional position in the conduct of the economy after World War II, a position they often called "social codetermination." German labor envisioned it as a step toward self-determination at all levels of the economy, capped by either socialization or corporatist economic management (depending on the faction involved). Under Allied influence, however, codetermination ultimately became an end in and of itself at the firm level.

From the perspective of virtually all German labor leaders, both kinds of restrictions threatened their hopes for more economic democracy.[24] To elements across the spectrum of German labor the moment had appeared ripe for a major transformation of labor's roles in German society. Such a transformation would have had far-reaching institutional implications. That the unions did not realize these ambitions can be attributed in no small part to the occupation forces, which insisted on industrial unionism, tightly controlled the scope of collective bargaining, limited works councils, suspended codetermination and socialization measures passed by German legislatures,

23. Thus, the union movements were different in the two zones when they were joined in 1947–48.

24. An overview of the German left in the postwar period is William Graf, *The German Left since 1945* (Cambridge: Oleander Press, 1976).

controlled union publishing possibilities, influenced the composition of union leadership bodies, and suppressed the antifascist committees. Yet the Allies' use of their own models of industrial organization led neither to the stereotypical apolitical American "business union" orientation nor to British craft union structures. Rather, the clash of Allied policies about functional ends with German unionists' ambitions for increased authority led to novel arrangements.[25] In short, the Allies drew upon their functional models, in conjunction with certain institutional legacies of Weimar, to defeat other Weimar legacies and lessons learned in wartime exile.

The broader aims of occupation officials help explain their use of institutional transfer. They saw unions as potential allies in the democratization of Germany, and the issue was how to maximize this potential. They went about it cautiously. On August 6, 1945, General Dwight D. Eisenhower proclaimed to the German people, "The full freedom to form trade unions and to engage in democratic political activities will be extended rapidly in those areas in which you show a readiness for the healthy exercise of these privileges. Your own actions will determine the time for removing remaining restrictions."[26] What Allied fears lurked behind these restrictions? Communism has been emphasized most, yet it is clearly misleading to see the Allied trade union policy as a simple reflection of anti-Communism.[27] Much more was at stake, including a desire for order and a particular view about democratization. Both "order" and "democratization" were vague enough to direct against Communists, but many of the organizational restrictions targeted fascists and also traditions of authoritarianism inside German trade unions.[28] Social order is a fundamental concern for any occupation force, especially one as inexperienced in "civil affairs" as was the U.S. Army.[29] The widespread attitude among

25. Paradoxically, the intervention of the occupation forces actually drew unions closer in their organizational features to those of the Weimar period than would have been true without the Allies. Johannes Kolb, *Metallgewerkschaften in der Nachkriegszeit* (Cologne: Bund-Verlag, 1983), 123.

26. Quoted in Samuel Liss memo, n.d. (probably November 1945), George Meany Archives, Box 12, folder 04:1, 2, Papers of the CIO International Affairs Division, RG18-002, Silver Spring, Md.

27. The leading revisionist argument, which heavily emphasizes Allied anti-Communism, is Schmidt, *Die Verhinderte Neuordnung*, esp. 34–36, 106–13.

28. Siegfried Mielke, "Der Wiederaufbau der Gewerkschaften," in *Politische Weichenstellung in Nachkriegsdeutschland, 1945–53, Geschichte und Gesellschaft*, ed. Heinrich Winkler (Göttingen: Vandenhoeck & Ruprecht, 1979), 81–83. See also Schmidt, *Die Verhinderte Neuordnung*, 36. Daniel Rogers, *Politics after Hitler: The Western Allies and the German Party System* (New York: New York University Press, 1995), also emphasizes concerns about public order in the licensing of political parties.

29. The army had struggled mightily with issues of public order in its occupation of Italy and was determined not to repeat such mistakes in Germany. JCS 1067, the early foundation for U.S. policy in Germany, had outlawed all political activity there; consequently, the military government exercised close controls over the process of union building. (For text of the Joint Chiefs of Staff document, see, e.g., appendix to Carl Friedrich et al., *American Experiences in Military Government in World War II* [New York: Rinehart, 1948]).

Germans that National Socialism had been a good idea badly carried out was only one indication of a real danger of resurgent fascism or civil unrest.[30] Occupation policy, therefore, demanded that German labor organizations prove their reliability.

To gauge the Allied impact, one first needs some sense of German labor's historical trajectory from Weimar through the Nazi period.[31] Weimar's early industrial relations pillars were four: the 1918 Stinnes-Legien Agreement on collective bargaining, the 1918 legislation on shop committees, the 1918 legislation on collective bargaining agreements and their mediation by the state, and the 1920 agreement on works councils.[32] Collective bargaining made a breakthrough in Germany only after World War I as heavy industries negotiated a variety of issues with trade unionists during the demobilization period.[33] In the wake of the socialist revolution the Stinnes-Legien Agreement recognized trade unions as the official representatives of the workers, legitimated collective bargaining in all branches, called for factory committees in firms with more than fifty employees, and established the eight-hour workday. These factory committees were the progenitors of works councils, which represent workers' interests inside firms but are not formally a part of the trade union.

In December 1918 further legislation laid the foundation for collective bargaining agreements, the possibility of their extension by the state to firms outside the negotiations, and the role of the state in mediating conflicts over wages. This last decision was fateful, for the state assumed a responsibility that overwhelmed its capacities in the late Weimar period: the so-called mandated-wage (*Zwangstarif*) became a symbol of the state's inability to help mediate the core interest conflicts in society. As the trade unions weakened, they came to rely increasingly on this state instrument; conversely, as the employers needed the unions less and less, they launched offensives against the *Zwangstarif* and indeed against the Weimar Republic, most notably in the Ruhr iron strikes of 1928.[34] Thus, private "wage autonomy," because it

30. In surveys of late 1945, 45% of respondents agreed that National Socialism "was a good idea badly carried out"; 41% said it was a bad idea. Moreover, during the next four years the number responding "good idea badly carried out" *rose* about 3% per year (Merritt, *Democracy Imposed*, 96–97).

31. The literature here is vast. A good starting point is the series edited by Gerhard Ritter (currently 12 vols.), *Geschichte der Arbeiter und der Arbeiterbewegung in Deutschland seit dem Ende des 18. Jahrhunderts* (Bonn: J. H. W. Dietz, 1984–   ).

32. For a summary of these different structures, see Walther Müller-Jentsch, "Lernprozesse mit konträren Ausgängen: Tarifautonomie und Betriebsverfassung in der Weimarer und Bonner Republik," *Gewerkschaftliche Monatshefte* 5 (1995): 320–25.

33. On the World War I experience and its relevance for Weimar institutions, see Gerald Feldman, *Army, Industry, and Labor in Germany, 1914–1918* (Princeton: Princeton University Press, 1966).

34. Christfried Seifert, "Die deutsche Gewerkschaftsbewegung in der Weimarer Republik," in *Geschichte der deutschen Gewerkschaftsbewegung*, 3d ed., ed. Frank Deppe et al. (Düsseldorf: Pahl-Rugenstein, 1981), 190–91.

was incomplete, actually burdened the state heavily.[35] The changing balance of power between capital and labor made the institutional framework established near the beginning of Weimar dangerously anachronistic by its end. As Walther Müller-Jentsch pointedly noted, "The system of autonomous collective bargaining was already dead by the time the Nazis officially suspended it."[36]

In part because of disappointment with the way works councils were neutralized by German employers, labor intellectuals sought other ways to democratize capitalism. The notion of *Wirtschaftsdemokratie*, or economic democracy, clearly meant different things to different parts of the labor movement. Common to all conceptions, however, was that formal political democracy had to be augmented with democratic control of the economy.[37] The program, proposed by the Social Democratic Party (SPD) upon its return to power in 1928, has been variously seen as an elaboration of earlier concepts of a corporatist Reich Ecomomic Council, or of the proposals of the union congresses in Breslau (1925) and Hamburg (1928), or as an SPD reaction against the earlier Independent and Communist Party proposals for council democracy, or as a tactic to justify union participation in the modest institutional reforms of Weimar.[38] Whatever the motives, however, the central proposition (which went back to Rudolf Hilferding) was that capitalism had changed its character from *individual* to *organized* capitalism. The result was the possibility of a parliamentary rather than revolutionary transition toward a socialism in which trade unions, alongside the SPD, would play a crucial role in the centralized management of the economy.[39] Advocates of economic democracy called for a multifaceted workers' infiltration of organized capitalism for the purpose of removing economic decisions from the strictly "private sphere."

The Weimar SPD did strengthen unemployment insurance, yet it could advance only very partial legislation toward fulfilling the broader agenda of *Wirtschaftsdemokratie*. This disappointment combined with earlier disappoint-

35. Hans Mommsen, "Das Dilemma der Tarifpolitik: Die Politisierung der industriellen Arbeitsbeziehungen," in *Geschichte als Möglichkeit*, ed. Karsten Rudolph and Christl Wickert (Essen: Klartext, 1995), 218.

36. Müller-Jentsch, "Lernprozesse," 321.

37. For the conception and reality of economic democracy in the late Weimar Republic, see Heinrich Winkler, *Der Schein der Normalitat: Arbeiter und Arbeiterbewegung in der Weimar Republik, 1924 bis 1930*, 2d ed. (Bonn: J. H. W. Dietz, 1988), esp. 606–28.

38. See Seifert, "Die deutsche Gewerkschaftsbewegung," 180–91; William Patch, *Christian Trade Unions in the Weimar Republic, 1918–1933* (New Haven: Yale University Press, 1985), 146–47; David Abraham, "Economic Democracy as a Labor Alternative to the Growth Strategy in Weimar Germany," in *The Political Economy of West Germany*, ed. Andrei Markovits (New York: Praeger, 1982).

39. Thus, with the rise of the economic democracy ideal, the SPD downplayed calls for socialization and increased its opposition to state regulation of trusts. Fritz Naphtali, *Wirtschaftsdemokratie* (Berlin: Verlags-Gesellschaft des ADGB, 1928).

ments on works councils and on the ability of state arbitration to promote desirable and sustainable collective bargaining outcomes.[40] On top of the Weimar setbacks came German labor's bitter experience in the Nazi period: forced union dissolution into the Deutsche Arbeitsfront (DAF), imprisonment of labor leaders, the transformation of works councils into *Vertrauensräte*, the dismantling of unemployment insurance, the significant extension of working hours in a wartime economy.[41] All these grievances left deep impressions on German labor.[42] Whatever their internal divisions, most wings of the postwar labor movement shared a strong sense that the time for an institutional new beginning had arrived. That new beginning would require not only the elaboration of old concepts under new political conditions but also the development of ambitions never before realized. To this end, a wide variety of concepts of labor participation became important in the wartime thinking of German trade unionists.[43] These concepts, though often vague, involved an insistence that labor have legitimate institutional prerogatives at the highest levels of society as well as the nuts-and-bolts level of economic management.

Rebuilding Unions: The Focus on Collective Bargaining

In looking at questions of union structure and function, one must recall the difficult situation of German labor in 1945.[44] The immediate material concerns that dominated the day-to-day activities of the German population also shaped the tasks of union building, since the unions had to develop organizations that could speak to at least some of the immediate problems. The destruction of German cities, combined with the huge flows of refugees from eastern territories, had resulted in a serious housing shortage. In cities such as Hamburg, Bremen, Dortmund, and Cologne some 50 to 70% of apartments had been destroyed. In the American and British zones there were about 23% fewer dwellings in 1945 than in 1939, although within two years

40. Detlev Peukert, *Die Weimarer Republik: Krisenjahre der klassischen Moderne* (Frankfurt: Suhrkamp, 1987).

41. In the period after January 30, 1933, union leaders maneuvered to reach an accord with the National Socialist Party. These attempts to "prevent organizational death by committing political suicide" concluded on May 2 for the Allgemeiner Deutscher Gewerkschaftsbund (ADGB) and on June 24 for the Christian unions: Michael Schneider, *Unterm Hakenkreuz: Arbeiter und Arbeiterbewegung 1933 bis 1939* (Bonn: J. H. W. Dietz, 1999).

42. My formulation does not deny that some workers benefited from Nazi policies; my point here is simply that as the war ended, the significant disadvantages labor had suffered came to dominate the evaluations of surviving labor leaders. See Dan Silverman, *Hitler's Economy: Nazi Work Creation Programs, 1933–1936* (Cambridge: Harvard University Press, 1998).

43. Siegfried Mielke and Peter Rütters, "Die DAF: Ein Organisationsmodell für den Neuaufbau der Gewerkschaften nach 1945?" *Gewerkschaftliche Monatshefte* 5 (1995): 305.

44. This paragraph and the next draw on Siegfried Mielke's introduction to *Organisatorischer Aufbau der Gewerkschaften, 1945–1949*, ed. Mielke (Cologne: Bund-Verlag, 1987), 28–32.

Table 2. Trade union membership development in the U.S. zone, 1945–48

	Bavaria	Hessen	Würtemberg-Baden	Bremen	Total
Dec. 1945	95,000	40,000	122,000	6,000	263,000
Dec. 1946	359,000	300,000	291,000	63,000	1,013,000
Dec. 1947	647,214	371,126	399,629	88,844	1,506,813
Sept. 1948	773,949	409,586	443,118	103,544	1,730,197
Density June 1948	32.5%	36.0%	41.0%	50.1%	37.0%

Source: Matthew Kelly, "The Reconstruction of the German Trade Union Movement." Reprinted with permission from *Political Science Quarterly*, vol. 64, no. 1 (1949), pp. 40–41.

the population of the two zones had increased by about 20% as a result of immigration that substantially exceeded war deaths. Officially, food consumption stood at 1,550 calories per day, but many Germans were eating much less as General Clay struggled with Washington for funds to feed a hungry population.

If destruction drove some parts of a union agenda, low production threatened other parts. Production had been halted in many factories, and in the spring of 1945 it stood at some 12% of 1936 levels in the U.S. zone and 15% in the British zone. These figures rose to around 30% in the first quarter of 1946, and to 50% and 37%, respectively, by the end of that year.[45] The combination of low production and the loss of many blue-collar males in the war confronted the unions with a difficult membership situation, one compounded by the entry of refugees into local labor markets. Refugees posed new organizing challenges for the unions and also reduced union bargaining power by slackening labor markets. Moreover, union organization was hampered by the absence of higher levels of German political authority, as the Allies did not allow the unions to grow at a rate faster than the state. With France utterly committed to decentralized state structures, this limitation on union organization was very significant. In addition, local MG authorities in Germany often placed bureaucratic obstacles in the way of trade unionists, making application processes exercises in strict formality.

Nevertheless, as Tables 2 and 3 show, membership grew rapidly in the newly constituted unions. By September 1948 membership in the U.S. zone was 1,730,197, representing a union density among all salaried workers of 37% and among all "employable" persons registered at labor offices of 24%. The corresponding figures for the British zone were 2,547,243 members, or 27.1% of the employable population.[46]

45. Only near the end of military occupation did it reach 1936 levels, and real wages remained below 1936 levels until the mid-1950s.
46. In the Soviet zone the numbers were 3,675,900 (49.7%); in the French, 402,400 (16%). In each case, figures exclude membership in Berlin. Matthew Kelly, "The Reconstruction of the German Trade Union Movement," *Political Science Quarterly* 64 (1949): 40–41.

Table 3. Trade union membership development in the British zone, 1946

	Hamburg	Hanover	North Rhine	Westfalen	Schleswig-Holstein	Total
Jan. 1946	103,171	37,593				140,765
April 1946	138,847	183,332	301,366	25,486	16,857	655,888
June 1946	141,996	198,288	311,265	84,647	24,007	760,203

Source: Monthly report of the Control Commission for Germany (British Element), No. 1, June 1946, in Joseph Keenan Papers, lot 75, box 2, folder 8, Catholic University of America, Washington, D.C.

Manpower officials in both MGs watched with satisfaction as union membership levels grew. Yet with this growth came questions about what kind of union movement was being built. Even before organizational density climbed, wartime concerns about the vulnerability of German unions to Communist or fascist influences mingled with postwar concerns that the MG keep its monopoly on political authority in Germany, as mandated in JCS 1067. Consequently, the Allies imposed tight restrictions on trade unions, restrictions whose effect was to channel union activity in certain directions while foreclosing other possibilities.

To this point, I have suggested that the concept of Allied institutional transfer can offer a fuller account of processes of institutional change than can overreliance on the concept of learning on the part of German elites. My claim has been that institutional transfer, rather than being a story about the "power of ideas" (again, American-style labor relations were mysterious to most German unionists of the time), was one of "ideas backed by power." And yet the unlimited *formal* authority of the MGs had very real *practical* limits, obliging them to cultivate de facto partnerships with certain German leaders and organizations. The transfer concept privileges state policy elites, for it is their efforts to codify imitation through law that leads to a case of attempted institutional transfer. Of course, if the lessons of Weimar learned by German leaders informed their actions and their ambitions, one might wonder how to separate the learning of German leaders from the teachings of the Allies. My answer is that the utility of the institutional transfer concept grows as the gulf widens between state (here, MG) and societal (here, German labor leadership) preferences.

I begin where that gulf is its narrowest. Two organizational options for labor—the return to separate unions for different political affiliations (like the Weimar *Richtungsgewerkschaften*) and the continuation of the DAF structure of the Nazis—were rejected by both the Allies and the majority of German unionists. From the American perspective the Weimar pattern of separate unions for separate political movements was disconcerting. Joseph Keenan, longtime secretary of the Chicago AFL and General Clay's deputy for labor affairs in the Organization of Military Government, U.S. Zone (OMGUS), later recalled, "There were four unions: social democrats, Christian democrats, . . . the *Einheit* [unitary] unions, and then there were the communists. . . . I went to Clay and said, 'Well, General, this is a mix up, and I would like to reorganize these unions along the lines in the United States. They have these four different political unions which is not just right.' Well, he [Clay] said, go ahead."[47]

The social engineering implied by Keenan was simply never needed, however. German labor leaders wanted one unified union movement to avoid the fragmentation that had made labor's resistance to fascism so ineffective during the Weimar Republic. Thus, whereas in the Weimar period the social democratic unions had linkages with the SPD, the Christian union federation with the Catholic Center and other bourgeois parties, and the Hirsch-Dunker unions with the German Democratic Party, virtually all unionists agreed in 1945 that strict party affiliations should be ended. This consensus against party affiliation did not require Anglo-American models (indeed, TUC–Labour Party connections in Britain were and are tighter than any such links in post–World War II Germany). At most, it is possible that American ideals helped strengthen the German rejection of the *Richtungsgewerkschaften* and sent a discouraging message to those who pondered reviving them.[48]

The decision against reforming the DAF was somewhat more controversial, so the institutional transfer concept is more useful here. Although decisively rejected by the Allies, DAF features still functioned for a time as a kind of conceptual building block for many of the German union leaders who were rebuilding regional unions in the early months after the war.[49] Fritz Tarnow was probably the strongest supporter of the conversion of the DAF into a trade union organization, having begun the discussion as early as 1939 in Sweden. But this and his later variants of the plan were generally opposed by the majority of the other exile leaders. The anti-Communist Tarnow saw in the DAF a mechanism for preventing a Communist takeover of the union movement by capturing its organizational high ground for social democrats.[50] Several other union leaders, including Hans Böckler, Albin Karl, Gustav Schiefer, and Markus Schleicher, even if they rejected the DAF itself as an appropriate foundation, found some of its organizational features interesting. These

47. Keenan interview with George Hrenuni, Joseph Keenan Papers, lot 75, box 1, folder 2, 9–10. Catholic University of America, Washington, D.C.

48. Since noncontroversies leave thin paper trails, evidence on this point is indirect. Certainly, anti-Communist leaders such as the AFL's Irving Brown worried well into the occupation that political divides might reappear. See Brown to Jay Lovestone, April 7, 1947, in Jay Lovestone Papers, Meany Archives, box 11, folder 7. In the French-occupied Saar some unions linked to parties *were* established, and today the Saar is a stronghold of Christian trade unionism in the FRG.

49. Fichter (*Besatzungsmacht*, 76–80) suggests that SHAEF might have accepted a reformed DAF structure until the Morgenthau Plan made such a policy unthinkable.

50. See Dieter Lange, "Fritz Tarnow's Pläne zur Umwandlung der faschistischen Deutschen Arbeitsfront in Gewerkschaften," *Zeitschrift für Geschichtswissenschaft* 24 (1976): 150–67.

features included the centralized organizational design augmented by *non-autonomous* industrial groups. The central organization would control union finances and would have very wide competence vis-à-vis the industrial groups and regional organizations. Some considered the possibility of mandatory membership (with dues to be paid by the employer), arguing that mandatory membership reflected democratic principles "because the working conditions generated by union activity are a benefit to all."[51] Although one motivation here was the need to finance the organization, it was also an effort to deny free riders the "fruits of union labor." Another motivation was clearly the hope of using mandatory dues to prevent competing unions from appearing alongside the "unitary" union toward which the several leaders were clearly working.[52] But whatever the outcome of the continuing debate between proponents of industrial and unitary unionism, the Allies were unwilling to accept this "lesson" learned by some Weimar labor leaders about the costs of division and therefore unwilling to accept a reformed DAF.

In the DAF case the weight of Allied authority was significant, yet Allied reliance on any sort of "functional equivalent model" remains unclear. In order to see the real significance of transfer, one must back away from the DAF tree and look at the labor forest. The three most important Allied influences on German union organizations were the limitation of unions to collective bargaining functions, the choice of industrial rather than unitary structures, and the procedures adopted for union organization. Anglo-American models and MG influence were important in all three decisions.

The end of party-affiliated unions did not mean that trade unions wanted to end their political activity. Yet although the large majority of German trade unionists were committed to some form of economic democracy, the Allies proposed fairly strong divisions between economic and political activities and rejected specific attempts to "democratize" economic relations. Allied policy encouraged unions to focus all their organizational efforts instead on collective bargaining, which, as AFL internationalists such as Irving Brown constantly claimed to European labor leaders, had secured for American workers the highest living standard in the world.[53] Keenan expressed this policy in

---

51. Gottlob Sigmund, quoted in Mielke and Rütters, "Die DAF," 305. A small group around Adam Stegerwald was also attracted by the notion of labor unions as a quasi-public association like the chambers of commerce and industry; for the historical roots of this line of thought, see Patch, *Christian Trade Unions*.

52. Following convention, I translate this now extinct version of the *Einheitsgewerkschaft* as "unitary union." Another contemporary description of this proposed form was *eine allgemeine Gewerkschaft*, "one general union." Although contemporary German unions are also referred to as *Einheitsgewerkschaften*, because they include all workers in a sector within one union, the following pages demonstrate that this form of "industrial unionism" was an *alternative* to unitary unionism in the post–World War II debate.

53. On July 10, 1951, the Marshall Plan administration's William Foster testified to the House Foreign Affairs Committee that U.S. income per capita was about $1,700 per annum, whereas in

a 1946 letter to the CIO's James Carey: "The more responsibility we put on the trade unions to secure their own objectives by economic strength rather than by legislation, which had been the practice in Germany for many years, the better it will be for the working people. By the old method, they were dependent more on the passage of laws than on their own ability to achieve improved working conditions, higher wages and every day [sic] functions of trade unions."[54] In addition to the material benefits of collective bargaining for workers (secured in the United States as a right almost two decades later than in Germany), New Deal and wartime American experience with collective bargaining suggested its value in stabilizing wages and maintaining purchasing power.[55] The same concern with protecting labor's right to free collective bargaining occupied Britain's Labour government, which was backing away from the quasi-corporatist Joint Productivity Councils forged during wartime.[56]

If there was Anglo-American agreement that legitimate union activity should be centered in the economic domain, the Americans took the lead in promoting rapid party development to dominate the political domain. General Clay especially pushed the parties to develop quickly, even when the wisdom of his decision to set local elections for early 1946 was doubted by his own staff and by many party leaders in Germany.[57] As the parties grew in importance as a locus of political decision making, union hopes for a central political role began to fade.[58] Both MGs justified their narrower visions of labor's role in rebuilding German society with the claim that unions would need flexibility in bargaining for changes in wages and working conditions. The implication was that unions should focus on private-sector bargaining and eschew legislative goals, which might prove inappropriate for society's further development. This understanding of unions frustrated German labor's agenda for inclusion in a broad range of questions about the society and the economy through local, regional, and national levels of an "economic council." The rapid reintroduction of party competition and the building of

---

France it was still only about $525. In Germany, annual income remained below $300 per capita at this point.

54. Keenan to James Carey, July 30, 1946, Meany Archives, box 12, folder 03.

55. Christopher Tomlins, *The State and the Unions: Labor Relations, the Law, and the Organized Labor Movement in America, 1880–1960* (Cambridge: Cambridge University Press, 1985), 99–102.

56. Jim Tomlinson, "Productivity, Joint Consultation, and Human Relations in Post-War Britain," in *Management, Labour, and Industrial Politics in Modern Europe*, ed. Joseph Melling and Alan McKinlay (Brookfield, Vt.: Edward Elgar, 1996), 29–37.

57. See the diary entries for September 2 and 26, 1945, and January 20, 1946, in James Pollock, *Besatzung und Staatsaufbau nach 1945: Occupation Diary and Private Correspondence, 1945–1948* (Munich: R. Oldenbourg, 1994), 80, 86, 147.

58. See Gewerkschaftlichen Zonensekretariats (British Zone, Abt. Wirtschaftspolitik), "Wirstchaftsdemokratie—Vorschlaege zum Aufbau einer wirtschaflichen Selbstverwaltung," Düsseldorf, January 1947, reprinted in *Nachkriegsdeutschland, 1945–1949*, ed. Peter Bucher (Darmstadt: Wissenschaftliche Buchgesellschaft, 1990), 263–71.

state legislatures quickly outpaced the growth of unions. Most factions within the unions supported parliamentary democracy, but their expectation that it would be augmented with "economic democracy" was mistaken.

To the extent that the focus on collective bargaining was designed to ensure that wage setting was not the responsibility of the state, there was no disagreement between occupiers and occupied. As in the matter of the *Richtungsgewerkschaften*, Allied aims dovetailed smoothly with this lesson of Weimar learned by the German social partners. Allied Control Authority's Law 35 set the basic framework, in which it was clear that responsibility for wage setting would lie with the social partners alone.[59] The FRG's 1949 law on collective bargaining clearly attributed responsibility for mediation to the social partners themselves, a principle reinforced by subsequent decisions of the high court.[60]

The real issue was whether collective bargaining would be all that unions could do. The Allies' exclusive focus on bargaining was contradictory as well as unpopular. Unions had a difficult time establishing themselves as economic actors: first, because the MGs controlled wages and work time along with prices, and second, because firms appeared so weak that unions feared that an aggressive push for economic benefits would cause the firms to fail.[61] When OMGUS authorized wage increases of up to 15% in April 1948, Clay allowed the unions to use collective bargaining to arrive at the actual figure, writing, apparently without irony, that now "German trade unions had a real issue in which they could represent their members in negotiations with employers."[62] Both MGs insisted that the unions act the way a "normal" union should, even if times were so obviously abnormal.[63] Unions were told to act "flexibly" by forgoing institutionalized legal protections (in light of the "unusual nature" of the tasks of reconstruction) but, at the same time, to orient their organizational construction around the normal tasks of labor. The two

---

59. A proposal by authorities of the embryonic German state (Economic Council) in late 1948 for a wage "conciliation law" was rejected by both the unions and the employers associations as too interventionist. Instead, each association would stand behind the deals it had made rather than blaming the state for faulty mediation. In this way, the inevitable friction of economic change would not destabilize the national economy. George Phillip Dietrich, "The Trade Union Role in the Reconstruction of Germany" (OMGUS) Visiting Expert Series 6 (March 1949), 16.

60. Helmut Liesegang, *Gewerkschaften in der Budesrepublik Deutschland* (Berlin: Walter de Gruyter, 1975). In practice, the state has made any number of threats that a failure of the social partners to solve their own problems might lead to state intervention.

61. Fichter, *Besatzungsmacht*, 260–64. Chapter 5 discusses a related dilemma after reunification in 1990 in which unions chose differently on the wage pressure problem.

62. Lucius Clay, *Decision in Germany* (New York: Doubleday, 1950), 298. After the end of wage controls with ACA Ordinance 58 on November 3, 1948, collective bargaining once again became a meaningful acitivity for German unions. In December 1948, Ordinance 68 permitted the extension of a collective bargaining agreement to the entire industry. But as U.S. officials noted, limiting recourse to this tool encouraged unions to commit organizational resources to developing institutions of collective bargaining; see Dietrich, *The Trade Union Role*, 13–14.

63. See Liss memo, 12.

MGs, with their AFL, CIO, TUC, and NLRB personnel, had specific ideas about what was normal.

But what did German labor leaders want? The two principal competing union models in post–World War II Germany were industrial and unitary unionism.[64] The key principle of *industrial* unionism was that one union would organize all the workers in a single sector.[65] These industrial unions would be largely autonomous actors with control of policy, wage bargaining, strikes, and finances. The concept of *unitary* unionism was that each geographical area (rather than each industrial sector) would have one union, which would then contain industrial or craft groups. Policy autonomy and the control of finances would clearly lie with the central body, as had been the case with Sweden's Landesorganisationen (LO) Congress (established in 1941) or Austria's Österreichischer Gewerkschaftsbund (ÖGB) (founded in April 1945).[66] Advocates of unitary unionism foresaw local, regional, and ultimately national levels of operation. Among both the Germans and the Allies there were proponents of each form, but Allied policy quickly and clearly came to favor industrial unions, whereas unitary unions had majority support among Germans. Again, as the divide between competing Allied and German aims grew larger, the concept of transfer became central.

German proponents justified unitary unions mostly with reference to concrete challenges: the concentration of labor's forces to push for economic democracy and prevent future divide-and-conquer tactics, the hope of a powerful counterweight to the Communist unions in the Soviet zone, and the realization of social functions such as educating youth and retraining adults in democratic concepts. Yet if new challenges invited new structures, old concerns about concentrated authority seemed especially relevant in the immediate aftermath of Nazi centralization. The Allies variously worried that unitary structures could be taken over by fascists or by Communists, or simply used as bases of political power in their own right. Proponents of unitary centralization defended their plans against these charges of excessive power with an argument that Johannes Kolbe characterized as the "tyranny of proven

64. I treat supporters of craft unionism—*Berufsgruppen*—as advocates of industrial structures. Although advocates of craft unionism had long struggled against industrial unionism and its "one plant, one union" philosophy, the new enthusiasm among German union leaders for centralization quickly turned these old adversaries into allies.

65. Thus, organized workers in Germany's auto sector are members of the metalworking union, whether they stamp fenders, fit windshields, or make seats.

66. For a discussion of the centralized power of the Swedish LO federation over its industrial and craft union members, see Lars Ekdahl and Alf Johansson, "The End of a Historical Compromise? The Labour Movement and the Changing Balance of Power in Swedish Industry, 1930–1990," in Melling and McKinlay, *Management, Labour, and Industrial Politics*, 81–85. On the strongly centralized Austrian trade unions, see Ferdinand Karlhofer and Anton Pelinka, "Austria," in *European Labor Unions*, ed. Joan Campbell (Westport, Conn.: Greenwood, 1992), 17–19.

democrats."[67] Their claim was that trade union leaders, more than officials of other organizations, could be trusted not to abuse authority.

These leaders had little chance to test their claim. The prevention of a central unitary union organization was one outcome of an alliance between occupation authorities and German proponents of independent industrial unions. The principal tool of both MGs was the issuing of licenses to individual unions. They maintained strict licensing procedures, and several existing unions reestablished in the immediate postwar period were dismantled for not following the rules.[68] Yet although the Allies made no secret of their strong preference for industrial unionism, both MGs allowed many unified unions to form, especially in 1945. The explanation of this apparent contradiction lay in a second aspect of the Allies' view of what legitimated a union— namely, shop elections—and reflected Anglo-American understandings of organizational democracy. OMGUS especially laid substantial importance on the legitimation of unions in individual firms through shop elections and established detailed processes with strong similarities to NLRB certification elections. Works council representatives elected by secret ballots were allowed to construct a committee to apply formally for recognition of a union at firm level (and this step simultaneously disallowed an application in that locality by those *not* connected to a firm). The Americans insisted that the workers then express their desire for a union by acquiring written support from 25% of their numbers.[69] After submitting their application to OMGUS, local officials could begin building the union by recruiting members, electing a board, and generating a program. Generally, only then would OMGUS grant approval, and this process of certification had to be repeated for firm-level unions to join together in either industrial or unitary organizations. During 1945 many unitary unions were thus certified.

In the British zone the process was similar, and strict adherence to requirements meant that many union foundings were delayed and several declared void.[70] Former Weimar unionists who were active in establishing unions clearly struggled with the regulations. For application purposes these leaders generally built a committee from networks that had remained intact

67. "Herrschaft der bewährten Demokraten," quoted in Mielke and Rütters, "Die DAF," 309.

68. Fichter, *Besatzungsmacht*, 112–18; Rolf Steininger, "England und die deutsche Gewerkschaftsbewegung, 1945–46," *Archiv für Sozialgeschichte* 18 (1978): 89–90. American unions had their own ambivalent experience with state licensing of trade unions, especially when the Wagner Act replaced the National Labor Board with the NLRB. On these battles, see Tomlins, *The State and the Unions*, 103–47.

69. In NLRB elections the administrative threshold for a so-called showing of interest has historically been 30%.

70. Franz Hartmann, "Entstehung und Entwicklung der Gewerkschaftsbewegung in Niedersachsen nach dem Zweiten Weltkrieg," (Ph.D. diss., Göttingen, 1977), 252–60; Mielke, "Der Wiederaufbau," 77–78.

at home and abroad over the fascist period. Then, while the MG investigated their application, they went to work recruiting members and building a program. As in the U.S. zone the process of legitimating union organizations reflected not only ideas about democratization but the actual practices in the society of the occupying power. As one skeptical MG official noted to a TUC officer in 1945, the elections in the British zone involved a "miniature parliamentary election complete with nomination by eight sponsors, election of a returning officer, division of the factory into constituencies and a number of other purely English practices."[71] The Allies' restrictive regulations forced unionists to spend considerable time on the internal democracy of their organizations, occasioning delays that were consequential because they occurred while the political power of German capital was at a low ebb. By the time organizational prerequisites were fulfilled, the domestic environment for programmatic changes had grown much less hospitable to labor.[72]

I have been portraying the disputes about the function and form of German unions in terms of "the Allies" versus "most German unionists." Yet during the first year of the occupation the key disputes within the German trade union movement about form and function were actually reproduced inside OMGUS itself. This is hardly surprising, given the wide range of views within the U.S. labor movement and the remarkable evolution in labor practices between the New Deal years and the 1947 Taft-Hartley Act. AFL officials in Germany, working closely with several officials from the Manpower Division of OMGUS, pushed for "free trade unionism." The OMGUS officials also enjoyed the active support of George Meany, Irving Brown, and James Riddleberger back in the United States. The AFL position, which emphasized apolitical business unionism and strong control by unions over works councils, also advocated U.S. support for labor leaders from the old Weimar union federation. The AFL saw these older union leaders, who had often lived in exile during the Nazi regime and had established their own contacts with the American, British, and Scandinavian labor movements, as the foundation for a new union movement.[73] And the AFL linked the programmatic content of free trade unionism to a top-down approach to constructing labor organizations. An example is the Württembergischer Gewerkschaftsbund, founded in May 1945 by a handful of social democratic and Christian trade union functionaries. It consisted of a central body of fifty to one hundred officials who established a network of local and industry-affiliated unions through which they recruited members.

---

71. E. A. Bramalls letter to H. Tracey, September 15, 1945, reprinted in appendix to Steininger, "England und die deutsche Gewerkschaftsbewegung," 98.

72. Mielke and Rütters, "Die DAF," 25.

73. Julia Angster, "Konsenskapitalismus und Sozialdemokratie: Zur ideellen Westorientierung der deutschen Arbeiterbewegung, 1945–1965" (Ph.D. diss., University of Tübingen, 1999).

Neither the free trade unionism approach nor the dependence on Weimar labor leaders was uncontroversial. Influential members of the Manpower Division, including its leader, Major General Frank McSherry, advocated instead a grassroots approach.[74] Doubting that the very union leaders who had proved themselves unable to help the nation resist fascism the first time would be able to do so the next time, they proposed that the labor movement build substantially on the local antifascist committees—the so-called antifas—that had grown up in the last weeks of the war.[75] The antifascist committees and shop locals themselves did not share the widespread notion that only a centralized labor movement could protect workers' rights. But although the Allies made occasional use of the antifas in denazification efforts, the MGs (and SHAEF before them) also distrusted them as potential competitors to political parties. The antifas, organized in at least eighty cities in the U.S. and British zones, had been immediately limited by the Allies to apolitical functions inside individual firms, where they made up the bulk of the movement for grassroots unionism.[76] As articulated by their key proponent in the Manpower Division, Mortimer Wolf, the grassroots position

> turned upon the use of the elective, rather than the appointive, process in trade union organization. It contemplated that the German people, including workers, required elementary exercises in the use of democratic processes at the lowest and simplest levels; that in the formation of trade unions, popular initiative and participation should be encouraged; that for the emergence of democracy in Germany a new elective leadership was required, which might prove a liberalizing influence and source of leadership beyond the trade union field; and that the indefinite continuance of an appointed leadership would necessarily impede the development of a democratic trade union movement.[77]

State Department officials and the supporters of free trade unionism in the AFL rejected a strict requirement that all union certifications grow out of shop elections and sought successfully to open up some possibility that trade unionists could restart locals prior to developing firm-based organizations. But they argued that since the personnel who could start such unions

74. The best account of the "free trade union" versus "grassroots unionism" dispute is Fichter, *Besatzungsmacht*, 76–89, 128–75.

75. See Lutz Niethammer et al., eds., *Arbeiterinitiative 1945: Antifaschistische Ausschüsse und Reorganisation der Arbeiterbewegung in Deutschland* (Wuppertal, Germany: Peter Hammer, 1976). The group of officers so inclined enjoyed support outside OMGUS from Sidney Hillman of the CIO; Ernest Bevin, leader of the Labour Party in Britain, was also supportive of the grassroots ideal. See Steve Fraser, *Labor Will Rule* (New York: Free Press, 1991), 550–52.

76. Niethammer et al., *Arbeiterinitiative 1945*, 639–40; for figures on antifa density, see 721 (map).

77. Mortimer Wolf memo to J. H. Hilldring, February 1946, reprinted in *Quellen zur Geschichte der deutschen Gewerkschaftsbewegung*, 6:198–202.

were often returning from exile and were unknown in the firms, the grass-roots demands were unrealistic and would promote Communism. A bitter intra-division fight developed around the free trade union faction's approval of the aforementioned Württembergischer Gewerkschaftsbund. Officials from that faction argued that it would be unfair to force the organization's dismantling, even though its earlier French certification clearly contradicted OMGUS procedures. Wolf, in communications back to Washington, fed the fire by accusing the works councilors of being merely "self-appointed union officials" and comparing the union elections in Stuttgart to DAF elections under the Nazis. Not until late 1945 and early 1946 did the free trade union faction persuade General Clay to replace the OMGUS officers who supported the grassroots position. The key factors in the demise of the grassroots position were external pressures brought to bear on Clay by AFL and congressional leaders and internal contradictions of efforts to cede key areas of political activity to the labor movement (once its democratic bona fides were established through elections) at a time when the MG was still consolidating its own authority.[78]

Yet OMGUS still faced a dilemma: the Weimar unionists who benefited from the victory of the free trade union backers over the grassroots faction had their own ideas about institutional design, and these visions often did not match those of OMGUS. Older Weimar union leaders generally did not share the victorious free trade union faction's enthusiasm for independent industrial associations rather than a unified union with strong central authority over relatively weak industrial, craft, and regional groups. An opinion poll of union members conducted in late 1946 by the OMGUS Information Control Division found that 69% preferred unitary unions against only 22% for industrial unions. Among new members the proportions were even more striking: 75% versus 12%.[79] Still, not all local union organizations developed as unitary locals, although clearly most did. In Bavaria, as in the other *Länder* (states) of the U.S. zone, some had been developed around one principle and some around the other.[80] The Munich, Augsburg, Regensburg, and Würz-burg local organizations were all built as federations of industrial unions. In addition, some that followed unified unionism as their organizational form also contained strong industrial unions as members. Such was the case, for example, in Hof, Fürth, Ingolstadt, and Rosenheim. In short, industrial unionism, though a minority tradition, was a robust one, and under Allied tutelage and control it became an increasingly acceptable option to erstwhile proponents of unitary unions.

---

78. Fichter, *Besatzungsmacht*, 171–75.
79. Ibid., 197.
80. Siegfried Mielke, "Grenzen und Motive der Einflussnahme der amerikanischen Militär-regierung auf den Aufbau und die Organisationsstruktur der Gewerkschaften in der amerika-nischen Besatzungszone," *Internationale Wissenschaftliche Korrespondenz zur Geschichte der deutschen Arbeiterbewegung* 14 (1978): 187–202.

Institutional transfer, I have argued, is not a decision but a process—a feedback loop of policy decisions, societal countermoves, and adaptations. Making the Allied position in support of industrial unionism more palatable were some problematic experiences with unified unionism. For example, in Bavaria the unified Bayerischer Gewerkschaftsbund, established in March 1947, was designed to have control of union finances and even to pay all the full-time employees of the subordinate unions out of its own budget. Neither principle proved unshakable, however: four unions negotiated successfully for exemptions to the policy of central financial control, and at least two other small unions hired their own officials because of concerns that the central organization was neglecting their sector's needs. A similar confrontation with difficulties inherent in unified unions occurred in Württemberg-Baden, where, by the time of the first *Land*-wide conference in December 1946, the central organizational authority had been so much reshuffled to the advantage of the industrial unions that only one-third of the funds were still flowing to the center.[81] Starting in 1946, with the end of its internal dispute, OMGUS plus AFL and CIO officials offered strong and constant support for industrial unionism and material support in the form of newsprint and "care packages" for its German advocates.[82] In 1945–47 they increasingly found converts to their principles. Thus, industrial unionism in the U.S. zone was introduced through a long, slow construction of an alliance between OMGUS officials and an ever growing minority of German union leaders. Without OMGUS intervention, U.S. zone unions would have looked very different. Nevertheless, the American approach to transfer took a long time and relied on German partners.

The British influence on the decision for industrial unionism was more focused but also depended on minority voices. Franz Spliedt, who headed the industrial union movement in Hamburg, was the strongest supporter of the British MG in this endeavor. Although many of the unitary unions founded in Germany were motivated by such pragmatic considerations as organizational economies of scale in localities with few members, the North-Rhine and Lower Saxonian unitary movements were clearly driven by ideological conviction. As their leaders articulated time and again, they considered the unitary union the only organization that could concentrate working-class interests to prevent any return to fascism and to push toward a new economic and social order. Once that new order was established, there would be much less need for classic trade union functions such as strikes against particular firms or sectors. The unitary union was also thought to help represent class interests in major social issues of the moment, such as housing and food. As

81. Ibid., 192–93.
82. The many notes from German unionists received by AFL officials combine expressions of gratitude and entreaties for more; see, e.g., "Care Packages," 1947–48, Lovestone Papers, Meany Archives, box 17.

in the American zone, only a minority of trade union officials agreed with the MG that such a union organization would be incompatible with democracy, initiative, and a lack of bureaucracy.[83] Throughout the fall of 1945 the British MG attempted to dissuade German unionists, especially Hans Böckler in North-Rhine and Albin Karl in Lower Saxony, from the unitary approach. As noted, the primary mechanism for doing so was the imposition of legal restrictions on union organization. As long as unitary unionism remained the guiding principle, few new unions were allowed, and many existing ones were disbanded. Böckler, Karl, and many others were confronted with the possibility that insisting on a particular organization would mean that the movement simply could not go forward.

The other key MG tool turned out to be the Trades Union Congress. In the fall of 1945 the TUC, to that point a peripheral participant in trade union policy, was approached about going on a "mission" to the British zone.[84] The MG objective was to convince TUC officials that German preferences for unitary unionism not only were incompatible with democratic development or effective interest representation but also reflected cultural inclinations toward authoritarian organizations. The TUC delegates, after a handful of stops inside the zone, fell into line behind the MG and wrote on November 27 to Hans Böckler of their strong disapproval of the unitary union. Böckler read the letter to other North-Rhine union leaders, remarking, "I don't see any other choice besides, with a heavy heart, to drop our plans and to orient ourselves along the advice of our foreign friends."[85] On December 7, 1945, the North-Rhine union officials officially though reluctantly abandoned efforts to build the unitary union. Böckler noted that it "was time to finally get recognition so that we can move forward with our work. How can we do this? It will be possible if we change our plans. This means that we must for now build autonomous unions without losing sight of our longer term plans."[86] But his obvious hope of revisiting the issue was dashed; although Albin Karl held out for some time in Hanover, the unitary union was finished in the British zone.[87] It is perhaps not surprising that a government headed by Labour—a party founded by unions to prevent the encroachment of politics into the sphere of collective bargaining—was so hard on German union leaders' institutional aspirations.

If the influence of the British MG on this point is clear, the issue of institutional transfer is less clear than in the U.S. zone. The motivations for Allied

---

83. Mielke, Introduction to *Organisatorischer Aufbau*, 45.
84. The definitive account of the mission is in Steininger, *England und die deutsche Gewerkschaftsbewegung*, 69–87.
85. Quoted in Schmidt, *Die Verhinderte Neuordnung*, 41.
86. Quoted in Steininger, *England und die deutsche Gerwerkschaftsbewegung*, 85.
87. Karl finally switched to industrial unionism under pressure from the British MG after a zonal conference in August 1946; see Barbara Marshall, *The Origins of Post-War German Politics* (London: Croon Helm, 1988), 118–21.

policies toward unions (military control, democratization, and, especially later in the occupation, anti-Communism) were complex and often contradictory; additionally, the British MG was pushing a policy of industrial unionism that looked very different from the predominantly craft-oriented British system. Yet the very ambiguity of national models of industrial relations was used by the British to suggest that they had faced many of the same issues as the Germans and had found a superior form of organization. One official's criticism of Albin Karl's appeal for the unitary union acknowledged centralism's temptations even for the TUC yet urged Karl to resist them:

> In the [mission's] experience, a heavily centralized organization inevitably becomes bureaucracy. The British Trades Union Congress fought bureaucracy in this country during the war and succeeded, to some extent, in breaking down centralized direction into regional organisation in order to widen the base of consultation and discussion. The General Council of the [TUC] agree that there are too many Unions in Great Britain at the present time, but they would strenuously resist any attempts to create one Trade Union from the organisations at present affiliated to [the TUC]. And however much you may differ, the fact undoubtedly remains that if one centralised organisation handles all finance then those who have control of funds will dictate policy and can lead to bureaucracy.[88]

At essentially the same moment, however, the TUC was *supporting* unitary unionism for Czechoslovakia and Austria. Defenders of this "apparent contradiction" in policy noted that their visits with those union leaders had inspired confidence, whereas they were simply less sure that all German trade union leaders, present and future, could be similarly trusted.[89] The TUC, then, was not convinced that the industrial model was always preferable but seemed to argue rather that there needed be an appropriate fit between structural models and the particular social actors who would be using them. The British used the functional equivalent approach chiefly to justify policies chosen for a mix of other reasons. Here, the British model of industrial relations was strategically invoked (in the sense highlighted by the policy-borrowing literature), rather than functioning as a consistent guide to MG policy.

Restrictive Practices: Allied Limits on Codetermination

German labor leaders were less divided about union participation in economic management than about unitary unions, for almost all advocated some form of codetermination. Thus, the codetermination case involved in-

---

88. E. P. Harris to Albin Karl, January 8, 1946, reprinted in Steininger, *England und die deutsche Gewerkschaftsbewegung*, 117–18.
89. Ibid., 85.

stitutions strongly favored by the German labor movement but opposed by the allied MGs. The Allies not only faced a more unified front but in this matter, unlike the collective bargaining case, initially had no *programmatic* alternative to offer from their own models. They did, however, use their own domestic models in a *negative* way: namely, as evidence that responsible unions did not need codetermination.[90] But if they clearly tried to transfer their own structures, the fact that German unions did eventually prevail in efforts to institutionalize codetermination—little known in American and British industrial relations of that period—raises the question of how effective their transfer effort was.

Codetermination has often been damned by German *employers* as an "Allied creation," but the facts show a much more complex story. In telling that story, this section makes three points. First, it complements the account of Allied transfer efforts in union structure and collective bargaining. From the perspective of Allied policymakers—the perspective privileged in this analysis—promoting certain functionally equivalent structures presupposed restricting other kinds of functional efforts. With regard to collective bargaining, restrictions were linked to a positive role for unions: hence, the notion of "constitutive" transfer employed above. Effective transfer required turning minority wings of the German labor movement into dominant ones. In the case of codetermination, however, a "restrictive" mode of transfer prevailed initially; a positive Allied vision for unions in economic management came only very late, under the administration of the Marshall Plan. And the Allies had few available partners because on the basic demand for union participation in economic governance, whether in individual firms or in making economic policy, German labor was more united than in the debates over industrial versus unitary unionism.

Second, therefore, this section demonstrates that the process of restricting institutional ambitions can play a central role in larger processes of imitation. This point is especially relevant to discussions of economic liberalization, where the emulation of "best practices" often seems to require some deregulation in the form of removing institutional protections. The transfer of "leaner" foreign models can mean *forgoing*, rather than *adopting*, certain practices.

Third, the politics of the case reveals that what was nevertheless effective about Allied policies was the way both their programmatic and negative policies endured over time and came to be ratified by both state and society in Germany. In the face of a stronger labor consensus—which extended to substantial parts of the Christian Democratic Union (CDU)—the Allies fought a

---

90. My distinction between positive and negative integration mirrors the distinction in supranational regimes. See Fritz Scharpf, "Negative and Positive Integration in the Political Economy of European Welfare States," in *Governance in the European Union*, ed. Gary Marks (Thousand Oaks, Calif.: Sage, 1996).

rearguard action, defending their restrictions with references to their own societies and with appeals about what was "good for Germany." They did ultimately allow limited forms of codetermination even when it had been their intention not to. But the limits they set, though undoubtedly frustrating labor's broader agenda, did not halt this agenda so much as channel it in particular directions, especially toward an appreciation of "productivity."[91]

German unions did not drop their effort to exert a broader influence over German society just because the two MGs sought to limit them to collective bargaining. Their most visible effort to achieve a political role came through attempts to acquire legal rights to codetermination. This effort can be divided into three overlapping phases, during which Allied influence moved from restriction to adjudication to channeling.[92] German codetermination resulted from a series of struggles in which labor's vision of codetermination was revised from a *provisional* step toward self-determination to a goal in and of itself.

In the first phase, unions struggled in the immediate postwar months to rebuild their organizations and carve out a sphere of authority in a political economy highly regulated by the occupation. Though they gradually recognized that the Allies would not permit outright socialization of industry, they continued to advocate some form of increased democratization of the economy. Union demands for "societal codetermination" grew out of many of the aspirations behind the economic democracy in Weimar.[93] A range of codetermination proposals circulated among labor elites, but the core idea was that unions should gain the legal ability to influence a broad range of social, political, and economic questions. The Deutscher Gewerkschaftsbund

91. Space considerations prevent explication of the similar case of Allied restrictions on postwar works councils, codified in ACA Law 22 of April 10, 1946, and bitterly criticized by both unions and works councils as a weakening of labor's voice in firms. The law on works councils finally passed by the Bundestag in 1952 was far weaker than labor had expected in the immediate postwar years. For an extensive bibliography on the works councils in this period, see the notes in Karl Lauschke, "Industrielle Beziehungen im Betrieb nach 1945," in *Unternehmen zwischen Markt und Macht*, ed. Werner Plumpe and Christian Kleinschmidt (Essen: Klartext, 1992).

92. There has been a growing interest in occupation policies toward codetermination: Horst Thum, *Mitbestimmung in der Montanindustrie: Der Mythos vom Sieg der Gewerkschaften* (Stuttgart: Deutsche Verlags-Anstalt, 1982); Volker Berghahn and Detlev Karsten, *Industrial Relations in West Germany* (Oxford: Berg, 1987); Gloria Müller, *Mitbestimmung in der Nachkriegszeit: Britische Besatzungsmacht-Unternehmer-Gewerkschaften* (Düsseldorf, 1987); Eisenberg, "The Limits of Democracy"; Michael Fichter, "HICOG and the Unions in West Germany," and Diethelm Prowe, "German Democratization as Conservative Restabilization: The Impact of American Policy," both in *American Policy and the Reconstruction of West Germany, 1945–1955*, ed. Jeffry Diefendorf, Axel Frohn, and Hermann-Josef Rupieper (New York: Cambridge University Press, 1993); Christoph Dartmann, *Re-Distribution of Power, Joint Consultation, or Productivity Coalitions?* (Bochum, Germany: N. Brockmeyer, 1996); Anthony Carew, *Labour under the Marshall Plan: The Politics of Productivity and the Marketing of Management Science* (Detroit: Wayne State University Press, 1987).

93. And as with "economic democracy," the vagueness of "codetermination" allowed each leader to see what he wanted in the slogan. See Franz Neumann, "The Labor Movement in Germany," in *Germany and the Future of Europe*, ed. Hans Morgenthau (Chicago: University of Chicago Press, 1951), 103–4; Kerr, "The Trade Union Movement," 553.

(DGB), especially the secretariat around Ludwig Rosenberg, was clearly the center of these theoretical elaborations of economic democracy. As the DGB's Böckler put it in 1946, "We must be represented in the economy in completely equal terms, and not just in individual organs, not just in chambers, but in the economy as a whole."[94] Such an agenda for labor clashed with the Allied understanding of proper union prerogatives, and the rapid consolidation of party competition in legislatures also undercut the unions' proposals for economic governance "councils," even when the unions advocated them as complementary to parliamentary democracy.

While societal codetermination was being pursued unsuccessfully at the macro level, German labor leaders began to explore other routes to codetermination.[95] In this second phase, especially after the DGB's Bielefeld conference in August 1946, the older emphasis on labor's voice in controlling monopolies and cartels was superseded by a stronger emphasis on controlling individual large enterprises.[96] The unions concentrated their efforts on heavy industry—historically, the site of significant labor strength and determined managerial resistance. Distinct from the council-centered notions of societal codetermination, the newer ideas called for the appointment of labor representatives to supervisory and management boards of individual firms. In this the unions could rely on some degree of sympathy from the Allied forces, who saw a need to balance the power of oligopolistic business. The American diagnosis of the German (as, for that matter, of the Japanese) steel sector was that it was an unholy alliance between large, nearly monopolistic producers of standard steel and pig iron—Yahata in Japan and Vereinigte Stahlwerke and the Hermann Göring Werke in Germany—and an array of smaller specialized producers attached to the bigger firms by ties of ownership or contract.[97]

Accordingly, decentralization of Ruhr steel firms was a pillar of occupation policy. But the Allies also remained skeptical—though to different degrees—of putting labor on the boards of the entities that emerged from restructuring. Had the Manpower Division been the sole Allied protagonist in the British zone, restriction would have been quite severe.[98] British Manpower did prefer union representation on firms' supervisory boards to the concept of works councils, but the British shared OMGUS skepticism about putting a la-

94. Quoted in Berghahn and Karsten, *Industrial Relations*, 174.

95. Space considerations prevent the elaboration of proposals on socialization of industry. For these debates, see Thum, *Mitbestimmung in der Montanindustrie*; and Müller, *Mitbestimmung in der Nachkriegszeit*.

96. For details, see Dartmann, *Re-Distribution of Power*, 95–102.

97. Gary Herrigel, "American Occupation, Market Order, and Democracy," in *Americanization and Its Limits: Reworking American Technology and Management in Europe and Japan after World War II*, ed. Jonathan Zeitlin and Gary Herrigel (New York: Oxford University Press, 2000).

98. Müller, *Mitbestimmung*, also emphasizes the British role in restricting codetermination to the iron and steel sectors.

bor representative on management boards.[99] But the British skeptics were not the key actors in the momentous decisions around worker participation in the steel sector. Rather, an ad hoc organization only loosely integrated into the British MG, the North German Iron and Steel Control (NGISC), was the site of several key decisions.

The NGISC efforts to dismantle iron and steel firms delivered a second key impetus to the establishment of firm-level codetermination. The threat of Allied dismantling made German managers' traditional antagonism to unions seem less pressing, and some managers began to see the possibility of recruiting unions to their side in persuading the occupation forces to limit industrial dismantling. It was clear that the price for this cooperation was to give labor more voice in the operations of firms. Fleshing out this demand challenged union leaders in the British zone. At first, even the key DGB officials around Böckler (who were working with industrialist Heinrich Dinkelbach and the NGISC's William Harris-Burland on the details of what became the special form of codetermination for the coal and steel industries, *Montanmitbestimmung*) were uncertain as to the competencies of a labor representative on the management board.[100] But over several months of negotiations the sides developed a model of codetermination in which labor had equal representation on the supervisory board and in which each management board included a single labor representative approved by the unions. Significantly, this form of codetermination applied only to firms in the iron and steel industry and was not codified by parliamentary legislation. Concurrent British MG efforts to restrict worker participation in management were motivated by efforts to model German industrial relations on British ones, but NGISC's isolation from most of the British MG seems to have played a key role in its incubation of this exceptional and important agreement.[101]

In the U.S. zone, where no such major deconcentration program brought unions and employers to the table over codetermination, the development of state parliaments offered labor a chance to establish codetermination through legislation. As the unions' numbers and organizational strength grew, they began pressing state governments for codetermination laws. Despite Clay's warnings, in 1948 state governments in Hessen, Bremen, and Württemberg-Baden passed legislation—albeit weakened through negotiations with the Christian Democrats in all three parliaments—allowing some codetermination in firms. In Hessen, 72% of voters confirmed their support for this provision in a referendum. Whether the vote reflected popular enthusiasm for a new role for labor or frustration with the occupation forces,

99. Berghahn and Karsten (*Industrial Relations*, 176–77) suggest that the British MG backed codetermination, in part, as an alternative to the radicalism of works councilors. For a different view, see Dartmann, *Re-Distribution of Power*, 129–30.

100. Dartmann, *Re-Distribution of Power*, 116–17.

101. Ibid., 258–70.

the suggestion of a considerable level of mass acceptance implies that American restrictions were not welcomed. Nevertheless, Clay—echoed by the OMGUS Economics Division—publicly argued that decisions affecting the German economy as a whole had to be left to the entire German nation to decide.

U.S. labor leaders who had worked closely with the American occupation urged Clay not to suspend the German states' legislation. They and many Manpower Division officials tried to convince Clay that some democratization of German industry was inevitable and desirable and that codetermination was a better alternative than socialization.[102] In some cases, union sympathizers inside Manpower fed information to AFL and CIO officials for use in putting outside pressure on Clay, whom they often referred to as "antiunion."[103] But in the fall of 1948 the general did suspend the state legislation, explicitly invoking the American model: "Trade union forces seem to survive very well in America without such a law."[104] As Clay said later, both socialization and codetermination "were foreign to my way of thinking—and to the American way of thinking. . . . As long as I was there, I was going to try my best to prove that in encouraging free enterprise we were encouraging a more rapid recovery for Germany than would have occurred otherwise. Certainly, I came from a free enterprise country, and I represented to the best of my ability the advantages of free enterprise."[105] One cannot explain away American restrictions by attributing them to ignorance of German traditions and aims. That charge may hold for Clay, but it certainly does not for Franz Neumann, who went from helping draft societal codetermination legislation during Weimar to opposing it as a member of the U.S. occupation. Neumann argued that since state officials would be involved in such a process, the antidemocratic German civil servants would render such models ineffective for promoting the social democratic goals that he shared. To be sure, his reasoning was different from Clay's, but like the more conservative general he argued that legal privileges could not substitute for a lack of union "militancy."[106]

102. Clay disagreed: "In point of fact, national ownership might well form a better pattern than economic codetermination as the latter is, in my opinion, much more apt to retard the German economy." Letter to William Draper, January 18, 1949, in *The Papers of Lucius D. Clay*, 2 vols., ed. Jean Edward Smith (Bloomington: Indiana University Press, 1974), 989.

103. Henry Rutz memo to Jay Lovestone, Lovestone Papers, Meany Archives, box 56, folder 12. Similar dynamics were at work in British Manpower, as its head, Reginald Luce, helped persuade Lord Pakenham, the government minister responsible for the British zone, that British-style restrictions would go too far to curb German labor's prerogatives. Dartmann, *Re-Distribution of Power*, 116–17.

104. Quoted in Eisenberg, "The Limits of Democracy," 77.

105. Quoted in Jean Edward Smith, *Lucius D. Clay: An American Life* (New York: Henry Holt, 1990), 393; after Clay retired from the army, the Continental Can Company, which he headed, was indicted by the U.S. Department of Justice for antitrust violations (11).

106. Neumann, "The Labor Movement in Germany," 103–4.

Lacking legal guarantees, German unions hoped that *Montanmitbestimmung* would be a foot in the door of broader codetermination rights in other sectors. Such hopes were not fulfilled. Rather, growing Cold War tensions shifted the Allies' calculations to the means of coexistence with the Soviets. With the occupation forces thinking much more about promoting German and European economic recovery, employers saw less and less need to secure labor's cooperation. These changes in the international environment and in the strength of business interests narrowed labor's opportunity for broader participation rights in firms. By the late 1940s labor's gains appeared tenuous: Clay had suspended the codetermination laws of democratically elected states; developments in the British zone appeared unstable, given the lack of a legislative basis. The pressing question became whether the gains of the late 1940s could be defended against renewed attacks from business interests.

At the same time that OMGUS disallowed formal codetermination, it continued to promote informal contacts along the lines of the social partnership widely thought to have played an important role in wartime America. Indeed, what Charles Maier has termed the "politics of productivity" established a larger policy framework for the issues of institutional redesign pursued by the Allies.[107] A joint statement of the American and British military governors to both employer associations and unions emphasized in several places the central importance the Allies attached to consultation with "workers, employers and farmers" and made clear that they expected the future German government to follow that policy as well. The statement continued:

> Moreover, it almost goes without saying that in matters which concern employers and workers jointly, and there are very few occasions when their interests are separated, the work of government will be facilitated if the joint voice of employers and workers can be heard. We need hardly stress, therefore, the supreme importance which we attach to a body or bodies which will enable employers and trade unions to get together, to iron out their differences, and concert plans of action not only in matters which may be the concern of governments but in those for which the authority and responsibility remain with the partners in industry.[108]

Talk of "partners in industry" was controversial inside a labor movement still searching for a legal basis from which to influence broad economic decisions. Given the way that consumer prices outstripped growth in real wages after

---

107. Charles Maier, "The Politics of Productivity: Foundations of American Economic Policy after World War II," in *Between Power and Plenty: Foreign Economic Policies of Advanced Industrial States*, ed. Peter Katzenstein (Madison: University of Wisconsin Press, 1978).

108. This plea for togetherness was read separately to the employers' associations (on February 15, 1949) and trade unions (February 28, 1949). Lucius Clay, *Decision in Germany* (Garden City, N.Y.: Doubleday, 1950), 295.

1948, such rhetoric was a hard sell indeed.[109] In fact, not until 1954 did real wages reach the levels of 1938.[110] The British MG too energetically promoted such social partnership but, unlike the U.S. authorities, had neither the inclination nor the organizational leverage to link codetermination to the issue of productivity. And it was this linkage that held the key to an effective use of American influence on German labor's determination to achieve participation rights, as well as an enduring set of organizational structures to protect those rights.

Debate on the legal status and scope of codetermination continued past the transition to the era of civilian occupation and the founding of the Federal Republic in late 1949. In this third phase, divisions *within* the occupation, as U.S. actors chose sides in the German codetermination debate, ultimately emerged as important in channeling the unions' efforts in a particular direction. Although AFL support for the DGB position was minimal—in part, no doubt, because many U.S. union leaders were highly skeptical of codetermination—the AFL did urge U.S. High Commissioner John McCloy to advise Konrad Adenauer to establish national legislation on codetermination or face the lifting of the retired Clay's suspension of the state laws in Hessen and Baden-Württemberg. After much dithering, McCloy did so. When talks between unions and employers then broke down in the spring of 1950, he carried out the threat and lifted the suspension. Because this reinstitution raised the specter of different laws in different states, McCloy's actions may have helped spur the German government and employers in their negotiations.[111]

As the Germans jockeyed over legislation in 1951, however, the U.S. National Association of Manufacturers (NAM) also entered the fray, warning that American capital could not be expected to flow into Germany if the protection of stockholders' rights could not be assured.[112] In the subsequent debates the AFL and the German unionists lined up on one side, the NAM and the German industrial federation on the other. The NAM defended its interest as an effort to "determine what US industry might do to halt the spread of this [codetermination] scheme in its extreme form"; it also maintained that the German political right needed help, as it was "paralyzed" by its inexperience in dealing with the public, its association with Nazism, and its fear of

109. The key labor proponent of a more "expansionary" wage policy was the DGB's Viktor Agartz, who in this period was still a close ally of Böckler. On Agartz, see Hans Willi Weinzen, *Gewerkschaften und Sozialismus: Naphtalis Wirtschaftsdemokratie und Agartz Wirtschaftsneuordnung* (Frankfurt: Campus, 1982).

110. Volker Gransow and Michael Krätke, *Viktor Agartz: Gewerkschaften und Wirtschaftspolitik* (Berlin: Verlag die Arbeitswelt, 1978), 30.

111. Because he favored holding out for federal legislation, Böckler was actually lukewarm to the idea of lifting the suspension; thus it would likely not have happened then without AFL involvement.

112. Until 1950 the State Department had generally disallowed new U.S. investment in Germany.

reprisals for public action should the Soviets later come to occupy West Germany.[113] Yet the NAM intervention came across as a heavy-handed foreign intrusion, concerning even some key CDU officials who were committed to passing a bill based on a deal between employers and unions and brokered by Adenauer.[114] By portraying codetermination as a strictly economic instrument, U.S. labor officials, working through the State Department, put pressure on U.S., British, and French officials to remain neutral in the parliamentary debates on the issue. At the same time, these officials pressured the NAM to discontinue its campaign and urged German employers and the CDU to consider codetermination as an instrument for productivity rather than a political tool of labor. After a great deal of parliamentary and extra-parliamentary maneuvering—including significant intervention by Chancellor Adenauer himself—the German parliament passed a codetermination law in May 1951 which guaranteed for heavy industry (this time including the coal sector) the essential features of the model developed in the British zone, as well as a significantly weaker form for other sectors.

With the legal basis of codetermination secured, at least for the coal and steel industries, efforts turned to elaborating that legal model. Here, yet a third U.S. actor entered the debate, the Labor Division of the Marshall Plan's Economic Cooperation Administration (ECA).[115] On the initiative of the ECA's Clint Golden (affiliated with the United Steelworkers of America), the Labor Division sought to transform existing codetermination arrangements in iron and steel into a basis for labor's participation in efforts to enhance productivity.[116] American unionists such as Golden and Meyer Bernstein, also of the steelworkers' union, used instruments of the Marshall Plan in waging a highly effective campaign to recast codetermination as a means for unions to deliver "immediate benefits" to their members by raising the productivity of the firms in which they worked.[117] Sponsoring visits to the United States for union leaders helped break down German skepticism about American industrial relations. For example, after returning from such a visit, Markus Schleicher spoke with twenty-five groups in the next three months, helping thereby to shift some of the weight from Allied negation to German emula-

---

113. Werner Link, *Deutsche und amerikanische Gewerkschaften und Geschäftsleute, 1945–75* (Düsseldorf: Droste Verlag, 1978), 49.

114. Dartmann, *Re-Distribution of Power*, 276.

115. Ibid., 318–27.

116. See Clint Golden memo to William Foster, reporting on trip to Europe January 3–February 5, 1951, Golden Papers, box 4, file 18:6–8, Historical Collection and Labor Archives, Pennsylvania State University, University Park.

117. On the ambivalence of German labor toward "productivity" during the Weimar period, see Mary Nolan, *Visions of Modernity: American Business and the Modernization of Germany* (Oxford: Oxford University Press, 1994); on the more modest effects of U.S. efforts to increase French productivity, see Richard Kuisel, *Seducing the French: The Dilemma of Americanization* (Berkeley: University of California Press, 1993).

tion. Marshall Plan officials enticed organized labor with visions of American workers' affluence, easier working conditions, and more humane and trusting relationships on the job. According to Werner Link, "Above all, the possibilities for influence held by the American trade unions were recommended as a model—they were much larger than in Germany and were based on excellent cooperation between labor and management; the German workers and their unions would be happy if they could exchange their shop steward committees, suspended by the military government, for such political influence as the trade unions had in the US."[118]

ECA labor officials relentlessly invoked such comparisons in evaluating German labor's aims. Bernstein, who sent back detailed reports on German labor from Düsseldorf, was particularly appalled by the way the striving for codetermination seemed to take precedence over the drive for wages and safer working conditions. Calculating that German steelworkers' wages amounted to only 18% of industry turnover, he reported, "This is a shockingly low share for labor. In the United States labor costs in the steel industry amount to approximately 40%." Moreover, the problematic divide between unions and works councils meant that labor had a weak voice in safety: Bernstein compared the rate of 84 accidents (including an average of 16 fatalities) per month in a large German plant in 1949 with the record of a U.S. plant that had "approximately the same number of employees" but had run for 175 days without an accident.[119] Since the ECA, like OMGUS, was unable to dissuade German unions from their pursuit of codetermination, it tried to redirect those aims. Above all, it needed a vehicle for promoting productivity and found one in codetermination.[120]

In forging this new connection, the Labor Division had some credibility with the DGB because of its support during the 1951 codetermination debate. As Christoph Dartmann has demonstrated, Golden's insight linking productivity to codetermination was taken up by the AFL's Nelson Cruikshank and Helmuth Kern, working inside the ECA.[121] ECA officials strove to ensure that productivity gains would translate into higher wages and lower consumer prices instead of only higher profits or, worse, unemployment.[122]

118. Link, *Deutsche und amerikanische Gewerkschaften*, 35. Fritz Tarnow, Schleicher's colleague in the Weimar woodworkers' union, had visited the United States before the war and written an enthusiastic book about the relationships between high wages, rationalization, and purchasing power: *Why Be Poor? (Warum arm sein?)* (Berlin: Verlagsanstalt des ADGB, 1928). Compare the similar reaction of many non-Communist French unionists reported in Kuisel, *Seducing the French*, 92–94.

119. Bernstein letter to Otis Brubaker, August 24, 1950, Bernstein Personal Correspondance, series D, box 4, Historical Collection and Labor Archives, Pennsylvania State University.

120. Carew, *Labour under the Marshall Plan*, 104–6.

121. Dartmann, *Re-Distribution of Power*, 328–35.

122. These efforts helped cement an explicit linkage between wages and productivity growth—a linkage that still informs German wage bargaining. Peter Hall and Robert Franzese, "Mixed Signals: Central Bank Independence, Coordinated Wage Bargaining, and European Monetary Union" (discussion paper of the Wissenschaftszentrum Berlin, 1996).

Where Bernstein focused mainly on the squalid conditions of German workers, Golden's main motivation was the desire to win the workers for rearmament as part of a growing competition with the Soviet Union. As he put it,
"Historically, rearmament in Western Europe has meant a lowering of living
standards. . . . Lack of enthusiasm concerning rearmament and defense is
clearly evident until it is pointed out that by increasing productivity through
the introduction of new work methods and techniques it is possible to rearm
and at the *same time* not only *maintain* but *improve* current living standards."[123]

The German unions, then, having begun the postwar era with hopes of codetermination on social, economic, and political levels which could be translated into constitutional prerogatives, saw those high hopes disappointed.
The Allied intent to limit the juridification of labor's role in society and the
economy was evident throughout this period. Restriction was not the only
component of Allied influence in this case, however; in the end, although the
military occupation refused to allow German labor an instrument that British labor distrusted and American unions "survived very well without," the
civilian occupation, impelled by U.S. domestic interests, actually helped to restore pressure on the FRG government to produce modest codetermination.
The Labor Division of the ECA then sought successfully to channel codetermination by linking it to productivity gains. Thus did restrictive transfer set
real limits on German labor's ambitions for societal codetermination, shape
the particular form of firm-level codetermination later codified in federal
law, and finally—with the deepening of the Cold War—weld to the structure
of codetermination the Allied interest in productivity. Nor did American
influence end there, for even after the formal Allied powers ended, private
actors continued to focus on persuasion. Both the AFL's Department of International Relations under Jay Lovestone and the CIO's Department of International Affairs under Mike Ross sustained active networks of American-
German labor contacts into the early 1960s.[124]

Rolling Back Economic Autocracy?

As in the area of labor, occupation policies toward business organizations
used Allied models in both constitutive and restrictive fashion.[125] At various
times the Allies tried to prevent the reemergence of traditional business organizations and replace them with new structures and practices. In imme-

---

123. Clint Golden memo to William Foster: 10 (original emphasis). The productivity-rearma-
ment linkage was emphasized by Golden's boss, Robert Oliver, in a memo to the ECA's Public Advisory Board on March 8, 1951. See Golden Papers, box 4, file 18:4–6.

124. Angster, "Konsenskapitalismus und Sozialdemokratie," details the American and British
roles in the slow ideological reorientation of the German left in the 1950s.

125. I use "business organizations" as a catchall term for three different kinds of organizations
of capital: employer associations, business associations, and chambers of commerce.

diate terms these efforts were less effective than was their intervention with labor. Business organizations showed a striking degree of personnel, organizational, and policy continuity, and the lack of transnational actors on the business side comparable to labor's AFL and CIO clearly resulted in less sustained Allied reform efforts.[126] Moreover, Allied plans for business organizations involved a complicated, multifaceted shift of competencies—a shift that broke down in its first step and never recovered momentum. In the longer term, however, the fragmented reform efforts had some significant effects on the organization of German capital, and the changes that endured were, again, those for which German supporters could be located.

Unlike labor, the leaders of German capital were not seeking major institutional discontinuities in their traditional models of self-organization and influence on public policy. Rather than comprehensively describing Allied policy toward German business, therefore, I focus here on those policies that did include reference to American or British capitalism. As D. F. MacDonald of the British National Association of Port Employees wrote in his 1949 review of Allied policies toward business organizations, "The Allied authorities in Germany have been more or less influenced by the experiences and the politics of their own countries, although large differences were still possible."[127] Three Allied efforts were the promotion of "occupational freedom," a human resources approach to firm management, and anti-cartel policies. In the first case the Allies understood the victims of business autocracy to have been potential market entrants; in the second case, the trade unions, which had not been accepted as legitimate bargaining partners; and in the third case, consumers. The Allies' efforts to change business practices followed the same basic logic as their dealings with labor: restrict private organizational inroads into politics, and encourage private dealmaking though collective bargaining.

In the Weimar period there had been three main forms of business organizations, all significantly distinct from their American and British counterparts. First, business and sectoral associations, later headed at the peak level by the Bundesverband der deutschen Industrie (BdI), mainly represented the interests of industrial employers in economic policymaking.[128] Second, employer associations, headed at the highest level by the Bundesvereinigung der deutschen Arbeitgeberverbände (BdA), primarily engaged in collective bargaining with unions. Although American employers' organizations were important in sectors like aircraft production, where their main function was to lobby the government to continue purchasing planes, they performed sub-

126. Recall that the NAM became involved only in the early 1950s. Earlier, the ban on new investment in Germany by American companies surely contributed to NAM indifference.
127. D. F. MacDonald, "Arbeitgeberverbände in Westdeutschland," OMGUS Visiting Expert Series 8 (August 1949), 3.
128. The peak association, BdI, has only industry-based member associations.

stantially fewer functions than their German counterparts. Most important, wages in the United States were generally negotiated between unions and individual firms, not between unions and employer associations.[129] Third, chambers of commerce and industry were, unlike those in the United States, organizations with mandatory membership for all firms. Further, the chambers—in conjunction with some business associations—had control over who qualified to open a business.

These German business organizations, which all sought reestablishment in the immediate postwar period, appeared not only unfamiliar but also threatening to the occupation powers.[130] They seemed to provide a basis for protectionist cartels even during peacetime and were widely supposed to have been the financial power behind the rise of Hitler.[131] As Volker Berghahn has shown, the American conception of cartels sprang not from firm size alone—indeed, many American corporations were larger than their German competitors—but from an ideology of competition explicitly challenged by the division of markets practiced by German cartels since the mid-1920s.[132] In wartime the alliance between cartelized domestic industry and expansionist foreign policy had seemed eminently clear in the plunder and use of slave labor that followed Nazi conquest in both Western and Eastern Europe.

Alongside this Allied skepticism, the German ordo-liberal tradition or so-called Freiburg School also advocated reducing the power of organized business in Germany.[133] In the context of British and American influences, ordo-liberalism had two important features. Although its influence on policy was modest in the early period of military occupation, its growing influence, especially in the person of Ludwig Erhard, made many American proposals seem somewhat less foreign. Moreover, the reform initiatives pushed by German liberals often satisfied occupation authorities' demands for changes in German structures and practices. The Allies leaned most heavily on functional equivalent transfer initiatives in those cases where German actors took no reform initiatives of their own. Thus, Allied flexibility was not limited to

129. Over the course of the postwar period American collective bargaining did indeed become increasingly centralized.

130. In the Nazi period, German employer associations for collective bargaining had been forced into the DAF; the business associations and chambers of commerce had been integrated into the *Reichswirtschaftsystem*. Henry Ashby Turner, *German Big Business and the Rise of Hitler* (New York: Oxford University Press, 1985). See, more generally, Walter Simon, *Macht und Herrschaft der Unternehmerverbände* (Cologne: Pahl-Rugenstein, 1976); Ingo Tornow, "Die deutschen Unternehmerverbände, 1945–50: Kontinuität oder Diskontinuität?" in *Vorgeschichte der Bundesrepublik Deutschland*, ed. Josef Becker et al. (Munich: Wilhelm Fink, 1979).

131. On American views of German politics in the 1930s and 1940s, see Merritt, *Democracy Imposed*, 23–48.

132. Volker Berghahn, *The Americanization of West German Industry, 1945–1973* (Cambridge: Cambridge University Press, 1986).

133. On ordo-liberalism, see Fritz Holzwarth, *Ordnung der Wirtschaft durch Wettbewerb: Entwicklung der Ideen der Freiburger Schule* (Freiburg: R. Haufe, 1985); Razeen Sally, *Classical Liberalism and International Economic Order* (London: Routledge, 1998).

its own institutional initiatives, and even where ordo-liberal reforms were novel, the Allies tended to accept them and to back them.

The functional equivalent of American practices would have been to weaken the role of employer associations in collective bargaining, end the dualism of employer and business organizations, and push chambers of commerce toward strictly private and voluntary organization. British and American MGs both sought to do these things. The Allies tried to end the business organizations' influence over occupational freedom and to promote competition among "free organizations" for member firms, rather than allowing the organizations to divide up member firms (just as the member firms divided up markets). In the most important statement of these efforts, U.S. MG Regulation 13-120, the principles of functional equivalence were evident. According to the "basic views underlying MGR 13-120," OMGUS personnel, hoped to prevent business organizations from having public law status, exercising "governmental powers," or prohibiting new entrants into their occupation.[134]

Yet a gulf remained between the dominant American and German conceptions of the legitimate functions of business organizations. For example, within eighteen months OMGUS had decreed that the German states must liberalize their licensing laws, which required that "persons desiring to open new businesses or to enlarge existing businesses [must] establish the 'economic need' for their proposal, as well as their 'personal reliability,' and to prove that they owned 'sufficient' capital, and other similar requirements."[135] As with labor organizations, the clearest statements of what I have called functional equivalence principles came in response to worrisome developments on the ground. Here too the Allies used institutional transfer defensively more than proactively. What developments in postwar Germany had given cause for such concern?

Although the Allied authorities in the first months of the occupation were wary of German industrialists, they did allow a fairly rapid reconstitution of local business associations in individual economic branches.[136] At the end of the war these associations, the so-called Organisationen der gewerblichen Wirtschaft (OGW), were initially banned by the Americans and the French. The British, noting that they had not been deemed Nazi organizations by Control Council Law 2, allowed them to remain, and this position was later accepted by the other two powers, provided that mandatory membership

---

134. For a thorough, and still cautiously optimistic, review of how these restrictions were holding up in Bavaria, see John Holt memo to OMGUS Economics Division, September 1947, OMGUS Papers, Bavaria, Economics Division, admin. Sec., box 1, folder 2, 13-75-3, RG 260, National Archives.

135. Charles Jeffs report, OMGUS Papers, box 9, folder 8, 11-2-1. The highly sarcastic quotation marks are in the original.

136. Klaus-Dieter Henke, *Die amerikanische Besetzung Deutschlands* (Munich: Oldenbourg, 1995), 497–507.

Table 4. Bavarian firms organized in business associations, September 1947

Sector	Total firms in sector	Number of member firms	Percentage organized
Machinery	350	300	86
Optics/fine mechanics	500	147 (full members)	29
		200 ("cooperating")	69
Metal manufacturing			"virtually all"
Chemicals	450–500	423	90
Retail sales	230,000	77,000	33
Wholesale	5,000	2,150	43
Ceramics			"nearly 100%"
Textiles			90

Source: John Holt, memo to OMGUS Economics Division, September 1947, OMGUS Papers, box 1, folder 2, 5, RG 260, National Archives; author's calculations.

ended and all public functions ceased.[137] Then, on October 30, 1945, the British officially allowed business associations (*Fachverbände*) to form; U.S. authorization came a month later, on November 30, 1945. These organizations could not make membership compulsory, were limited to one branch only, and had to list their functionaries for cross-checking with denazification processes. Given the steps the Allies took to promote democratization inside the trade unions, denazification of personnel within the associations was minimal.[138]

Besides Nazi ties, a second concern had to do with the concentration of market and political power. A key Allied objective was to restrict the size and scope of the associations, above all forbidding them market regulation functions. But OMGUS also vetoed multisectoral associations to avoid "too great a concentration of economic power which might easily dominate the very inexperienced and weak governmental authorities."[139] The Americans did eventually allow some multisectoral associations to form but forbade any organization above the *Land* level.[140] Here, however, the industrial importance of the British zone came to the fore: the British MG allowed associations to form more quickly there, to be multisectoral, and to exist not just at *Land* but at zone level.[141] Yet as Table 4 demonstrates, by the fall of 1947 business asso-

137. Since the new associations were deemed to be "functional descendants" but not the legal descendants of the OGW, it took until 1956 to transfer OGW property to the business associations; see Tornow, "Die deutschen Unternehmerverbände," 238.

138. Berghahn, *Americanization*, 48–51.

139. Otto Brodnitz memo to Bipartite Control Office, December 16, 1947, OMGUS Papers, box 7, folder 5, 11-1-3.

140. This changed only with the February 1948 decision to allow the new German Economic Council to authorize bizonal associations.

141. MacDonald, "Arbeitgeberverbände," 5, 11–13.

ciations in the U.S. zone were making rapid headway in organizing member firms.

Employer associations were initially even more restricted, and because of the limits that wage controls put on collective bargaining, their policy functions were carried out by the business associations.[142] In the British zone a few employers had received tacit MG approval to restart employer associations in 1945, and many were multi-industry (as most union organizations still were at that time). The British then formally allowed single-sector business associations but disallowed multisector business and all employer associations. The employer association leaders, however, argued that fusing business (lobbying) and employer (collective bargaining) associations would replicate Nazi practice. Additionally, some union leaders sought a partner in industry with whom collective bargaining could take place on social issues beyond wages, issues for which the unions had to depend on firm-level agreements. Since the unions had very uneven strength in individual firms, and especially since the strongest firm-level organizations were Communist, moderate union leaders hoped to reestablish bargaining at a higher level. On May 5, 1947, therefore, the British Manpower Division finally agreed to allow employer organizations. One month later, metal employers in the British zone founded working groups of all metal employer associations in order to remove them from the control of the business associations.[143]

OMGUS officials followed these developments with some concern and worried openly that multi-industry organizations would restore "the old employer associations which we understood we intended, at least for the present, to prohibit."[144] The obvious concern was that such a *centralized* organization could exercise undue influence on *industry*-level wage bargaining, which OMGUS was promoting. When the Americans finally followed the British lead and allowed employer associations to form in October 1947, they still denied permission for a bizonal peak association of all employer associations.[145] But in February 1949, with collective bargaining once again in the hands of Germans, Walter Raymond, the head of the Central Secretariat of the Employer Associations, met with the two military governors to negotiate permission for a peak association. Clay and Robertson informed him that if such an organization was formed, they would change the law to allow its continuance. It was, and they did.[146]

The final plank of the star-crossed Allied effort to roll back what they saw

142. Tornow, "Die deutschen Unternehmerverbände," 243.
143. Luitwinn Mallmann, *100 Jahre Gesamtmetall* (Cologne: Deutscher Instituts-Verlag, 1990), 2:241–42.
144. A. Kramer memo to Manpower Division, September 15, 1947, OMGUS Papers, box 7, folder 43a, 11-1-3.
145. See Hannaman Report, November 28, 1947, OMGUS Papers, box 7, folder 5, 11-1-3.
146. D. J. McCutcheon and Walter Mather report to Bipartite Board, March 24, 1949, OMGUS Papers, box 7, folder 4, 11-1-3.

as the business community's appropriation of public functions had to do with chambers of commerce and industry. This was a purely American campaign. OMGUS sought unsuccessfully to transform chambers into quasi-American organizations with voluntary membership, no control over market entry, and no public functions in, for example, distributing scarce raw materials and labor; chambers could then have performed a number of the functions previously carried out by the employer organizations that the Americans hoped to prohibit.[147] Chief among these functions would have been negotiation with trade unions on local issues of economic importance. It was on this basis that OMGUS allowed chambers to reopen immediately after the war. In the last months of the war German industrialists in many cities had built informal circles to coordinate transport and energy, and beginning in June 1945 some of these "commissions of industry" functioned as protochambers, with American approval. In other places the old *Gauwirtschaftskammern* were denazified at the very top and then used as a liaison to the business community.[148] Not until the fall of 1945 did the U.S. authorities move to reorganize the chambers. Their plan, however, besides running into fierce resistance from the chambers themselves, ultimately disintegrated under the ambitions of the unions to transform the chambers into corporate, bipartite bodies of economic democracy.[149] Against this backdrop OMGUS moved toward allowing the old employer associations to return as "working groups for social rights," and it was these organizations that began to reestablish collective bargaining functions. With this step and the earlier decision to allow the business associations to reconstitute, the road was clear to restore the traditional forms and functions of German employer organizations.[150]

Although efforts at fundamental reform of the business organizations quickly went awry, the Allies did develop a range of other policies to balance capital's power and thus try to reduce economic autocracy. Three mechanisms stand out. First, as noted above, labor unions were encouraged to concentrate their energies on collective bargaining and to build capacity to mobilize their members in support of narrowly economic goals. As the occupation went on, the MGs not only allowed strikes but, in some U.S. cases, actually encouraged them if they were the only way to deliver better benefits to

147. A good general source is Diethelm Prowe, "Im Sturmzentrum: Die Industrie- und Handelskammern in den Nachkriegsjahren, 1945–1949," *Zeitschrift für Unternehmensgeschichte* B53 (1987): 91–122.

148. Henke, *Die amerikanische Besetzung Deutschlands*, 497–509.

149. See Walter Mühlhausen, *Hessen, 1945–1950* (Frankfurt: Insel-Verlag, 1985), 205–17.

150. The bitter fight over chambers of commerce and industry continued until, in 1956, the German government rescinded the American-mandated restrictions on chamber functions in order to homogenize FRG regulations. The British had never tried to enforce similar changes, and the French occupation, with similar structures in France, perceived quasi-public chambers as entirely unproblematic; see Gerda Wuelker, *Der Wandel der Aufgaben der Industrie- und Handelskammern in der Bundesrepublik* (Hagen: Linnepe Verlagsgesellschaft, 1972); Gary Herrigel, "Industrial Organization and the Politics of Industry" (Ph.D. diss., MIT, 1990), 483–88.

workers.[151] Second, the Allies tightly restricted levels of German industrial output. Disputes about precise "level of industry" allowances eventually came to occupy a central place in their broader discussion of the role of Germany in the European recovery, but from the beginning of the occupation, controls also served as a check on the organized power of employer organizations.[152] Third, the Allies, especially the Americans, made a concerted effort to move the Germans toward a laissez-faire competition policy that emphasized tough antitrust legislation. In short, the Allies did not dismantle the traditional dualist structure of employer organizations but did rely on unions, output restrictions, and decartelization to help modify the influence of employers.

To be sure, the hope of using antitrust provisions to ban cartels and promote an American view of competition policy was only partially realized. Challenging the highly cartelized and often monopolistic structure of German industry, an important plank of Allied policy, was enshrined in JCS 1067. Yet as in the struggle over unions, the Allies confronted a range of reactions to their proposals. The Americans sought to prohibit the reintroduction of the traditional "abuse clause" system, favored by cartel supporters, under which cartels were legal in principle, and only certain extreme practices were outlawed; they preferred a ban on cartels with, if necessary, a few exemptions. Thus, instead of making cartels generally legal with some exceptions, the Allies sought to make them generally illegal with some exceptions.

Berghahn's study leaves no doubt that the occupation's antitrust policy was driven by reference to American laws and traditions and that the gulf between this policy aim and the wishes of the majority of German industrialists was very large indeed.[153] But efforts to achieve American-style antitrust law were not made in ignorance of the German economy. Centered in the Justice and State Departments, the designers of the deconcentration program for Germany did not ignore German cartel law but "discarded it as inappropriate to deal with the concentration established under Hitler."[154] Most postwar German industrialists were intent upon reestablishing some form of traditional cartel arrangements. The peak business association, the BdI, was dominated by heavy industrialists in the Ruhr, who had at least traditionally been strong supporters of cartelization, plus a number of small-firm-dominated industries that also depended on cartels to stabilize their markets.

---

151. Dartmann, *Re-Distribution of Power*, 329.

152. The British MG generally opposed tight limits on industrial production as it was the only way its zone could pay for food imports; see Marshall, *Origins*, 198–99. Clay too became an ardent opponent of strict controls.

153. See Berghahn, *Americanization*, 178 ff.

154. Graham Taylor, "The Rise and Fall of Antitrust in Occupied Germany, 1945–48," *Prologue* 11 (1979): 29; Herrigel ("Industrial Organization," 495–96) has shown that the Americans were in fact ignorant of the dependence of *small* firms on cartels.

As the OMGUS Economics Division recognized, however, not all Germans were hostile to American concepts of production.[155] Parts of German industry had flirted with internationalization and mass production in the 1920s, when firms such as Bosch, IG Farben, and Siemens had used export markets to increase economies of scale in production.[156] Hoping to build on these interests, American policy aimed at encouraging the coming national government to continue the occupation's competition policies and to institutionalize in law its strong antitrust provisions. In so doing, OMGUS and, after 1949, the U.S. High Commission found supporters both in the German state and in civil society: Ludwig Erhard referred to the antitrust bill introduced by Adenauer's government as a "seedling" (*Pflänzschen*) from America, and Berghahn's biography of Otto Friedrich shows how the industrialist used his position in the BdI presidium to win hardliners over gradually to grudging acceptance of the principle of a cartel ban.[157] In addition, the employers' collective bargaining body, the BdA, came under the influence of export-oriented producers such as Hans Bilstein, an auto-parts supplier and the longtime head of Gesamtmetall, BdA's largest member association. Bilstein and a number of others had traditionally been both more accepting of labor unions and less dependent upon cartels to stabilize their markets than most German firms.

In loose coalition with German liberals such as Erhard and with the support of key factions inside the BdA, the Economics Division and later the High Commission exerted steady pressure on the BdI to accept a legislative program restricting the use of cartels. Threatening (though never imposing) their own legislative solution, U.S. occupation officials expended substantial effort to bring about such legislation under the Adenauer government. The BdI, however, resisted Erhard's antitrust proposals and stalled until 1957, when the Bundestag finally passed a ban on cartels—albeit one watered down with significant exemptions.[158]

Although German industry blocked the transfer of the extremely restrictive American antitrust practices, it is equally important to note that the oligopolistic competition of the postwar years bore little resemblance to the tightly organized private monopolies of the early twentieth century. Once again, a functional principle—this time the principle of a ban on cartels—was wielded by the Allies in a restrictive and reactive fashion and drawn upon by German supporters to make significant changes in the institutions

155. In general, the OMGUS Economics Division was considerably more business oriented than Manpower, which oversaw trade union reconstruction. It was Economics that began by 1947 to push the development of employer organizations as part of a broader interest in supporting German economic reconstruction; Fichter, *Besatzungsmacht*, 250.

156. Berghahn, *Americanization*, 22–23; Nolan, *Visions of Modernity*.

157. Volker Berghahn, *Otto A. Friedrich: Ein politischer Unternehmer* (Frankfurt: Campus, 1993).

158. Berghahn, *Americanization*, 170–73.

of German economic regulations. And as in the case of unions, the outcome was neither a simple "return to Weimar" nor a reproduction of American structures.

Notwithstanding the tension arising from U.S. efforts to promote strong antitrust legislation, America's "cooperative" labor-management relations attracted the attention of many German industrialists. Against the backdrop of their country's traditional authoritarian practices, many German managers became interested in the "socially responsible manager" associated with Fordist U.S. firms.[159] Exposed to "Training within Industry" courses offered in the U.S. zone and a flood of articles in *Der Arbeitgeber*—the official publication of the BdA—advocating the diffusion of U.S. management methods, BdA members came to frame the debate about industrial relations institutions not in the BdI's terms of "capitalism versus socialism" but in terms of "socialism versus community."[160]

At the same time, German managers were the targets of a larger American effort to export the politics of productivity. As CIO treasurer James Carey said:

> The idea of simultaneously increasing production and the capacity of the community to consume is the most typical American product we have to export. It is, to my way of thinking, the best answer Democracy has to the Communist charge that conflict and collapse are the inevitable products of our type of economic society. Communism is fighting Democracy not only with guns but with ideas as well. We have found in our American experience the answer to Communism. Our friends in Europe want to explore this idea and adapt it to their own environment. I do not believe we should fail them even though some timid souls may call it "interference."[161]

German businessmen's study visits to the United States, sponsored by the European Reconstruction Program, often focused on industrial relations practices. As the German Marshall Plan ministry noted after the initial trips: "This relationship is founded on the common goal of increased productivity. Both partners start with the recognition that every increase in productivity benefits the employees as well as the management; such an increase brings with it lower prices simultaneously with higher production and wages, a rise connected to the shorter production time. In scientific and practical research into all problems connected with the concept of productivity, as the German

159. Throughout the immediate postwar period, most industrial elites remained quite authoritarian; Heinz Hartmann, *Authority and Organization in German Management* (Princeton: Princeton University Press, 1959).

160. Berghahn, *Americanization*, 247–49. Thus, the business organization that OMGUS tried hardest to repress became the most important conduit for "human relations" approaches to management.

161. Quoted in Link, *Deutsche und amerikanische Gewerkschaften*, 83.

specialists were able to determine, the US has made considerable advances especially in recent years."[162] Allied pressures at the institutional level gained credibility each time German actors actively pulled in American practices from the private sphere. At the firm level, a growing body of historical research documents these trends. For example, the synthetic fiber producer Vereinigte Glanzstoff strategically imitated Dupont's technology, pricing structure, marketing program, and even some of its factory décor.[163]

More cooperative management practices reinforced accommodationist shifts within the labor movement. With the growing marginalization of Communists, many German Communist Party (KPD) members left the unions and stayed only in the works councils, giving the unions more maneuvering room vis-à-vis moderate managers. The relative weight of the American production model in this gradual evolution, however, has not been precisely specified. Alongside the emerging hegemony of the American production model were indigenous German traditions of mass production, and a judgment about the relative influence of these two sources awaits further empirical analysis.[164] Nevertheless, Berghahn's demonstration that a "generational change" inside the German employer associations led to a much less contentious form of industrial relations suggests that the American model was a constant point of reference for the modernizing faction. There is little reason to believe that the resurgent influence of older German traditions would have evolved *over time* in this fashion; the continued success of the Fordist production model throughout this period seems more likely to have captured German interest. But that this trajectory was dependent upon actively sustaining transnational links in the business community is suggested by the comparison to labor, where the networks built in the 1940s and 1950s declined significantly during the 1960s.

In sum, narrowing industrial relations issues to economic ones helped change the calculations of a substantial group of employers as to the possibility of accepting unions as equal partners in shaping the economy. Even though the concerted American attempt to gain strong antitrust legislation in Germany was unsuccessful, the more diffuse effect of the American pro-

---

162. Quoted in ibid., 84. The full story of the effects of these missions remains to be written. As Luc Boltanski has said of similar French "productivity missions" to the United States, "importing social technology had priority over transferring material technology"; see Boltanski, "Visions of American Management in Postwar France," in *Structures of Capital: The Social Organization of the Economy*, ed. Sharon Zukin and Paul DiMaggio (New York: Cambridge University Press, 1990), 345. On the other hand, Kuisel (*Seducing the French*, 84–89) implies that "material technology" held great interest for the French visitors and that organizational innovations tended to dwindle in isolation once brought back to France.

163. Christoph Kleinschmidt, "An Americanized Company: The Vereinigte Glanzstoff Fabriken AG in the 1950s," in *The Americanisation of European Business*, ed. Matthias Kipping and Ove Bjarnar (London: Routledge, 1998). See also V. Wellhöner, *Wirtschaftswunder, Weltmarkt, Westdeutscher Fordismus: Der Fall Volkswagen* (Munich: Westfälisches Dampfboot, 1996).

164. For the steel industry, a beginning is provided by Herrigel, "American Occupation."

duction model had a lasting effect on the balance of power within the associations. The case for institutional transfer as an analytical device is less strong here than in the case of labor organizations, because the one truly "constitutive" effort—toward chambers of commerce—was ultimately rejected by the Germans after the occupation ended. Yet in the form of "restriction," the concept helps clarify the relative weight of external and internal forces in reorganizing the interest representation of capital in occupied Germany.

CONCLUSION: MODELS IN AN ESTABLISHED SYSTEM

Rather than a technique used by technocratic elites to make narrow changes, imitation appears to have been a route to the transformation of the structures and tasks of the two main organized interests in capitalist society. Subject to certain conditions, foreign models clearly can have a significant impact even on long-established systems of industrial relations—provided that the policy elites in charge identify and nurture potential partnerships with existing social actors (such as those advocating industrial unionism or the business organizations most open to productivity partnerships with unions) *and* that the means to achieve those ends be subject to negotiation with those partners.

The Allies were in a high-stakes, low-expertise situation. They were dependent upon German elites not just for local knowledge but also for the maintenance of their changes after the occupation ended. Where the stakes were highest—namely, in questions of foreign and military power—the Allies simply retained all formal authority.[165] But in virtually all other policy areas they sought to return control to the Germans. The prerequisite for this step seemed the establishment of a solid foundation for further democratic development. The cases in this chapter show the Allies using a functional equivalent approach to help shift the balance of power within existing groups of labor and capital, to the benefit of those Germans whose institutional visions were most compatible with the Allies' own. Their measured pace and their resistance to restarting the German economy immediately gave them leverage over economic actors and provided a framework for a dialectical approach rather than a purely didactic one.

In the face of an organized civil society, flexibility was crucial; indeed, in those areas of industrial relations where the Allies tried to force specific organizational forms (as opposed to broader functions) on the Germans, their work was undone after they left, as in the chambers of commerce case. This

---

165. The last of it was returned to Germany only during the "2+4 talks" (among the two German states and four Allied powers) of 1990.

finding leads to a paradox about the politics of transfer: any indigenous actor strong enough to support a foreign design is also strong enough to try to
turn that design to its own purposes. The Allies were not averse to using force,
however. To the contrary, their functional equivalent approach was predicated on the strategic use of force to transform minority German traditions
into majority ones. As U.S. Manpower's Leo Werts wrote to the CIO's James
Carey, OMGUS wanted "the German trade unions to have freedom of decision . . . [but] this does not mean that we will not attempt to create conditions
which will influence them to voluntarily choose affiliations which will, in our
judgment, contribute to the building of a force for peace and democracy."[166]
Believing that democratic forces in Germany were weak and that authoritarian ones—whether fascist remnants or Communist vanguards—were strong,
the MGs used controls to force a dialogue with leaders of German capital and
labor and to structure German "choices."

A creative synthesis arose from the interplay of the Allies' efforts to replicate the rough structures of liberal capitalism and the Germans' more corporatist traditions. The institutions that resulted, though certainly not mir-
roring the American or British industrial relations systems, were shaped in
crucial ways by those models. The restrictions imposed by the Allies on German unionists' plans for economic democracy helped change the system of
economic regulation. The central features of the postwar system were private
collective bargaining with employers instead of novel forms of economic democracy, and decentralized industrial unionism instead of the centralized
union movement (like those consolidated in Scandinavia and Austria during
this same period) which was envisioned by most German union leaders.

Both the unions and the business and employer associations complained
bitterly that their own organizational progress was impeded because the occupation forces favored the interests of the other class. Each side was right
about its own experience but wrong in its interpretation of Allied policy. In
reality, because the Americans and the British were committed to models of
decentralized industrial relations, they placed restrictions on *both* kinds of organizations, allowing them to retain some of their familiar organizational
forms but channeling them toward functions that better matched Anglo-
American understandings of democracy and capitalism.

These restrictions mattered because of the critical juncture at which they
were applied. By the time a German state regained sovereignty in 1949, German capitalists had also regained much credibility. As a result, their willingness to expand labor's participation rights in economic regulation quickly
faded, while CDU hegemony in Bonn and, later, the "economic miracle"

---

166. Quoted in Fichter, *Besatzungsmacht*, 228–29. The issue was whether or not the German
unions could join the CIO-supported World Federation of Free Trade Unions.

helped cement the basic contours of liberal economic regulation. The moment of real openness was over by the end of military occupation in 1949, and incremental changes thereafter had to take place against principles anchored in both statute and constitution. Such a "window of opportunity" argument as this emphasizes contingency and choice more than do path-dependent arguments. The latter, more structural approach risks perpetuating a myth of noninterference by implying that German actors built these institutions independent of outside influence, a claim that does not square with the evidence.

Because many institutions are the results of long, slow historical processes, the technocratic or top-down efforts of outsiders to promote institutional change are often ineffective. Yet the concept of transfer used here mirrors the political reality that not all cases of transfer are truly top-down or technocratic. Ironically, it is because some Germans were willing partners in implementing the kinds of changes the Allies desired that the Allied role has been so obscured. The institutions that virtually no one desired (such as private and voluntary chambers of commerce) became political flashpoints; the ones that many found useful (such as industrial unionism) were accepted *with relatively less attention.* Moreover, the character of their intervention was not always evident even to the Allied officers. Given their ignorance of Germany, the restrictions they proposed were often portrayed in MG documents as the prevention of what were, to them, self-evidently undemocratic structures rather than the promotion of Allied preferences.

Each skeptical view about transfer noted at the outset of the chapter is only partly accurate. Even taken loosely, the first claim, that the transferred designs *already existed,* is most incomplete. Like the related claim that all reform was the result of German learning, strict path-dependency arguments must ignore the evidence of Allied intervention into union foundings, structures, functions, and leadership. The second claim, that transfer was actually *rejected* by the Germans, is confirmed in some cases but not others and thus will not do as a generalization. The third claim, that *macroeconomic* circumstances made institutional changes moot, cannot account for the fact that German industrial relations were first reformed under very difficult circumstances—well before living standards appeared even tolerable, let alone the outcome of an economic "miracle." Interestingly, the final rejection of the American design for the chambers of industry and commerce occurred *during* the economic miracle, confirming that macroeconomic success could not automatically legitimate existing institutions.[167]

Of course, in pointing to the incompleteness of other explanations, it is crucial to note that the institutional transfer explanation is also incomplete.

---

167. Recall that OMGUS had immediately reopened chambers *before* reforming them; the next chapter shows how a similar decision helped doom American efforts at school reform.

The cases discussed are useful examples of transfer, but the heuristic itself cannot account for all their important political dynamics. Transfer is always likely to be embedded in a broader set of policies: strategies of institutional transfer were often explicit or implicit ways of operationalizing prior policy choices such as "democratization."

To emphasize the utility of the concept, however, several points about transfer bear repeating. First, although the functional equivalent approach was sometimes envisioned during wartime *planning* for the occupation, it was much more often a tool used by the MGs in *reaction* to developments in Germany. As such, it was an instrument born of revulsion as much as of vision.

Second, different Allied actors drew on different conceptions of their "home" institutions. Recall that General Clay and the AFL each actively invoked the American model of industrial relations yet in 1948 came to *opposite* views on the issue of *Land* laws on codetermination. This echoes the point about the opportunistic use of foreign evidence, but the deeper point is that the same institution can have very different meanings to different actors. Chapter 5 shows how the same structures can have very different meanings in different regions.

Third, although the functional equivalent approach provided a useful template through which the AFL internationalists could negotiate the complexities of foreign industrial relations, no actors relied exclusively on this approach. Indeed, it is tempting to see functional equivalence as a compromise strategy that was almost no actor's initial or dominant choice. The State and War Department forces that sought rapid reconstruction of German economic power were often annoyed by the time-consuming institutional meddling of the functional equivalent approach; those in the Morgenthau camp who sought a harsh occupation came much closer to the "anti-model" position identified with French policy in Chapter 2. Even the proponents of supporting the "good Germans" thought to look first to Germany's own democratic traditions rather than to emphasize ones that seemed to work for the United States or Britain. Again, the evidence in this chapter (and the next) shows that the functional equivalent approach was often a recourse and a compromise rather than a plan.

Finally, the same functional principle can have different effects in different political contexts. One reason industrial unionism so appealed to the Allies was that it promoted organizational decentralization. Yet in imperial and Weimar Germany, industrial unionism had been a powerful tool of *centralization*. The Social Democratic union federation had generally tried to promote industrial over craft unionism, and so reduced its number of affiliated unions from fifty-five in 1891 to thirty in 1931.[168] The organizational principle that

168. Müller-Jentsch, "Lernprozesse," 319.

had led to centralization during Weimar could be used for decentralization after World War II because the German *aspirations* for centralization had grown so dramatically.[169] Chapter 5 demonstrates again that in a new political environment even well-established institutions produce very unfamiliar results.

---

169. Indeed, many German trade union leaders continued to see industrial unionism as a tool for promoting centralization, since it eliminated competition for members inside firms and branches.

CHAPTER FOUR

Education after the War:
Germans Confront "the One Best System"

> Where anything is growing, one former is worth a thousand re-formers.
> —HORACE MANN, as quoted by John Dewey

The U.S. authorities tried to transfer institutional designs inspired by American schools into postwar Germany. The German educated elite, American reformers believed, used schools to promote authoritarianism and perpetuate their own advantages. The proposed antidote was common schooling: ending the German track-based system or, at the very least, maximizing the years before separate academic and vocational tracks commenced; ending tuition and fees for pupils; and requiring all primary and secondary teachers (not just those whose students made up the tiny cohort of the university-bound elite) to have university training. American efforts were ineffective. Of these goals, only the removal of tuition and fees was accomplished.

Yet the Americans were flexible and an organized civil society clearly existed, so why did no substantial reform take place? I argue that American strategy negated the reformers' flexibility and ultimately helped weaken the very reform tradition in German education that they had come to encourage. Institutional transfer was not impossible in this case, but achieving American aims would have required a fast start, a strong organization, and an effort both to engage traditional organized supporters of school reform and to win new supporters.[1]

---

1. The British began with many similar objectives in their zone, but by the beginning of 1947 they had largely returned control of education to the Germans. OMGUS, on the other hand, chose this moment to launch its "school reform" program.

Modest Proposals: U.S. Planning for Reeducation

In his interviews with German educators in the early 1960s, Robert Lawson discovered that most of them believed the Americans had arrived in Germany with extensive and ready-made reform plans. In fact, the opposite was true.[2] U.S. society was especially interested in the links between schools and democracy, and Americans generally agreed that schools could strengthen democracy's promise and its practice. Thinkers such as John Dewey had been explicit: schools had the responsibility to teach democracy by "teaching democratic living." In a heterogeneous society it was crucial that people have contact with groups and classes, races and religions, other than their own. OMGUS education officers translated John Dewey into German and distributed his writings around the U.S. zone.[3] What features of German schools so concerned them? Why did they think reading Dewey might help?

The three-track German schools were and are unusual in Europe in the breadth of their differentiation and in the duration of their tracking. The outlines of German primary and secondary schools have remained remarkably constant across the twentieth century, although the names of the tracks have changed over time. For the postwar period I use the then contemporary German terms *Volksschulen, Mittelschulen,* and *Gymnasien*. The first, the "school of the people," had comprised since Weimar a four-year elementary phase for all children and another four years for the great majority. Well over 80% of German youth who finished these eight years in the *Volksschule* then left full-time schooling; most entered the dual system of vocational training (part-time classes combined with firm-based apprenticeship), and others joined the labor force as unskilled workers. The "higher schools" began with grade five: the *Mittelschulen* generally for pupils oriented toward the professions, and the *Gymnasien* for university preparation.[4]

The Nazis had not fundamentally restructured this system, though some of the changes they did implement threatened the privileges of the traditional elite.[5] Their most important changes were the closing of parochial schools (*Bekenntnisschulen*), a reduction in the number of humanistic *Gymnasien* (although not a reduction in their total number), and a shift of decision-making from parents to the state and from the localities to the central state. In all these areas, Nazi rhetoric about equality and Party control of education far exceeded actual alterations. But since the Nazis had *talked* of changing Ger-

---

2. Robert Lawson, *Reform of the West German School System, 1945–1962* (Ann Arbor: University of Michigan Press, 1965), 105.

3. James Tent, *Mission on the Rhine* (Chicago: University of Chicago Press, 1982), 6.

4. After 1964 the elementary schools were separated from the *Volksschulen. Hauptschule, Realschule,* and *Gymnasium* were then adopted as the standard names for the three secondary branches.

5. Hermann Schnorbach, *Lehrer und Schule unterm Hakenkreuz* (Königstein: Athenaum, 1983); Rolf Eilers, *Nationalsozialistische Schulpolitik* (Cologne: West-deutscher Verlag, 1963).

man education, educational conservatives after 1945 could claim to be simultaneously tearing down Nazi structures and restoring traditional ones. Like many other groups, the educational administration and faculty painted themselves as victims of the Nazis, despite overwhelming evidence of their broad complicity in the rise and rule of fascism. Indeed, the percentage of teachers with membership in the Party or its organizations was higher than that of any other occupational group except judges and police.[6]

Notwithstanding widespread criticism of Nazi schools, the United States initially decided *against* attempts to transfer American-style educational institutions to Germany.[7] The official doctrine of the State Department and War Department—which were jointly responsible for planning occupation policies—was that Germans should be encouraged to reform their own educational institutions. The occupation therefore concentrated only on the pragmatic problems of reopening schools in the fall of 1945, reflecting the more fundamental policy decision not to attempt a major school reform in Germany.

The failure to act early to achieve major changes resulted from a stalemate in policy-planning discussions between different ideas about how the Germans should be treated after the war. Advocates of harsh measures proposed either closing German schools and reducing German education to minimal levels or, in the softer version, conducting an elaborate reorganization of the system. The various Morgenthau plans of 1944 said little about education except that it must be denazified and that schools should not reopen immediately. Morgenthau himself argued that no German should have "higher technical education" and mused in August 1944 about having Allied personnel reeducate the children of Nazis: "Do not you think the thing to do is to take a leaf from Hitler's book and completely remove these children from their parents and make them wards of the state, and have ex-US Army Officers, English Army Officers, and Russian Army Officers run these schools, and have these children learn the true spirit of democracy?"[8]

Reconstructionists, on the other hand, proposed either denazification alone or a "wait and see" approach to allow the Germans maximal reform initiative. Most important, the German Country Unit (GCU) of SHAEF in London produced a draft handbook for the occupation. John Taylor, an army captain who had done his doctoral work at Columbia Teachers College on Weimar youth groups and who had practical experience teaching in

---

6. Wolfram Grams, *Kontinuität und Diskontinuität der Bildungspolitischen und pädagogischen Planungen aus Widerstand und Exil im Bildungswesen der BRD und DDR* (Frankfurt: Peter Lang, 1990), 219.

7. My discussion of American planning for the occupation follows Tent's careful reconstruction in his *Mission on the Rhine*.

8. Quoted in Hans-Joachim Thron, "Schulreform im besiegten Deutschland: Die Bildungspolitik der amerikanischen Militärregierung nach dem Zweiten Weltkrieg" (Ph.D. diss., University of Munich, 1972), 22.

Berlin, headed the GCU's education staff of ten.[9] Isolated in London from the many policy fights within Roosevelt's administration, they produced a reconstructionist proposal that Morgenthau promptly attacked for its leniency toward the Germans. GCU called for a rapid reopening of schools with little change in structure. Its plan gave, in James Tent's words, "maximum initiative to the Germans in all phases of reform, including denazification and, at a later date, the activities associated with structural and curricular reform."[10] When FDR vetoed the general plans that lay at the base of the GCU plan, the much harsher SHAEF handbook—tougher in all respects, including education—became the official War Department plan for the occupation. But the education officers who began operations in Germany followed the spirit of the handbook they had drafted as part of the GCU rather than SHAEF's.

Archibald MacLeish, assistant secretary of state for cultural affairs and coordinator of State's plans for postwar German education reforms, pondered ways to reconcile the department's core conviction that Germans must be involved in the active reconstruction of their own educational system with the growing awareness that there would be no central government in Germany once the war ended. The anticipated lack of a central government naturally raised the question of who in Germany might be able to reform German education. MacLeish himself was not sure that sufficient German personnel for thoroughgoing reforms would be available: "The basic question of the reeducation of Germany probably cannot be approached intelligently until we have occupied Germany and have learned whether or not the civilian personnel we need for our assistance actually exists [sic]."[11]

MacLeish's focus on "civilian personnel" hints at the tendency to define the need for German partners in technocratic terms rather than in avowedly political or coalitional ones. Planners generally had a normative view of education as an apolitical endeavor, and they were looking not for groups or parties as allies but rather for enlightened individuals who could be entrusted with specific tasks. Uncertain about the availability of such individuals, MacLeish put detailed planning on the back burner, and the State Department developed the Long Range Policy Statement for German Reeducation, or SWNCC 269/5. In essence, this statement proposed to delegate maximum educational control to the Germans, foreseeing only a minimal and rapidly receding control function for U.S. occupation forces. By the eve of occupation both the War Department (implicitly) and the State Department (explicitly) were planning to reopen schools immediately and return control of educational reform to the Germans. Unable to decide what reforms to undertake, the United States essentially avoided the question by turning over

9. Tent, *Mission on the Rhine*, 23–24.
10. Ibid., 26.
11. Quoted in ibid., 31.

the job to the Germans themselves. The very weak organizational status of the Education and Religious Affairs Section (ERA) of OMGUS flowed directly from these modest policy ambitions.[12]

Yet if reconstructionists controlled actual education policy early on, the punishment faction controlled the airwaves. When OMGUS announced an effort to install committed antifascists—whether returning exiles or those surviving inside Germany—this personnel policy contributed to an early blitz of anti-Nazi information which was also a channel for disseminating American suggestions that the occupation be thorough and harsh.[13] Exiles such as Alfred Döblin and Lion Feuchtwanger suggested that the "German disease" was incurable even by reformed institutions and called for permanent U.S. occupation of Germany. Although this view never drove official occupation policy, it did reflect a certain mind-set that found expression in the U.S.-controlled press. "Reeducation" thus quickly got a bad name in Germany, and that reputation likely made opposition to later efforts at school reform much easier to mobilize.[14]

Like the American and British unionists (see Chapter 3), the professionals who staffed the occupation brought with them their own biases about how institutions should be structured. OMGUS tried to find American specialists to fill its positions, and the education officers—the few hundred men and the handful of women who oversaw school reforms from 1945 to 1949—brought insights from their professions as American teachers and administrators. But because ERA's low organizational status always made difficult the recruitment of adequate personnel, virtually none had experience in school reform, and their general level of knowledge about German education was modest at best. Erich Hylla, a Prussian educational official who became an OMGUS consultant, reported in 1947 that of the eighty educational specialists in Germany, only three or four spoke German well enough to exchange ideas with German teachers.[15]

Below the top layer, few OMGUS officials had expertise on German education; most were familiar only with the American system. Since the core of Allied policy as articulated in JCS 1067, the Potsdam Accords, and SWNCC 269/5 did not foresee an active school reform, however, this deficiency appeared unimportant.

---

12. Within OMGUS, ERA was small and weak, a subordinate organization struggling for resources yet generally responsive to OMGUS goals. Thus, unless the context implies otherwise, I attribute U.S. policy goals to the two organizations interchangeably. I also include *Land* detachments of the U.S. military government in the designation "OMGUS."

13. Harold Hurwitz, *Die Stunde Null der deutschen Presse: Die amerikanische Pressepolitik in Deutschland, 1945–1949* (Cologne: Verlag Wissenschaft und Politik, 1972).

14. Jutta Lange-Quassowski, *Neuordnung oder Restauration? Das Demokratiekonzept der amerikanischen Besatzungsmacht und die politische Sozialisation der Westdeutschen* (Opladen, Germany: Leske + Budrich, 1979), 266.

15. *The Smith-Mundt Group Collection* (National Security Archives, Washington, D.C.), 2 (1947): 77–78.

In short, the American failure to build a coalition to support German school reform had its roots squarely in the uncertainties and contradictions of the planning process. Education officers (although their differences did not reflect allegiances to different U.S. interest groups, as was the case in the AFL and CIO factionalism that played such an important role in German industrial relations reform) were not homogeneous in their reform philosophies. Contentions inside the planning apparatus were important in two ways. First, there was a potential tension between a thoroughgoing reform of schools and the effort to rebuild Germany quickly. Second, the reconstructionist faction, which was most inclined to ally with German reformers, was least inclined to push for institutional change, whereas the faction insisting that institutional change was necessary was committed to a view of Germany suggesting that appropriate partners would be few. Even when institutional change did belatedly move to the forefront of American policy, it was not accompanied by a concerted effort to persuade and recruit a variety of German partners. Instead, OMGUS held to the broader modus operandi of working directly with German elites inside government ministries—often people originally appointed by OMGUS. The obvious question then is whether suitable partners for school reform were available among these elites.

New Players, Old Plans: German Parties and School Reform

Whether hoping for indigenous German reforms or pushing actively for common schools, American school reformers in each *Land* dealt primarily with the two major political parties, the Christian Democratic Union–Christian Social Union (CDU-CSU) and the Social Democratic Party (SPD). Doing so conserved scarce organizational resources by allowing OMGUS to work directly with state Ministries of Culture, but it left OMGUS with the problem of constructing an alliance for school reform between parties that were either opposed in principle (the CDU) or uncertain in practice (the SPD).

Postwar CDU education policy was something of a paradox in that cultural policy was an obsession, yet school reform was barely mentioned. The newly formed party welcomed both Catholics and Protestants and thus welded together quite diverse world views. As it had not yet developed a consensus on education, it spoke of promoting "Christian values," a slogan both vague and vibrant. Party leaders invoked these values in all elements of policy formation but left the question of educational reform quite underspecified. CDU dialogue depicted National Socialist education as the *extension* of perverse liberal and socialist notions of progress, secularism, and human perfectibility.[16] The

16. Alfred Hoffmann, "Die Bildungspolitische Vorstellungen der CDU und SPD" (Ph.D. diss., University of Erlangen, 1968), 52–53.

party's education experts generally gave religious education clear priority over intellectual and vocational education, calling for the separation of state schools by religions, for additional state funding for "private" (church-run) schools, for the constitutional anchoring of parents' rights, and for guarantees that clerics (not the teachers) give religious instruction in any public schools that were co-religious.[17]

Accordingly, the CDU preferred "internal reform" of schools to institutional reforms. Internal reform was seen as a way to reconcile the party's mission to establish Christian values in all spheres of public life with a defense against the further extension of state control of education. (The slogan that captured party demands for limits to state prerogatives was "parents' rights.") Despite some CDU plans in North Rhine-Westphalia to roll back state authority and put education back into private hands, the party majority was content to defend traditional educational institutions, provided they could be used to promote Christian values. In sum, the institutional reform debate inside the CDU in this period was muted by a fundamental satisfaction with traditional educational structures. The organizational divisions of the school system were seen to *reflect* natural differences of ability in the population but not to *perpetuate* such distinctions—which could, in any event, be transcended by common values.[18]

In the SPD, by contrast, American reformers had a potential school reform ally of long standing. SPD school politics in the Weimar period had reflected the party's division over whether revolution or reform was the immediate goal.[19] This internal division, combined with the challenges of building a coalition with bourgeois parties and solving the chronic financial problems of the Reich, left both the party's school reform utopias and even its more modest plans largely unfulfilled. Weimar SPD school goals were captured by the slogan "*Weltlichkeit, Staatlichkeit, Einheitlichkeit, und Unentgeltlichkeit*" (secular, public, unified, and free), and the party's central institutional demand was for common schools. The SPD dilemma was that when it allied with the left, early in Weimar, it could pass its school reform proposals (including a four-year common primary school) but could not keep parliamentary democracy intact; yet when it allied with bourgeois parties, it could not get its reforms through the Reichstag.[20] The SPD also suffered from the lack of a strong base among professional groups and in civil society more broadly.[21]

17. Lange-Quassowski, *Neuordnung,* 179.
18. Hoffmann, "Die Bildungspolitische Vorstellungen," 64–66, 515. Lange-Quassowski (*Neuordnung oder Restauration?* 182) shows how CDU officials used pseudoscientific research on "giftedness" to counter arguments about the links between social class and educational opportunity.
19. This account of the SPD follows Wolfgang Wittwer, *Die Sozialdemokratische Schulpolitik in der Weimarer Republik* (Berlin: Colloquium Verlag, 1980).
20. Ibid., 20.
21. Ibid., 195–96.

For all the Weimar SPD's problems building a coalition for school reform, there was strong evidence that social class and educational opportunity were linked. In 1925–26 only 499 (1%) of the 49,000 students at Prussian universities were children of workers or farmers. At the technical universities the numbers were even more extreme: only 88 of 17,700 (0.5%). The links also extended to the secondary schools. In Berlin-Wedding, a heavily working-class section of the city, 90.5% of youth stayed in the *Volksschulen*, whereas in middle-class Zehlendorf and Wilmersdorf only 55.6% and 58.9% did so. And although the numbers of Germans going to higher schools and to universities exploded between 1911 and the late 1920s, the data show that there were few workers' children among them. In Bavaria in 1927–28 the higher schools had 8.2% workers' children and an additional 8.2% from "low-level employees"; in Saxony in 1927 only 7.73% were workers' children.

Moreover, to the limited extent that the SPD was able to promote the further education of workers, it was forced to do so through institutions constructed *outside* the regular educational system, as its efforts to change the system from within were consistently defeated.[22] With power shared between the working class and the liberal bourgeoisie, the same fights were fought out over and over, and Weimar ended up still making substantially the same education proposals in 1932 that it had started with in 1918. For the SPD the achievements were modest indeed: teachers gained more freedom from school administrators and were somewhat better paid; the four-year elementary school was established, extended, and made universal; vocational schools were improved (especially in some localities); and some efforts were made (usually outside the normal system) for advancing *Volksschulen* pupils to higher education.

During the Nazi years, however, common schooling became a touchstone of an otherwise physically and ideologically divided exile community. As Wolfram Grams's careful reconstruction of the exile left's thinking on education shows, the ten-year common school was a central demand of virtually all the groups.[23] The SPD thus emerged from World War II emphasizing education as a tool for changing individuals and society. Since the experience of Nazi dictatorship seemed to have discredited Marx's claim that historical progress stood on the side of the proletariat, in the SPD a sense of contingency and possibility, best articulated by Kurt Schumacher, took precedence in party discourse over notions of inevitability and control. As the SPD sought to move beyond strictly working-class circles, its old dogmas about education changing more or less hydraulically with changes in production gave way to a discussion about what kinds of institutions could really best promote the "free development" of each individual. There emerged a growing interest in the

22. Ibid., 219, 266, 278.
23. Grams, *Kontinuität*, 65–67, 173–81, 233–236.

pliability of institutions and the possibility that under democratic control they could reach down to the level of individual citizens.[24] Equally important, the postwar SPD's call for equal educational opportunity was flanked by a new acceptance of unequal outcomes based on differences in individual abilities.[25] This was hardly the same old SPD utopianism.

The revision of social democratic thinking on educational policy left little tension between the party's institutional goals and the hopes of U.S. occupation officials. If one could always find residual hostility in the SPD to seeing expanded educational opportunity used merely to promote individual talents and not to overcoming class differences, there was nevertheless a great deal of common ground concerning institutional reform. But the SPD, like OMGUS, initially gave little attention to implementing these goals.[26] Like the CDU, the SPD was attempting to unite diverse strands of support under the auspices of a single party. Unlike the CDU, the SPD was handicapped by a history of hostility to religion. The effort to expand the party beyond the working class led to ambivalence among party leaders about how to address issues of religious instruction and about the precise form the common school should take.

In short, in 1945 OMGUS faced an uphill battle with intransigence in one camp and indecisiveness in the other. Without decisive leadership to promote reformist agendas, dampen conservative resistance, and win the uncommitted in both camps, no school reform was possible. By allowing Germans to recruit personnel and reconstruct physical facilities along traditionalist lines, OMGUS closed off this possibility.

THE FIGHT FOR SCHOOL REFORM

The Political Consequences of Pragmatism

The occupation arrived in Germany with no detailed guidelines on education, far less a blueprint for Americanizing it. JCS 1067 called for full denazification and then a rapid opening of schools. As noted, the decision not to attempt a thoroughgoing reform of German secondary schools in time for the beginning of the 1945 school year reflected the disagreements around the question of punishing versus reconstructing Germany. Returning maximum control of education to the Germans was the practical outcome of this stalemate. The U.S. Army, given its experience in the occupation of Italy, also favored a pragmatic policy of concentrating on securing enough textbooks

---

24. Hoffmann, "Die Bildungspolitische Vorstellungen," 345–77.
25. Ibid., 393.
26. SPD's emphasis on capturing the economics ministries may have distracted its attention from cultural affairs.

and buildings and approved teachers so that schools could be rapidly reopened and children kept off the street. Thus, for both strategic and organizational reasons, schools were reopened quickly, and reform was left to the Germans.

Unlike its practice with unions, the press, and political organizations, OMGUS did not rely on a licensing process for schools but rather sought to reopen them all at the beginning of the 1945 school year on October 1. With that date looming, ERA's small staff went to work.[27] Although shifts in denazification procedures constantly disrupted their efforts at personnel recruitment, 20,000 teachers were cleared that first year—at best, however, only about half the number needed. Denazification resulted in the firing of half to two-thirds of all incumbent teachers, and in individual districts the proportion was often much higher.[28] In Würzburg, 90% of teachers were purged (although many returned soon thereafter).[29] Consequently, in 1945 the student-teacher ratio in the *Volksschulen* was over 80 to 1, and even then some 220,000 children between six and fourteen could not attend school at all for lack of buildings, teachers, and materials. In Hessen, for example, by December 1945, 75,000 of the 400,000 *Volksschüler* still had no school to attend, and in the higher schools only 2,400 of the 45,000 pupils were back in class.[30] Substantial energies were also invested in securing textbooks, often from the Weimar period, to replace those used under the Nazis.

OMGUS was well into its first year of operations before any formal mention of school reform was made. In keeping with the decision to return control over most aspects of educational affairs to German hands, it did act quickly to organize appropriate competencies. The United States began establishing state governments more rapidly than any other occupation power, Bavaria's first in May 1945 and the other *Länder* of the U.S. zone by September 19, 1945 (although the states did not receive any real authority until January 1, 1946). One of the first measures was the writing of *Land* constitutions—a process that OMGUS sought to influence indirectly through contacts with the drafting committees. Then in December 1945, Taylor announced to the Ministries of Culture ERA's interest in receiving short- and long-term goals and pro-

27. ERA personnel increased to about forty officers in the first year of operations, but by 1947 they still had filled only fifty of the more than eighty authorized positions. These few officers were totally employed with the initial denazification procedures and the reopening of schools. *Smith-Mundt Collection*, 2:77–78.

28. Ibid.; Tent, *Mission on the Rhine*, 69; Richard Merritt, *Democracy Imposed* (New Haven: Yale University Press, 1995), 273.

29. In late 1946 the Bavarian Ministry of Culture began allowing previously banned teachers to return to their jobs. By July 1948, 11,000 of the 12,000 Bavarian teachers originally banned had returned; see Herbert Schott, *Die Amerikaner als Besatzungsmacht in Würzburg, 1945–1949* (Würzburg: Freunde Mainfränkischer Kunst und Geschichte, 1985), 118–19. All SPD school reform plans were predicated on large programs to train "new teachers" (*Neulehrer*).

30. Walter Mühlhausen, *Hessen, 1945–1950* (Frankfurt: Insel, 1985), 465.

posals from the state governments, because "in the process of reviewing and approving such documents . . . the occupation authorities [can] exert their influence in the most effective manner."[31] With regard to education policy, however, the *Länder* constitutions were disappointing—an eye-opener for an organization hoping that education reform would come from within. That the constitutions said virtually nothing about school reform or even school organization dismayed the ERA, which had worked to persuade Germans that education should be reformed. Only the Hessian constitution really fulfilled most of the rhetorical minimums requested by OMGUS; those of Württemberg-Baden and Bavaria were much less satisfactory.[32]

The immense practical tasks of reopening schools have been cited as a reason for the relative inattention to institutional issues.[33] But it is precisely the sheer breadth of the physical destruction and the personnel limitations of the German schools that make the counterfactual so suggestive: instead of seeing the extent of the breakdown of the old system as a justification for rebuilding it, why was there not a policy of immediate institutional reform? Nothing could have helped justify the construction of *common* schools more than the stunning shortages of buildings and teachers. Consolidation of the system would have been easy to justify in urban areas, where physical infrastructure had been so badly damaged by war. And the moral discredit of teaching personnel may have been higher in rural areas, given the great pressures that had existed for local notables to join the National Socialist Party. It might even have been possible to use resources saved through physical and administrative consolidation to offset some of the costs of tuition, texts, and university teacher training. But concentrating on the broader OMGUS objectives of holding elections and encouraging constitutional development compromised American control over education reform just as ERA discovered that "indigenous school reform" would be an oxymoron.

The Shift to School Reform: When and Why?

Why did the idea of an aggressive American-led school reform—discussed and rejected in wartime planning—resurface during 1946? Quite simply, OMGUS was disappointed with the meagerness of German reform plans. In December 1945, Taylor called ERA staff together in Frankfurt to discuss the first six months of operations (which had, after all, contained their share of successes in reopening and equipping schools) and to look ahead. ERA

---

31. Quoted in Thron, "Schulreform," 41.
32. See the discussion in ibid., 84–88.
33. See, e.g., Dietrich Goldschmidt, "Transatlantic Influences: History of Mutual Interactions between American and German Educators," in *Between Elite and Mass Education*, ed. Max Planck Institute for Human Development and Education (Albany: State University of New York Press, 1983).

officers agreed that there were many Germans with whom they could work and that those people had been indispensable in the denazification process and in the nuts-and-bolts phase of getting the schools opened. The staff also discussed "positive" goals, and Taylor proposed that they could best bring change by requiring *Land* officials to prepare long-term reform plans for OMGUS to approve. Clay also seemed to share the view that practical obstacles plus denazification had simply taken first priority and that therefore, through 1945, there had been "little opportunity to implant our own teaching philosophies."[34]

But these internal deliberations alone cannot explain the substantial shift in U.S. policy toward German education which occurred in 1946. Rather, the very modesty of initial reforms was fuel for advocates of a harsher occupation. Reports in the *New York Times* and the *New Republic* about old Nazis in high places helped catalyze a second wave of denazification purges in education (much more inclusive than the first).[35] At the same time, the State Department began calling for an "education mission" to Germany by a group of American experts.[36] The U.S. delegation of American educational administrators arrived in August 1946, were briefed by ERA officials from Bremen and Berlin, and visited educational institutions in Bavaria, Hessen, and Württemberg-Baden. Determining that JCS 1067, the Potsdam declaration, and SWNCC/269/5 did not provide sufficient guidance for the actions of ERA officers, they issued a final report (a little over a month after their arrival) calling for an ambitious set of reforms in German schools. It was translated into German in October 1946, and 35,000 copies were circulated to teachers and other interested parties.[37]

The Mission Report (as it was commonly called) catalyzed a major shift away from the hands-off approach of SWNCC/269/5. It not only called for a common school but endorsed a larger system in which elementary schools would be six years in length and all the higher schools would be housed in the same building and consist of two consecutive three-year blocks. There were striking similarities to the U.S. system with its six-year elementary followed by junior and senior high schools. The reconstructionist State Department, which, ironically, had pushed for the mission, was dismayed by its rec-

34. Tent, *Mission on the Rhine*, 69–73, 78.
35. There was much to complain about. For evidence on the rapid return of purged teachers and the U.S. failure to build a reasonable program to train new teachers (as the Soviets did aggressively in the GDR), see Grams, *Kontinuität*, 173–81, 263. ERA did use crash courses to train "teacher's helpers" and placed them in schools in significant numbers, yet they did very little to retain them as full-time teachers. Such people—who might have served as an in-school clientele for reforms—soon moved on to other occupations as the purged teachers reclaimed their old positions.
36. General Douglas MacArthur had just hosted an education mission in Japan, and State seemed eager to repeat the plan in Germany.
37. Karl-Ernst Bungenstab, *Umerziehung zur Demokratie? Re-edukation-Politik der US Zone, 1945–49* (Düsseldorf: Bertelsmann, 1970), 52.

ommendation that OMGUS promote a modified form of the American school system in Germany.[38]

Nevertheless, Clay adopted the Mission Report as a guideline for school reform by quickly committing to a variant of the plan for a six-year elementary and a common higher school.[39] At the same time, though, his foreword to the German edition of the report warned that "real democracy cannot be imposed from outside. We will influence German education primarily through advice, encouragement and example." Even the Mission Report itself still explicitly endorsed the wartime decision to return postwar education to German authority, although it insisted that OMGUS retain veto power over education reform. It also called for a strengthening of the ERA, but this recommendation long remained a dead letter. Thus, as an entirely new and ambitious reform agenda was being prepared, the organization and its established mode of interacting with German partners remained essentially unchanged.

Giving Orders: The OMGUS School Reform Directives

There were three essential elements of the new American effort to advance institutional change in German schools: to promote common schooling both by increasing the years of elementary school and by reforming secondary schools, to make tuition and textbooks free, and to require that all teachers receive university-level training. The ERA saw these elements as mutually reinforcing steps toward a system in which children would be provided access to education, including higher education, independent of their class origins. Common schools would prohibit early differentiation of children into different tracks; the direct costs of public education would be reduced if not eliminated for all families; and all teachers would be given training of uniform quality to assure that pupils' later differentiation did not result in inferior instruction for that vast majority of German children who did not complete the *Gymnasium.* Franklin Keller spoke for many of his ERA colleagues when he said, "Democracy can never develop among a people who restrict their educated class to one per cent, and choose that one per cent from those who have money or social positions."[40]

In the wake of the disappointing *Länder* constitutions of 1945 and the critical Mission Report of 1946, the ERA sought to persuade each *Land* to pass legislation that would secure these three functionally equivalent goals. Its efforts were carried out in three waves of activity, involving increasingly angry

38. Tent, *Mission on the Rhine*, 110–19.
39. For a detailed comparison of the two plans, see Lange-Quassowski, *Neuordnung*, 206–8.
40. Franklin Keller, "Vocational Education in Germany," October 1947, OMGUS Papers, EDUC, Box 61, 5/299-2/9, 32, RG 260, National Archives.

demands on the part of ERA for school reform laws. The first phase was marked by the apparent divergence of the *Länder*; growing concerns about implementation and intransigence marked the second; unsuccessful threats of force, the third.[41]

OMGUS was far from inflexible. ERA officials did not expect overnight reforms, and in public forums they confirmed that they would have been happy with changes over five to ten years' time.[42] On the separate issue of the *content* of change, there is ample evidence that OMGUS was willing to accept, especially as time went on, a wide range of reform possibilities. In other words, American insistence on education reform grew out of broad claims about the democratizing functions of common schooling but not out of a fetish for particular institutional forms. Any "reasonable, wide forward step," as General Clay put it, would have sufficed.

The first round of school reform began on January 10, 1947, when Clay sent out a memo requiring each *Land*'s Ministry of Culture to submit by April 1 a list of general education objectives and by October 1 a more detailed long-term plan for achieving those aims.[43] The *Länder* were to submit plans for a common school in which different kinds of schooling merged in consecutive fashion rather than pursuing separate and exclusive tracks. Taylor and his deputy, Richard Alexander, fleshed out Clay's instructions in a series of strongly worded speeches at the Ministries of Culture in Bavaria, Hessen, and Württemberg-Baden.[44] They called for a six-year elementary education followed by a common higher school in which a six-year academic track would exist alongside—wherever possible in the same building, Taylor stressed—the general track that would enroll 90% of the pupils. The general track would continue through the pupil's fifteenth year of life; the academic track would proceed in two three-year blocks, only the second of which would be strictly differentiated and dedicated to preparation for university studies.[45] In addition to this 6-3-3 system, Taylor also called for an end to tuition and

41. Bavarian resistance to U.S. school reform efforts was the strongest; OMGUS experiences in Württemberg-Baden were not much better; and despite a promising start, Hessen and Bremen bitterly disappointed OMGUS in the end. Only in West Berlin, under a school law drafted in conjunction with the other Allied powers, were common schools maintained well beyond the end of the first phase of the American occupation, and even there the schools had largely returned to a three-track system by the mid-1950s.

42. Thron, "Schulreform," 95.

43. Extended from the original July 1 deadline.

44. Taylor had recruited Alexander, his old mentor from Columbia. Alexander succeeded Taylor as head of the ERA in April 1947, when efforts failed to find someone of higher status. See Tent, *Mission on the Rhine*, 125–31.

45. See "OMGUS-Telegramm vom January 10, 1947," in *Dokumente zur Schulreform in Bayern*, ed. Hans Merkt (Munich: Richard Pflaum, 1952), 53–54. Clay's memo reflected a decision not to follow the Mission Report's implicit recommendation to force the vocational schools, which offered the theoretical and general education portion of dual vocational training, into the comprehensive schools.

course fees and for university-level teacher training as prerequisites to the kinds of school organization OMGUS would accept.[46]

OMGUS officials had mixed feelings about the resulting *Länder* education proposals. They saw Bavaria's plan not as fundamental reform at all but simply as window dressing of the old system.[47] Württemberg-Baden's plan, proposing a six-year elementary as the basis for a 6-3-4 system, appeared too vague to be confidently evaluated. OMGUS was enthusiastic about Bremen's original plan, which called for a 6-3-3 system in which a six-year common elementary school would lead into three- and six-year tracks for vocational and academic preparation, respectively. Since even the three-year *Mittelschule* would be internally differentiated (although under the same roof as the academic track), the differences from U.S. high schools were plain enough, again indicating that ERA was not insisting on an exact replication of the American model. All levels would be tuition free, and training for *Volksschulen* teachers would be extended from two university years to three. The plan was to be experimental at first, with full implementation set for the beginning of 1948. OMGUS was willing to accept the proposal, provided that it could be implemented, saying it was "certainly outstanding in the soundness of its aims, its clarity of presentation, and the evident understanding and appreciation of the best of modern education."[48] Hessen's first school reform plan, a 4-4-4 system, also seemed to ERA officials a very good start.

Thus, as the deadline for submitting detailed long-range plans approached, OMGUS was confronted with two quite distinct sets of responses. It had suggested publicly that it was willing to tolerate a range of designs, but the Bavarian plan was clearly beyond the pale, and that of Württemberg-Baden only somewhat better. The Bremen and Hessian plans looked promising but were still merely paper reforms, and as OMGUS was about to discover, talk was cheap.

In June 1947 the most important Allied document pertaining to postwar educational reform, known as ACA 54, was promulgated jointly by the United States, Britain, France, and the Soviet Union. Pushed by the United States, the document contained a list of principles to guide institutional reform in German education in all four zones. Since "democratization" of German education was a goal shared by all the Allied powers, several tenets of ACA 54 are too broad to be characterized as functional equivalents; they are better seen as vague areas of international agreement: educational opportunity for all; compulsory full-time school attendance until the age of fifteen and at least part-time attendance until eighteen; a curriculum to promote international goodwill and understanding; a democratic school administration

46. Tent, *Mission on the Rhine*, 124–25.
47. Thron, "Schulreform," 102; Tent, *Mission on the Rhine*, 129–32.
48. Thron, "Schulreform," 100.

sensitive to the wishes of the people; and the teaching of civic responsibility and democracy through both the curriculum and the organization of the school itself.

At a greater level of specificity, however, all three core tenets of the American functional equivalent approach are codified in ACA 54: free tuition and materials for all primary and secondary pupils; the abolition of fully separate academic and vocational tracks in favor of consecutive levels of instruction; and university-level training for all teachers, not just those in the *Gymnasien*. Thus, the functional equivalent strategy was embedded in a range of other mechanisms to promote institutional change. Yet as the school reform struggle escalated, the institutional transfer component came to dominate the OMGUS agenda: it pursued institutional changes differing both from educational practices in other European states of the time and from policies pursued by the other Allied powers in Germany.

Again, in pushing transfer, OMGUS did not insist that Germans exactly reproduce American institutions. Payne Templeton, the head of ERA in Württemberg-Baden, spoke out repeatedly on this subject, remarking, "We understand that every educational system must be related to the culture and history of the particular *Land*, indeed we believe that the atmosphere of every locality ought to be tangible in its own schools. Nevertheless, we also believe . . . that the American program of democratic education has certain advantages which, when modified, can and should be built into the German education system."[49] Still, ERA officials occasionally reminded themselves to focus on the core mission of educational reform and not to substitute smaller modifications for the key structural changes desired. E. F. Lindquist, an OMGUS "visiting expert" from the Iowa State University, argued forcefully for this position at an ERA conference:

> [OMGUS's] exclusive educational goal . . . is the democratization of Germany. . . . Anything done by American educational authorities in Germany must be justified in terms of its direct or indirect contribution to this one all-important objective. There are many ways in which German education could be "improved," in the sense of being made more efficient or more effective with reference to other educational goals. Many of these ways must seem almost painfully obvious to the American educator—ways, for example, of "improving" the teaching of arithmetic, or of home economics, or present practices in vocational education, physical education, school building planning, etc. Many of these "improvements" could be readily effected, but even if effected, many of them would make no appreciable contribution to the one real objective. Nevertheless, the temptation to take the time to bring about such improvements appears to be very strong, particularly, perhaps, because of the frustrations that have been experienced in direct attacks on the major issue, and because of the natural desire to be able to point to some definite accom-

49. Quoted in ibid., 69.

plishments. It is a temptation, it seems to me, against which American educators in Germany must be constantly on guard, lest they lose the real campaign while winning minor skirmishes.[50]

The second round of school reform commenced with the October 1, 1947, deadline for detailed long-term plans. Despite constant negotiations with the Ministry of Culture, ERA had clearly failed to convince Bavaria to develop a common school. The Bavarians proposed to provide tuition help for children of poor parents, but they were unwilling to budge on textbook costs or teacher-training issues. In fact, the second Bavarian plan was judged by OMGUS to be "in many respects . . . even more reactionary than the first." The Bavarians countered that "internal (pedagogical renewal)" reforms were much more essential than "merely external (organizational) changes."[51] OMGUS officials in Bavaria judged that Minister of Culture Alois Hundhammer "does not want a single track school system and real educational opportunities for all children. He does not want equality between secondary and elementary teachers. He does not want Catholic and Protestant children in the same classroom. . . . The Minister furthermore does not want free education for all children, still less free textbooks and teaching materials. He does not want the masses of children in secondary schools, nor very large numbers in universities. . . . He does not want to disturb the stratified class structure of German society."[52] On December 23, 1947, OMGUS officially rejected the second draft in a letter to Bavarian Prime Minister Hans Ehard.

The Württemberg-Baden plan was seen as an improvement, though scant, over the goals submitted in April, but OMGUS worried that it lacked both specificity and a timetable for implementation. Appalled by the Bavarian plan and further disconcerted by that of Württemberg-Baden, OMGUS was also disappointed with the noticeable slowing of reform in the other *Länder*. Concern grew about the paucity of implementation measures being developed and about the lack of a concerted public relations effort on the plans' behalf. In Hessen, OMGUS officials had long considered the maverick CDU Minister of Culture Erwin Stein to be working in close tandem with Hessian ERA officials. Yet his October 1 plan was in some ways a step back from the April version and had also distanced itself from the recommendations of expert "working groups" formed to advise the ministry on school reform. The Hessian ERA saw in his proposal to reintroduce elective subjects—particularly Latin—as early as fifth grade a move back toward early differentiation for *Gymnasium* pupils.[53] In Bremen, a messy fight to finally ratify the *Land* constitution had included a rebellion by Catholics over provisions that

---

50. Quoted in Keller, "Vocational Education," 8–9.
51. Thron, "Schulreform," 108.
52. Quoted in ibid., 112–13. OMGUS believed that Hundhammer was attempting "to return the educational system to its 1913 pattern" (quoted in ibid., 90).
53. Tent, *Mission on the Rhine*, 177–79.

threatened public funding for privately run schools. Also, the demonstration effect of Bavarian resistance and of the fierce opposition to school reforms being implemented autonomously by the SPD in Hamburg and Schleswig-Holstein under British occupation had led Bremen's SPD senator for education affairs, Christian Paulmann, to slow his own reform ambitions.[54]

As 1947 drew to a close, then, the ERA saw intransigence from Bavaria and Württemberg-Baden and backtracking from Hessen and Bremen. In response, OMGUS officials authorized a third, desperate offensive that included a combination of threats, orders, and the avoidance of democratic processes that they had themselves established. The ERA ordered elected officials to implement the key elements of ACA 54. It backed off on some demands for the reform of the secondary school—angrily accepting that neither the *Gymnasium*'s importance nor its accessibility would be seriously changed—but held to its insistence on six-year elementary schools, free books and tuition, and university-level teacher training. In a battle for pride and principle, it sought to salvage what it could before the occupation ended.

Short sketches of the political disputes in the three U.S. zone *Länder* where OMGUS resorted to orders—Hessen, Bavaria, and Bremen—also serve to trace the ultimate outcomes of the institutional transfer attempts.[55]

The Endgame in Three Länder: *Variations on a Disappointing Theme*

State authority over education complicated U.S. efforts at institutional transfer. Issuing orders (and threatening to fire German officials who failed to carry them out) caused different reactions in different places. In Hessen, OMGUS attempted to engage the region's reform tradition in education by setting up "working groups" on school reform.[56] The experts in these groups, appointed by the ministry with ERA approval, were soon caught in a tug of war as Hessian ERA officials and Minister of Culture Stein both attempted to manipulate the structure of public participation. The ERA grew concerned that "uninformed" outsiders were dominating public discussions of the school reform drafts that had been the subject of long negotiation by the experts. Stein came under pressure from groups representing parents and teachers of *Gymnasium* pupils, and he resented the working committees' resistance to incorporating his suggestions for earlier differentiation of pupils. An organizational change to "streamline" the committees and reestablish them under the auspices of the ministry superficially appeared to meet the

54. Tent, ibid., 206–7.
55. Only in Württemberg-Baden was no recourse made to direct orders or explicit threats, because the director of military government there was opposed to such measures. The American efforts died quietly as seven bills were defeated before the end of the occupation in 1949. Ibid., 237.
56. Lawson, *Reform*, 67–77.

needs of both parties, but the opponents of school reform merely mobilized resistance in new ways. In the end the CDU's Stein was caught between the ERA's and the conservatives' demands. Next, his compromise proposal was blocked by a coalition of the Catholic church, the organization of secondary school teachers, and his own party.[57] By late 1948 Stein was still publicly promoting both "internal renewal" and institutional change but was also maintaining that "an imitation of foreign models would mean the stagnation of intellectual development in Germany."[58]

No six-year elementary school was achieved in Hessen. After exhaustive negotiations between ERA officials and Stein, OMGUS finally ordered the minister, on August 4, 1948, to ensure that no fourth graders in his jurisdiction would move directly into a higher school but would instead enter a fifth elementary year after 1948–49. Stein's first countermove, however, was to convince the parliament to postpone the beginning of the next school year by six months. Following this delay, he moved to negotiate with the ERA. OMGUS and the ministry each appointed four members of a negotiating board, a contrivance that allowed Hessen yet another year before extending the elementary schools as ordered—and by the end of that year the new occupation statute had ended U.S. authority over educational institutions. Further, although the Hessian constitution had called for an end to tuition and textbook charges, the law stipulating this provision was not passed until February 1949. After long negotiations, a complicated agreement did move teacher training to so-called pedagogical institutes; though they were not universities, this change represented a lone bright spot in the once promising ERA efforts in Hessen.

In Hessen the cultural minister was at least initially disposed toward school reform, but in Bavaria the ERA ran up against a committed opponent in Alois Hundhammer. Within a week of its official rejection of the second Bavarian plan, the ERA ordered both Hundhammer and Prime Minister Ehard to produce a satisfactory reform proposal by February 1, 1948. Ehard vehemently protested the shift from suggestions to direct orders, but Hundhammer proceeded to construct precisely the plan ERA had called for—simultaneously, however, beginning a public relations campaign to paint the reforms as the "Americanization" of German education. His primary themes were the purported cost of U.S. proposals and the destruction of the *Gymnasium* as a unique institution of learning.[59]

Moreover, as Bavarian officials had made no plans for curricular reform, OMGUS feared that they might try to sabotage the American-promoted legislation by passing all the provisions simultaneously before any preparations

57. Tent, *Mission on the Rhine*, 195–99.
58. Erwin Stein, "Comments on School Reform," October 30, 1948, reprinted in *Neubeginn und Restauration, 1945–1949*, ed. Hans-Jürgen Rühl (Munich: dtv, 1982), 318.
59. Tent, *Mission on the Rhine*, 143.

had been made for implementation. Consequently, the ERA demanded preliminary steps and even set up a fund to pay for them.[60] In vocational education too, OMGUS officials noted, although organizational reform plans had been laid out for demonstration projects in Bavaria, "care [was] required to prevent the use of demonstration schools as a method of 'stalling.'"[61] While OMGUS discussed removing Hundhammer, the ERA in Bavaria tried to select those parts of their reform that could be implemented even with a hostile ministry in place. This process led to a decision to back off on changing the elementary school structure and to focus instead on teacher training.

In the end, however, the Bavarians refused even to introduce the proposed legislation into their parliament during most of 1948. In April, under pressure from Military Governor Murray van Wagoner, Hundhammer and Ehard agreed to a plan to remove fees for tuition and texts for the 1949 school year and to establish a commission to plan for a six-year elementary school and university-level teacher training. But Hundhammer reneged on the deal within a month. After the further delay of the tuition and text bill until July 1948, the currency reform that had just been conducted then undercut *Länder* finances to such an extent that even the SPD voted against the bill in the Bavarian parliament's budget committee.[62] The situation worsened when the ERA brought in General Clay to declare that tuition and text charges would simply be billed to the Bavarian government as occupation costs; Ehard nearly resigned in protest. An agreement between Clay and Ehard on tuition and texts was finally passed by the parliament—against the protests and maneuverings of Hundhammer—on December 15, 1948. But although the ERA continued to pressure the Bavarians on the other issues, no further movement proved possible.

In Bremen the political momentum to implement school reform was slowed by a bizarre institutional factor: the last Nazi law (1938) codifying Bremen's traditional school structures. The Bremen constitution required any law that replaced an existing one to be passed by a two-thirds majority, and even the fact that Bremen was controlled by a leftist SPD and KPD coalition and had quite reform-oriented education officials was insufficient in itself to create the basis for statutory reform. Given this constitutional hurdle, Chris-

---

60. Thron, "Schulreform," 128–29.
61. Keller, "Vocational Education," 45. Consistent with the logic of the functional equivalent approach, institutional complexes without a significant American counterpart were underattended by ERA, so OMGUS reformed vocational training very little. It did not try to end the dual system of school and firm-based training, but it did intend to promote more class time and see that "social studies" were taught. The education mission (and ACA 54) assumed that modern industrial work demanded workers flexible enough to learn rapidly changing tasks quickly, instead of workers whose training was centered on one particular vocation; therefore, truly democratic (general) education was also the best industrial education. And if the goals conflicted, it was certainly "more important to be a good citizen than a good *Handwerker*" (Franz Hilker memo in Rühl, *Neubeginn*, 313–14).
62. Tent, *Mission on the Rhine*, 153.

tian Paulmann, the top education official of the SPD-KPD majority, could not immediately begin his ambitious plans for a common school. Paulmann asked the ERA to be patient until he could persuade the Bremer Demokratische Volkspartei—then in opposition with the CDU—to get on board and give him the needed two-thirds majority. In the spring of 1948, OMGUS agreed to a delay in order to make time for a "vigorous publicity campaign," and Paulmann promised a law by Easter 1949.

Yet, the opposition, if anything, hardened during the delay, leaving the minister in a quandary. OMGUS kept constant pressure on him, telling him that if no law was forthcoming before April, it would use direct orders to impose a reform.[63] Finally, on March 31, 1949, Bremen did pass legislation calling for six-year elementary schools and for secondary schools which, despite substantial internal differentiation (*four* different tracks), would at least house all the pupils in one building. The ERA officially called the plan "acceptable" and even expressed hope that other *Länder* would look to it for guidance. But Bremen SPD officials worried that thoroughgoing reform, if no other states complied, might expose their pupils to discrimination by other states, and the city parliament was slow to implement the legislation.[64] Paulmann, for his part, reported that with the May 1948 passage of the law for free tuition and texts and with the "internal reforms" of the school system, "all of the privileges of birth, vocation and property in the area of education had been done away with."[65] His self-satisfied comment reflected his party's waning interest in fighting school reform battles at the side of the Americans. In 1957 Bremen further softened even its modest reform by again allowing *Gymnasium* entrance after only four years of common elementary schooling.

THE FALLBACK TO "REORIENTATION"

In November 1947, Herman Wells, the president of Indiana University, replaced Richard Alexander as the head of ERA, and on May 1, 1948, ERA was upgraded to division status with four branches: education, religious affairs, cultural affairs, and group activities. These changes did not bring an immediate shift in education policy, for as Wells proclaimed, "The battle on school reform is so important that if we lose it we might just as well go home."[66] Wells's key contribution, however, was to lay the foundation for an ambitious set of cultural exchange programs financed through both private American donations and U.S. government funds. But Alonzo Grace, who soon replaced

63. Ibid., 216.
64. Thron, "Schulreform," 156.
65. Christian Paulmann, "Das Bremische Schulwesen im Umbau," *Schule und Gegenwart* 1, nos. 9–10 (1949): 11–12.
66. Quoted in Thron, "Schulreform," 136.

Wells, declared that the first three years of the occupation had focused far too much on institutional change and had been "more or less devoid of an educational and cultural relations effort."[67] For Grace, "the true reform of the German people will come from within. It will be spiritual and moral. The types of school organization or structure, for example, are of less importance to the future of Germany and the world than what is taught, how it is taught, and by whom it is taught."[68]

Grace immediately threw himself into building up the cultural exchange programs between Germany and the United States for which Wells had laid the foundation.[69] Clay, wary of the German reaction to school reform and now convinced of the possibilities of exchange programs, soon ended the school reform initiatives.[70] Thus, although Grace had a strong interest in American influence on German education, his emphasis on the cultural exchange approach marked a clear shift away from the functional equivalent approach to institutional transfer which had characterized the previous two years of efforts.

If their effectiveness is difficult to measure, the exchange programs certainly proved enduringly popular.[71] Richard Merritt argues that although elites raged against "Americanization," most Germans were indifferent to such charges and certainly thought they could learn something about democracy from the Americans. The public opinion data he employs generally suggest that average Germans favored OMGUS programs for promoting democracy and even if ignorant of those actually being implemented, would reply (when asked) that they thought such projects would work.[72] In any event, both laudatory and critical accounts of the exchange programs agree that their rise marked the end of a sustained effort at school reform.[73] Thus, whereas trips to America *complemented* the institutional transfer efforts in the industrial relations case, they were a *substitute*—a fallback position—in the education case.

67. Ibid., 140. Grace had been commissioner of education in Connecticut before joining the ERA.

68. Quoted in ibid., 142. Ironically, Grace resigned over the decision, codified in the 1949 occupation statutes, to relinquish control over education. Although he advocated empowering Germans—to justify the strategic shift away from reforming the school system along American lines—he rejected the idea that the occupation should relinquish all control of "cultural affairs." Clay, however, insisted that the document maximize German power and authority.

69. Tent (*Mission on the Rhine*) shows that previous efforts to establish exchange programs had largely foundered on Clay's reluctance; Clay feared that German students might not be accepted in America.

70. Ibid., 306–11.

71. Lawson's data (*Reform*, 105) suggest that in Bavaria they were the only part of the OMGUS agenda to enjoy any broad approval; even Hundhammer, archfoe of Americanization, took advantage of one such program to visit the United States.

72. Merritt, *Democracy Imposed*, 285–86.

73. Tent, *Mission on the Rhine*, and Lange-Quassowski, *Neuordnung*, respectively.

SILENT PARTNERS: THE OMGUS FAILURE TO RECRUIT
ORGANIZED ALLIES

How did the OMGUS agenda of encouraging German actors to develop
acceptable and enduring school reform degenerate into a frantic and failed
series of orders to conduct one version of it? Was there potential for such a
reform? If so, why did it go unused? To answer these questions, I look at ERA
efforts to measure and win support from German public opinion, intermediate associations, and political parties.

At least on the surface, the German public seemed open-minded about
U.S. proposals for school reform; polls conducted by OMGUS suggested that
the public was willing to consider them. Not surprisingly, though, education
reform was not seen as a primary consideration in a country devastated by
war and its aftermath. In a 1945 OMGUS study only about one-fifth of the
Germans who were asked thought there were *major* problems in education;
they tended to list such difficulties as teacher inexperience and shortages of
buildings and personnel.[74] A May 1947 OMGUS survey in Württemberg-
Baden, however, suggested that public perception of a need for reform had
shifted over time: although 62% of the 650 people queried thought the traditional schools and curricula were adequate to meet the needs of German
youth under normal conditions, 44% still thought that the education of the
child was dependent upon the wealth and status of the parents (12% agreed
with both statements). Even in this conservative stronghold only 30% of respondents thought no connection existed between socioeconomic background and educational opportunity.

Of course, such levels of concern did not necessarily mean that the German public was open to substantial institutional change. After all, even if
44% agreed that socioeconomic status affected educational opportunity, that
rather abstract connection was still a far cry from endorsing reforms that
could close the village school. Unfortunately, OMGUS had no way to measure
the strength of respondents' convictions and little sense of the stability of
German public opinion. As U.S. officials learned when the Catholic clergy began opposing school reform from the pulpit, other actors could shift these
opinions.

Yet the ERA did little to convince the German public about the importance
of education reform; its efforts were modest, late, and ineffective. Only with
the transition to cultural exchange programs was there a substantial increase
in "grassroots" work by the (then larger) Education and Cultural Relations
division.[75] Moreover, the ERA had difficulty getting Ministry of Culture personnel even in Hessen and Bremen to stump for their own reform plans be-

---

74. Merritt, *Democracy Imposed*, 275.
75. Lange-Quassowski, *Neuordnung*, 200.

cause, as confrontation grew, such actors often tried to distance themselves publicly from American policies in order to maintain their own legitimacy.

In distancing themselves, politicians were probably less impressed by the surface ambivalence of public opinion than by the focused opposition of certain organized interests. For if the public was largely indifferent to school reform, the many associations surrounding German educational politics clearly were not. Even in Bavaria, alternative school reform plans abounded: the Ministry of Culture, the main parties, the universities of Munich and Erlangen, the Bavarian Academy of Sciences, both Catholic and Protestant churches, the teachers' unions, and the chamber of commerce all developed school reform plans.[76] But although original U.S. planning laid education reform squarely at the feet of German actors, OMGUS developed few tools to encourage and influence the groups most concerned with education.

Even while it was still organizationally weak, the ERA did encourage *Länder* education officials to involve other "affected parties" (especially teachers) in formulating reform plans, but only in Hessen, with its long reform tradition, did such a step occur from the beginning. When OMGUS returned the first school reform drafts to each *Land* in the spring of 1947, it again repeated the instruction to consult affected social groups.[77] Württemberg-Baden's second draft was heavily criticized for not creating the local committees that were supposed to help devise curricular and organizational reform. Württemberg-Baden did not begin to institute such committees until after the third and most confrontational round of school reform. Bavaria, also a holdout in this regard, used the lack of curriculum committees as a way to retard progress.[78] In the end, OMGUS proved organizationally incapable of promoting an inclusive and democratic formulation of school reform policy. It was that failure which led to its undemocratic efforts to dictate such policies.

Within the educational establishment itself, associations of school psychologists and other agencies that provided services to schools tended to favor school reform but to be cautious in their support, often withdrawing from politicized issues into more narrowly professional ones.[79] The associations of *Volksschulen* teachers and of vocational school teachers too tended to support proposals for longer elementary and more common schooling, whereas the associations of teachers and administrators of *Gymnasien* and other higher schools generally opposed them. In Württemberg-Baden, after the *Volksschulen* teachers charged the higher school teachers with inciting the opposition of pupils—and, by extension, their parents—to reform proposals, the

---

76. See the versions reprinted in *Dokumente zur Schulreform in Bayern*, ed. Hans Merkt (Munich: Richard Pflaum, 1952).

77. Thron, "Schulreform," 104.

78. Ibid., 117.

79. Lawson, *Reform*, 98.

traditionalists accused these primary school teachers of being "collaborators of the occupation forces and therefore traitors to their fatherland."[80] The Association of Higher School Teachers in Hessen defended the traditional system as historically proven and biologically natural: far from its excluding children of certain classes (classes whose very existence in the wake of the war's destruction they often denied), the case was simply that the less gifted and less industrious excluded themselves. Association members rejected the charge of authoritarianism in pedagogy, arguing that too many groups and organizations had oversight or involvement in the modern school for injustice to go long uncovered. They also celebrated local control as an alternative to the dulling uniformity of a nationwide common school which, they said, ran counter to subsidiarity, the "grounding principle of the universe."[81]

Although Catholic and Protestant churches both opposed school reform, Catholic opposition proved most sustained and damaging. Occupation clashes with church officials seemed to bring out the worst on both sides. Incredibly, OMGUS appointed as chief U.S. negotiator on school reform in Bavaria an ex-priest who was married to an ex-nun; this move enraged the Catholic hierarchy and further undercut the legitimacy of American school reform efforts there.[82]

As conflicts grew, proponents of reforms similar to those called for by the ERA were careful to distance themselves from the Americans. For example, the Bavarian Teachers' Association (BLV), in the foreword to its school reform plan of 1947, emphasized that its proposal for a common school was not an opportunistic attempt to ride the American coattails but a plan that "grew rather out of the pedagogical traditions of the BLV and similar associations and for the realization of which distinguished pedagogues have long fought."[83] The shift from persuasion to threats of force also, at least in Bavaria, undercut the ERA's school reform allies in the SPD because the party then lost its active role in pushing reform in the parliament. Clearly, the Bavarian SPD was particularly weak, as evidenced by the CSU's ability to keep the bill out of the parliament for so long (indeed, in the final analysis the parliament simply approved a deal already struck between Clay and Ehard).[84] But the shift to threats of force left the SPD vulnerable to the "collaborationist" charge, leading it to distance itself visibly from OMGUS proposals.

When it came to school reform, unions were the dog that didn't bark. Though the secular unions had long advocated the democratization of schools as a complement to their efforts to democratize the economy, they

80. Quoted in Tent, *Mission on the Rhine*, 229.
81. *"Allgemeine Richtlinien"* of the *Landesverband Hessen für Höhere Schulen*, September 13, 1947.
82. Tent, *Mission on the Rhine*, 139–40.
83. Merkt, *Dokumente zur Schulreform*, 119.
84. Thron, "Schulreform," 120. The SPD had introduced a school reform bill on July 17, 1947; it included all of the provisions ERA was pushing, but it went nowhere: Merkt, *Dokumente zur Schulreform*, 94–107.

were reluctant to engage in school reform disputes, given their concerted efforts to organize religious workers in the new deconfessionalized unions. The U.S. occupation's education officers, drawn heavily from the ranks of U.S. school administration, seem never to have bothered to look for working-class support for their reforms, despite the long tradition of German union support for common schools. A glance at American education vis-à-vis labor offers an intriguing possible explanation for this oversight. In comparative perspective, America's early guarantee of educational access meant later difficulty in incorporating labor politics into educational supervision. The broader labor movement remained a weak player, and its already thin participation in American education—channeled almost exclusively through its role in municipal political machines—was fatally weakened after the turn of the century when schools were "progressively" insulated from municipal influence. As Ira Katznelson and Margaret Weir have noted, there was "no working class political movement or party system capable of successfully opposing the dissociation of school administration from municipal politics," a dissociation that "diminished the chances workers had to shape their children's schools." As a result, working-class capacities in this area quickly eroded after the Progressive era.[85]

Even when supportive German groups were identified, the ERA had difficulty using them to promote reform. The "working groups for new schools" in Hessen consisted of eleven expert committees in three broad areas (primary, vocational, and higher schools). The 229 members met 202 times in various groups and generally supported school reform.[86] It turned out, however, that these committees were more useful in encouraging smaller innovations such as student councils than in helping OMGUS and Minister of Culture Stein secure public support for school reform. When resistance stiffened, Stein channeled the working groups into a new form, the *Landesschulbeirat* (LSB). These "*Land* school councils" were subordinated to his ministry and devoted to curricular reform instead of institutional change.[87] Once pulled into the ministry, they largely ceased to be a source of original ideas for the structural reform of schools.

ERA officers concentrated their limited energies on alternately lobbying and threatening officials in the Ministry of Culture, but even "successful" lobbying was often just a prelude to later backtracking by the ministry. Stein's experience when he endorsed the inclusion of the six-year elementary school in the draft law of 1948 offered a stark illustration of the dangers of allying with OMGUS. Even though his government coalition partners in the SPD criticized the rest of the draft for not pushing the common school agenda

85. Ira Katznelson and Margaret Weir, *Schooling for All* (New York: Basic Books, 1985), 93.
86. The costs of these groups, which amounted to 40,000 reichsmarks, were paid mainly from American sources.
87. Mühlhausen, *Hessen*, 470–72.

more aggressively, his own CDU caucus publicly criticized the six-year elementary recommendation; moreover, the Catholic church, all four Hessian universities, and a number of parents' and teachers' associations opposed it outright.[88] In this case, the school working groups could offer scant support to the minister and little help in publicizing the plan and breaking down opposition. Thus, even in the *Land* where the ERA dedicated the most material and personnel resources to stimulating debate and contributions from civil society, the forum it created was too disconnected from the public to be able to support a CDU minister dedicated to school reform. In short, OMGUS efforts to engage German civil society proved inadequate, and waiting to act until the old system had been reestablished proved fatal.

OMGUS did engage political parties, but here too there were problems: by having to work through German parliaments (true to its original plan), it gave up crucial forms of control over education. Later, as a result, it had to engage in a difficult process of specifying vague lists of functions and then rejecting German drafts that did not provide for them. Personnel shortages go some way toward explaining the choice to work with ministry officials rather than directly with parties. The official fiction of noninterference in educational affairs also contributed to the reluctance to approach nonministry officials. But by the end, even the Bavarian SPD and Free Democratic Party (FDP) opposed legislation on free tuition and materials, in part because of ERA tactics. As OMGUS officials ruefully and rightfully acknowledged, "no party is going to lose votes in order to stand up for Military Government."[89]

In retrospect, ERA's tactics produced a kind of "democratic deficit" in which elite-level bargains turned out to be quite fragile when effects such as costs and the reorganization of local school systems filtered down to the public, interest groups, and political parties. The resulting confrontations were quite striking: OMGUS felt betrayed by the *Länder* ministry personnel whom they had trusted; conservative and progressive organizations alike felt ignored by politicians who were not willing to include them; and the public clientele of these organizations became politicized around misleading, often bizarre, descriptions of the proposals. In this context, change sounded risky and expensive, and the status quo easily prevailed. Further, it seems not to have especially mattered which party was in power, since any *Land* government inclined to try to sell a thoroughgoing school reform would have needed substantial help from OMGUS in doing so—help that the ERA was unable to provide, given its originally low organizational status.[90] Education "insiders" such as Christian Paulmann failed, whereas an education policy neophyte such as Alois Hundhammer succeeded in blocking school reform.

88. Ibid., 475–76.

89. John Elliot letter to Edward Litchfield, August 14, 1948, quoted in Thron, "Schulreform," 152.

90. That status, again, grew out of its original mandate simply to oversee German reforms.

At bottom, neither the Social Democrats, the reformist Christian Democrats, nor the Americans made education a high priority and devoted substantial resources to it; when they encountered organizations that did focus on education, they all ran into a buzz saw of opposition.

Skirmishes Won, Campaigns Lost

OMGUS efforts to achieve institutional transfer before the end of military occupation in 1949 clearly failed. Nor did these efforts appear to stimulate domestic proponents sufficiently to bring about indigenous reform thereafter. Through most of the 1950s the school reforms promoted by the Americans and long pushed by the SPD literally disappeared from the agenda. Already in its 1948 program the SPD had dropped its explicit opposition to the traditional three-track system, although it did continue to call for the six-year elementary and free tuition and materials. When Hessen returned a solid SPD majority in November 1950, the party made no moves toward further school reforms, and in its 1952 program even the demand for the six-year elementary school was removed. Unlike institutional innovation in industrial relations, which continued throughout the 1950s (especially on questions of codetermination), school reform gave way to a consolidation of the German three-track system.

Yet beginning in the late 1960s, common schools (*Gesamtschulen*) were introduced as experiments in several German states. By 1990 just under 10% of German secondary pupils were enrolled in *Gesamtschulen*. Did the breakthrough build upon the abortive efforts of the occupation period, or is it more likely that the occupation failures postponed and weakened the common school movement?

Since the ERA was at least able to change educational forms and practices less central than those of the school structures themselves, did its victories in what Lindquist had called "minor skirmishes," taken together, constitute a substantial American contribution to the reform of German education? Despite the ineffectiveness of institutionalized school reform, that a host of changes occurred in German primary and secondary education after the war is beyond dispute. For example, besides the end of tuition and materials charges and the upgrading of teacher training in Bremen and Hessen, during and after the American occupation the teaching of social studies was increased in scope and deepened in content.[91] Health education, as called for

91. Ibid., 237–40; here too, however, the Americans suffered many disappointments, including the discovery that often the most willing "multipliers" of their reform proposals were somewhat eccentric Christian pedagogues who had been pushing related ideas since the Weimar period.

in ACA 54, became a part of the accepted curriculum in most *Länder*. And at the university level the United States promoted the addition of social sciences such as political science, economics, and public opinion research—although in practice Germans continued to conceptualize social science as a part of German philosophy rather than American science.[92]

The only available data concerning the sources of these changes were gathered in 1962 by Robert Lawson, an American doctoral student in education. His surveys of teachers in Hessen, Hamburg (British zone), and Bavaria reveal the complexities of disentangling educational policy influences but shed much light on institutional transfer as a mode of institution building. Lawson first catalogued a range of changes in German education from 1945 to 1962. But although the changes correspond well to items called for in ACA 54, Lawson noted that this finding alone is no evidence that the Allies actually caused them. Consequently, he developed a questionnaire that he sent to teachers and administrators at fifty-six urban and rural schools in all three *Länder*: twenty *Gymnasien* and thirty-six *Volksschulen* or *Mittelschulen*. A total of 300 questionnaires brought some 150 responses from thirty-seven schools.[93] Lawson asked his respondents to list the five most important changes in the German school system since 1945, to designate the sources of those changes, and then to evaluate the overall influence of occupation policies.[94] The five changes judged most important by his respondents—university level teacher training, free schooling, free instructional materials, the introduction of social studies, and the reform of the upper level of the *Gymnasium*—reflected key American goals but did not include the central goal of increasing common schooling.[95]

Lawson then invited the respondents to code the changes they considered important as springing either from "educational thought before 1933," "foreign influence during the occupation period," or "new ideas independently developed by German educators after 1945." Interestingly, although some respondents complained that it was difficult to distinguish between pre-1933 and post-1945 developments, none apparently had difficulty sorting out post-1945 foreign-influenced developments from post-1945 "independently German" ideas. One possible explanation is that most respondents, like Lawson himself, saw the changes then afoot as driven by the necessities of mod-

92. David Staley, "In Whose Image? Knowledge, Social Science and Democracy in Occupied Germany, 1943–1955" (Ph.D. diss., Ohio State University, 1993).

93. All the Catholic secondary schools refused to participate, and Lawson received from several unwilling respondents written rebuttals to the presumption that such influences could be ascertained, if indeed they existed at all.

94. It is unclear how many respondents had taught prior to 1933 and were therefore in a position to judge "before and after" changes from personal experience.

95. Lawson, *Reform*, 114–15. The memory of the six-year elementary was good for thirty-first place, right after "whole word reading" and next to "international contact." Common secondary schools, of course, had never actually been implemented and did not make the list.

ernization, which Germans could presumably appreciate independent of foreign influences.[96] In actuality, though, the fact that German education during this period did not appreciably converge on that of other European nations makes it less plausible that Germans were part of a broad wave of simultaneous discovery, as their collective answers and Lawson's analysis often implied.[97]

Lawson's respondents generally thought that the Allies had had a positive impact (as opposed to negative or none) on German education, yet they considered the magnitude of that impact quite low. Further, they almost never attributed innovations solely to the occupation; rather, in those areas where foreign influences during the occupation were judged important, changes were always seen as also linked either to pre-1933 educational thought or to independent post-1945 ideas. In-school psychological assistance to pupils, for example, was regarded as "accepted" but attributed to older German precedents and to the evident needs of the postwar situation. The inception of local parent councils was likewise "credited to the occupation period but traced back to early German ideas." Student councils, on the other hand, ran up not only against teachers' authoritarian mores but also against their suspicion of organized young people after their experience of the Hitler Youth. In addition, the functions of the new student councils remained opaque, since German schools were not offering the range of activities that U.S. student councils help oversee.[98]

Lawson also acknowledged strictly voluntary institutional imitation: "All day schools [as opposed to the half-day German norm] were introduced before the war, but the new interest in them after 1945 was said [by his interview partners] to be stimulated by information on American practices. This is an example of an area where information on American practice was influential but unrelated to occupation plans." Lawson's respondents also noted the internal "liberalization" of authority relations in schools at both teacher-administrator and teacher-student levels. These improved relations too were attributed to older German ideas given new "impulse" by American efforts.[99]

Lawson's approach suggests that institutional transfer has two modes: ideas or influences from outside may be a catalyst to existing ideas that push those indigenous plans forward, or outside impulses may be truly new, in which case they must be adapted to local conditions.[100] Lawson's views on transfer are thus very much in line with the concept of pulling in foreign institutional

96. See ibid., 109–36.
97. On convergence, see Fritz Ringer, *Education and Society in Modern Europe* (Bloomington: Indiana University Press, 1979), 250–65.
98. Lawson, *Reform*, 42–43.
99. Ibid., 107.
100. Robert Lawson, "Das Berliner Schulwesen als Laborsituation 1945–1965," in *Schule in Berlin: Gestern und Heute*, ed. Benno Schmoldt and Hagen Gretzmacher (Berlin: Colloquium Verlag, 1989): 83.

models. But because his work is fundamentally a history of ideas, not of the political influence and strategies behind those ideas, it is susceptible to the tautology that institutional transfer worked when Germans accepted it. At this limit, institutional transfer becomes a purely cognitive phenomenon. For example, Lawson argues that "the points of [ACA] 54, inasmuch as they took up earlier German reform efforts, or respond to social-educational needs of postwar Germans, are still having an effect on German education. Thus, free schooling, uniformity of teacher training standards, extension of compulsory education, and international emphases in historical and political instruction are living issues in German education today. Where an Occupation aim reflected a particular American characteristic, such as the comprehensive high school, there is little residual effect."[101]

I have demonstrated, however, that the "social-educational needs of postwar Germans" were sufficiently in dispute to make that concept badly underspecified. There was a substantial reform tradition committed to comprehensive schools, but rather than trying to mobilize popular opposition to traditional schools, OMGUS merely leaned on German elites, insiders who had no desire to change the system. My analysis suggests that American efforts not only were not geared toward mobilizing indigenous reform forces but in fact actually discredited some of the Germans who did work with OMGUS.

The analysis can now move beyond the claim that institutional transfer was effective when Germans accepted it. First, "acceptance" in this case would have required political persuasion and a coherent strategy, not *ex ante* cognitive agreement. Second, failure mattered. America's modest catalysis of some German reforms must be weighed against the setback it dealt to the central goal of school reform. The argument that American efforts boosted the chances for subsequent reform, even if such attempts failed in the short term, has both intermediate and long-term variants. The intermediate variant begins from the accurate observation that in the western zones of postwar Germany the United States was the most active advocate of school reform. Without such an effort, the argument continues, virtually no reforms would have been conducted. The implication is that America strengthened the German reform movement.[102] Yet this conclusion seems unlikely, since the preliminary evidence is that during the 1950s both the SPD and the trade unions dropped efforts to reform public and vocational schools.[103] That the SPD moved much closer to the CDU on questions of school policy during the 1950s is clear. My suggestion that the OMGUS school reform fiasco ultimately damaged the longer-term prospects for increased common schooling

101. Lawson, *Reform*, 210.

102. Lange-Quassowski, *Neuordnung*, 206–7.

103. Michael Taylor, *Education and Work in the Federal Republic of Germany* (London: Anglo-German Foundation for the Study of Industrial Society, 1981), 134–37.

in Germany is speculative; to sustain it would require more research into the SPD's reasons for dropping reforms oriented toward achieving common schools. But that outcome may simply be overdetermined: besides the lingering bitterness of many actors and the public perception that identified common schools with "Americanization," economic growth and immigration in the 1950s both lessened reform pressures. Further, East Germany was taken as a negative example of the common school model.[104]

The long-term variant of the argument is that where the United States had strong ties to local actors, the failure of school reform was merely temporary. Tent points to Hessen, which emerged as a center of the *Gesamtschulen* movement in the late 1960s, as evidence that the United States helped build a community of reformers. But even though Hessen (and Bremen) did have strong reform traditions that rebounded in the 1960s and even if the United States built the Hessian reform community in small ways, OMGUS, by discrediting the reform project in large ways, had set it back. And when the *Gesamtschulen* were eventually started, their architects generally looked to British and Swedish models, not American ones.[105] The *Gesamtschulen* movement received strong boosts from public dissatisfaction with the traditional system, from political support in several *Länder,* and from demographic trends that allowed it to build its own new schools instead of trying to convert existing ones. Yet despite these advantages, the schools have attracted less than 10% of western German pupils. Complicated disputes about the vices of contemporary *Gesamtschulen* aside, the purported virtues of "common schooling" can never be tested when the schools enroll such a small residual of pupils.[106] The immediate post-1945 period was a unique moment of supraclass thinking among German political elites, with "union" parties, "unitary" unions, and the "politics of productivity." The window of opportunity for supporters of common schools in Germany may never again be as wide as in the first postwar months, and for those supporters any positive effects of trying are surely secondary to the larger disappointments of failing.

CONCLUSION: CULTURE AS A STRATEGIC TOOL

Rather than make a normative appeal for or against common schools, I have analyzed the *effectiveness* of policymakers' use of institutional transfer.

104. Grams (*Kontinuität,* 260–62) argues that anti-Communist scholars incorrectly painted the GDR common school as exclusively a product of "Sovietization" and ignored the virtually unanimous intent of the German exile left to implement common schools in the postwar period.

105. Goldschmidt, "Transatlantic Influences," 36.

106. Most studies show that *Gesamtschulen* pupils and their parents are satisfied with the education given in these schools. But of course their contribution to society-wide democratization and tolerance is impossible to ascertain with confidence when common schooling remains so uncommon. For criticisms of *Gesamtschulen,* see Heinrich Wottawa, *Gesamtschule: Was sie uns wirklich bringt* (Dusseldorf: Schwann, 1982).

What the Americans urged in the name of democratization, a coalition of German forces successfully resisted as a lowering of educational standards. In all its phases, U.S. school reform policy showed sufficient flexibility to allow a place for German traditions and the exceptional postwar circumstances, and potential partners for this project existed on the German left and center-left and among some elements of the right. Yet U.S. reforms failed because U.S. strategy was indecisive, inconsistent, and insufficiently directed at building partnerships for school reform. The American failure to secure institutional reform, in conjunction with the ensuing economic miracle and a growing labor supply, meant that German educational reform did not reappear on the national agenda in any serious way until the early 1960s.

Internal disagreements about the desirability of transferring U.S.-inspired structures to Germany foreclosed any chance OMGUS had for a rapid start. Torn between punishing Germany and rebuilding it, officials allowed a compromise position ceding the structural reform initiative to the Germans to dominate the crucial initial period. Only when it became clear that no substantial reform would be forthcoming did OMGUS respond; as in the case of industrial relations, institutional transfer was its reaction to what it saw as problematic or inadequate indigenous reforms. But for the Christian Democrats and the Catholic church, the notion of "organic" structures in which institutions reflected deeper features of human society (in this case, natural differences in human ability) quickly became a code to justify resistance to the American project of institutional reform.[107] Once OMGUS had surrendered the organs of control, devoted its few education resources to the physical reconstruction of the traditional system, left longtime reform supporters to their own devices, and made only small efforts to win new allies, all its later efforts—however determined—were deeply compromised. Thus, the flexibility shown during the subsequent attempt at institutional transfer (beginning in 1947) was neutralized, and the reform potential in civil society was largely ignored. In the end, OMGUS backed down from forcing changes on democratically elected governments, abandoned the effort for school reform by 1949, and shifted occupation educational policy to a focus on student exchange programs.

Recent work on the failed civil service reform suggests that the cases have much in common.[108] A late start—again in 1946—foreclosed some initial opportunities for change. There seems to have been at least some use of what I have called the functional equivalent approach: OMGUS—in the name of separation of powers—sought to prevent civil servants from holding elective office and to promote "the Anglo-Saxon model of a Civil Service Commis-

---

107. Hoffmann, "Die Bildungspolitische Vorstellungen," 171, 183 ff.
108. Curt Garner, "Public Service Personnel in West Germany in the 1950s," *Journal of Social History* 29 (1995): 25–80; Rebecca Boehling, *A Question of Priorities: Democratic Reform and Economic Recovery in Postwar Germany* (Providence, R.I.: Berghahn, 1996), 246–57.

sion."[109] But again, the occupation had great difficulty exploiting SPD support for its basic objectives, actually splitting the party, and engendered the hostility of the CDU. As in the case of education, traditionalists damned the proposals as destined to result in lower quality. In this case, too, OMGUS resorted to efforts to impose a legislative settlement (MG Law 15), which the Germans countered with endless delaying tactics. Finally, after continuing the struggle into the first Adenauer administration, the Americans gave up, and the result was a lack of institutional reform.

Did transfer in education policy fail as a result of cultural resistance? It is clear by now that such a conclusion runs the risk of conflating the interests of Catholic educators and the indifference of the general public. It seems more accurate to say that the German opponents of school reform attempted to define education as "culture" in order to protect it. In doing so, they made strategic use of an essentially tautological category: culture is anything that one does not wish to see changed. Weimar reform traditions and the reform ideas of the SPD in the immediate postwar period indicate that the U.S. proposals all had viable histories in the German education reform debate. Some had even found a statutory foothold in the Weimar Republic, although resistance from bourgeois parties and a lack of money had prevented their realization.

But if the crude version of the cultural argument, that culture determines national aspirations, is unhelpful precisely because the German culture was so divided on school reform, what about softer versions? Dennis Bark and David Gress, for example, link the lack of institutional reform to the Germans' tendency to look at their education system with pride and to regard it as a "symbol of identity and hope"; they were "unwilling to see that, too, disappear, and become something foreign and unrecognizable."[110] Did opposition to school reform thus grow out of the Germans' need for stability? This seems, at best, a very partial explanation. They could just as easily have concluded that the failures of German conservatism called for change, and indeed, many Germans did come to that conclusion. Moreover, Japan accepted far more institutional changes in education than Germany without a noticeable destruction of its unique culture.[111] It may indeed be true that weariness and the search for stability played a role for some in Germany, but other groups were ready to give Weimar and American reform ideas a chance. The coalitional approach shows why OMGUS, despite its intentions, did not help them do so. Timing, resources, and legitimacy were all important in building coalitions with civil society. Larger disagreements in U.S. foreign policy drove

109. Boehling, *Question*, 252.
110. Dennis Bark and David Gress, *A History of West Germany* (Oxford: Basil Blackwell, 1989), 1:169.
111. For more on Japan, see Arnold Heidenheimer, *Disparate Ladders: Why School and University Policies Differ in Germany, Japan and Switzerland* (New Brunswick, N.J.: Transaction, 1997), 55–57.

timing; budgetary concerns in the postwar demobilization limited funds for the occupation.[112] And against the backdrop of an inconsistent and under-funded policy, any legitimacy that American educational institutions possessed by virtue of their abstract association with the American democracy and economy was quickly negated by the kinds of concrete steps OMGUS took to implement the policy.

I hold that policymakers' flexibility and the prior organization of non-state actors are important prerequisites for building coalitions to support transferred institutions. Yet although the U.S. occupation forces found a reasonably well-organized set of German actors and used flexibility in urging them to adopt American functional designs, they still failed miserably. For a fighting chance at effective institutional transfer, OMGUS would have needed to make a fairly explicit—and partisan—coalition with the German left, the only consistent advocate of common schools.[113] This finding presents an opportunity to clarify my broader argument further, for it poses an obvious choice: add "partisanship" as a third independent variable, or be more clear that the two factors I emphasize have probabilistic weight but do not guarantee effective transfer. I prefer the latter approach for two reasons.

First, adding partisanship puts the cause too close to the effect: it comes close to saying that an institutional change occurs when powerful actors want it to occur. But rather than focusing just on how laws are passed—a formalist approach for which the partisanship variable is well suited[114]—I emphasize the messy complexity of actual institutional transfer attempts. Many times, it seems, even powerful partisans get something different from what they were aiming for. Second, partisanship can be quite ineffective. For example, in post-1990 Romania, where U.S. programs to promote democracy assumed that strengthening "civil society" meant supporting the opposition to the barely reformed Communist government, partisanship helped sink attempts at institutional transfer. Romanian ministries were understandably hostile to U.S. "foreign aid" programs designed to encourage organizations that sought to undermine the government.[115] In other words, the external validity of the partisanship hypothesis is low; only the contextual factors that I have already identified (especially the Cold War) make it important here.

These two chapters on postwar Germany have looked at institutional transfer in contexts where there were deep political disputes about the workability of foreign models. These political struggles among groups of Allies and

112. Especially after the Republicans took Congress in 1946.

113. This is, of course, precisely what the advocates of grass-roots unionism tried to do in the industrial relations reforms detailed in Chapter 3. That they were fired for their efforts is another indication that coalitions with the left fit uneasily within larger American foreign policy priorities.

114. For examples, see the diffusion literature reviewed in Chapter 1.

115. See Thomas Carothers, *Assessing Democracy Assistance: The Case of Romania* (Washington, D.C.: Carnegie Endowment, 1996), 64–74.

Germans, both before and during attempts at transfer, also overlapped to some extent with historical struggles from the Weimar period and earlier and so problematize what might be called the "essentialist" view of institutional transfer. In the essentialist view, imitation is an all-or-nothing prospect: it occurs if and only if policymakers are struck more or less out of the blue by the genius of a foreign design and then set about to replicate it from scratch in their own society. When one considers the old and varied historical roots of *prevailing* institutions, one might then conclude that imitation is very rare and that when it does occur, the object of imitation is likely to be quite small—a management technique "diffused" or, at most, a "borrowed policy." The political alternative I pursue here suggests rather that very important structures might be the object of imitation, provided one recognizes the broader context in which imitation is embedded—a context that includes the possibility of combining external influences and indigenous minority traditions. In turn, this allows one to see that in many policy areas the answer to the question "Were postwar institutions Allied impositions or a return to Weimar?" is a double negative.

In the very different context of German reunification, the conditions for imitation seemed good: a substantial common history and language, ample resources, functionally interdependent institutions available for quick transfer, and the enthusiasm of most eastern Germans for West German institutions.

CHAPTER FIVE

Industrial Relations in Eastern Germany: The Politics of Imitation

> No experiments!
> —Prominent slogan in the campaign for the first democratic
> GDR election, March 1990

In the immediate aftermath of World War II most Germans agreed that significant changes were in order, but opinions diverged on how to reform structures inherited from twelve years of Nazi rule. Since Allied functional equivalent transfer was mediated by postwar civil society, many of the results bore at least a resemblance to traditional institutions. This was certainly true in secondary schools, where transfer failed, but it was also true of industrial relations, where transfer was much more effective. After German reunification, expectations were different: the slogan "No experiments!" captured nicely the pervasive determination of eastern Germans to have the "real" West German system, not some third way between capitalism and Communism. And the West German government's ambitions for institutional transfer also were much higher than those of the Allies after 1945, for they sought not mere functional equivalent transfer but rather the exact transfer of virtually their entire system. Yet a process built on the exact transfer of institutions—"No experiments!"—has unexpectedly required widespread experimentation. Pulling in structures from the outside demands more than the enthusiasm of the populace; it requires actors rooted in society who monitor institutional problems and authoritatively call upon the energies and loyalties of citizens to fix them.

COLLAPSE AS PROBLEM, INSTITUTIONAL TRANSFER AS SOLUTION

Whereas the end of the Nazi regime had been widely foreseen since the Battle of Stalingrad, German reunification came with stunning swiftness (see

Table 5. Chronology of key initial events in the political economy of reunification

Date	Event
November 9, 1989	Berlin Wall falls
December 7, 1989	"Round Table" talks begin between GDR governing party and opposition; free elections are announced
March 1, 1990	*Treuhandanstalt* is established by GDR regime
March 9, 1990	Western employers (BdA) and unions (DGB) agree to help establish West German–style collective bargaining in GDR
March 18, 1990	Electoral victory of Alliance for Germany is widely seen as popular mandate for reunification
Spring–summer 1990	Wage agreements specify no layoffs until summer 1991
July 1, 1990	GEMSU takes effect
October 3, 1990	Reunification: five new states are formed on the former territory of GDR and accede under Article 23 of FRG Basic Law
Spring 1991	Wage equalization plans are developed in numerous sectors
Summer 1991	First wave of large layoffs begins
February 1993	Metal employers unilaterally cancel wage equalization contract
April–May 1993	Strike in metalworking sector; settlement after two weeks

Table 5).[1] Faced with growing external debt, stagnant economic production, and declining support from its own population, the East German state faced an immediate crisis in the autumn of 1989, when thousands of its citizens began leaving by way of Hungary and Czechoslovakia. The subsequent collapse of the Berlin Wall in early November led to a series of unsuccessful efforts by the Communist Party (SED) to retain its leading role. Meanwhile, East German emigration continued to surge.

In February 1990 the West German government offered East Germany an "economic and monetary union," ostensibly to forestall the step toward political union. On March 18, 1990, however, elections in the GDR returned large pluralities for the Alliance for Germany, which had close ties to West Germany's ruling CDU, and the election results were widely interpreted as a mandate for reunification. A partial step was taken with the Treaty for German Economic, Monetary, and Social Union (GEMSU), which was signed on May 18 and took effect on July 1. But as the economic decline of East German firms and the migration of East German citizens continued more or less unabated, Bonn decided to move quickly toward full political union under article 23 of the FRG's provisional constitution of 1949, still designated

---

1. The literature on reunification is now very large. One study that admirably combines internal and external aspects is Philip Zelikow and Condoleeza Rice, *Germany Unified and Europe Transformed* (Cambridge: Harvard University Press, 1995). See also Konrad Jarausch, *The Rush to German Unity* (New York: Oxford University Press, 1993).

modestly as the Basic Law. The choice of article 23 reflected a fundamental commitment to remake the East in the image of the West and rejected article 146, which foresaw the writing of a new, all-German constitution. The subsequent Unification Treaty, negotiated between representatives of the FRG and the GDR, was signed on August 31, 1990, and took effect on October 3.

The economic collapse that helped topple the SED did not end with reunification.[2] From the implementation of the currency union in July 1990 to April 1991, eastern German production collapsed to less than one-third of 1989 levels. Employment fell dramatically and has stayed low: the number of persons in paid employment dropped from just under 10 million in 1990 to around 6.1 million in 1997.[3] Registered unemployment has hovered between 1 million and 1.3 million since 1993. The actual unemployment rate in the East is twice the official rate of 18%, though masked by massive deployment of labor market policies (see Figure 3). Significant labor migration (including commuting) to western Germany has also eased pressure on eastern German labor markets. Without the huge transfer of western funds, estimated as 750 billion deutsche marks (DM) between 1990 and 1995, the situation in eastern labor markets would have been even more dire.[4] For example, in 1997, labor market programs reduced eastern unemployment by 635,000.[5]

These economic difficulties provided the backdrop for a second attempt to transfer institutions of industrial relations. The performance of industrial relations in eastern Germany has been a kind of Rorschach test for scholars who have commented on it. Admirers of German industrial relations can find evidence of strong firms, creative works councilors, hard-working union officials, and tenacious employer associations. Pessimists can point to deindustrialization, declining memberships, and the fragmentation of established practices. I find optimism and pessimism analytically unhelpful and instead pursue three other points. First, I trace the inherently politicized nature of institutional transfer by challenging other uses of the concept. Second, I explore the limits of the suggestive—but also potentially misleading—concept of the "organization set," which implies that institutions can be transferred only if packaged together with other, supporting institutions. Third, I evaluate empirically the notion of "exact transfer," which was closely approximated after German reunification. I develop these points to highlight a striking puzzle: namely, that reunification, supposedly an essentially conservative process (from the West German perspective), is helping catalyze the largest institutional changes in industrial relations in the postwar period.

---

2. Charles Maier, *Dissolution: The Crisis of Communism and the End of East Germany* (Princeton: Princeton University Press, 1997).

3. Hans-Uwe Bach et al., *Labour Market Trends and Active Labour Market Policy in the Eastern German Transformation Process, 1990–1997* (Nuremberg: Federal Labor Office, 1998), fig. 1.

4. Karl Lichtblau, *Von der Transfer- in die Marktwirtschaft* (Cologne: Deutscher-Instituts-Verlag, 1995), 400.

5. Bach et al., *Labour Market Trends*, 15.

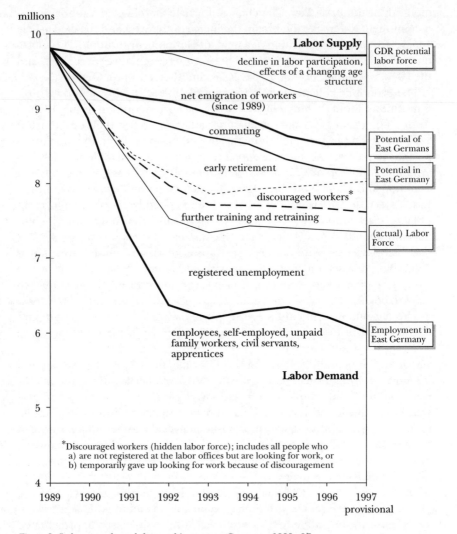

Figure 3. Labor supply and demand in eastern Germany, 1989–97

Source: Hans-Uwe Bach et al., *Labor Market Trends and Active Labour Market Policy in the Eastern German Transformation Process, 1990–1997* (Nuremberg: Federal Labour Office, 1998).

INSTITUTIONAL TRANSFER AS A COMPARATIVE CONCEPT

Scholars of the two periods considered in this book have made varied use of the concept of institutional transfer. Looking broadly at the question of Allied influence on postwar Germany, specialists on the occupation often conflated institutional transfer with a range of other actions—denazification, decartelization, reparations, the Marshall Plan, and so on—which the occupation forces used to influence Germany. Moreover, the accurate observation that there have long been German traditions in areas such as industrial unionism has unfortunately obscured the importance of Allied functional equivalent policies in nurturing and promoting those traditions while restricting competing designs. The preceding two chapters have argued against an essentialist concept, in which transfer is seen to implant a wholly new institutional design, and in favor of a political argument that emphasizes the impact of transfer on extant though perhaps weak minority traditions.

Although institutional transfer has emerged only partially from most discussions of the occupation period, the concept has figured prominently in discussions of reunification. I argue, however, that even the best descriptive work on reunification has been overly fixated on the East German case and has so narrowed the concept as virtually to empty it of comparative promise.

The idea of transfer has entered the debate about eastern Germany in three different (and inconsistent) ways. One common usage considers institutional transfer simply a tool wielded by West German actors to colonize the East—a technique for cutting off indigenous innovation in eastern Germany.[6] This approach tends to emphasize that the massive accompanying personnel transfers brought a range of benefits to West German citizens and that West German firms often purchased East German properties for a song. Although any useful concept of imitation must indeed be able to incorporate the interests of West German actors, this variant of the concept has two fatal flaws: it blends out the enthusiasm—however superficial their knowledge might have been—of East Germans for West German institutions, and it ignores the fact that West German cash transfers to eastern Germany—which have run at around $100 billion per year—constitute something of a reversal of the normal financial relationship between metropole and colony.[7] In sum, this image makes good copy but ignores those aspects of institutional transfer which appeared, from the East German perspective, to be desirable.

A second common view is that transfer is simply the *formal* process of establishing institutions and practices in the East.[8] The claim is that institutional transfer has worked very well because all the formal actors are present and armed with a legal basis for action. Problems may still abound, such arguments run, but the transfer itself was quickly and easily effected. My objection is that this use of the concept narrows transfer to a purely formal

6. Frank Unger, "Landnahme im Osten," *Neue Gesellschaft—Frankfurter Hefte* 40 (1993): 221–28. The most persuasive characterization of reunification as colonization is Bernd Schirmer's novel *Schlehweins Giraffe* (Frankfurt: Fischer Taschenbuch, 1994).

7. Much of this money has, of course, flowed back to the West German companies that provided East Germans with goods and services. "Annexationist Keynesianism" would no doubt be a more appropriate term than colonization.

8. An empirically rich example is Carsten Johnson, "Die Rolle intermediärer Organisationen beim Wandel des Berufsbildungssystems," in *Einheit als Interessenpolitik: Studien zur sektoralen Transformation Ostdeutschlands*, ed. Helmut Wiesenthal (Frankfurt: Campus, 1995).

process that consists of one or a few legislative acts or executive decrees in 1990 and perhaps 1991.[9] For example, the excellent article by Tobias Robischon and others on institutional continuity in the health, research, and telecommunications sectors during reunification shows that any efforts to transfer "reformed" West German structures to the East were blocked in all three sectors by the veto positions of other players in the sector; as a result, in all three cases the state and reunification treaties foresaw the 1-to-1 duplication of the western system.[10] Although these authors document well the intense intrasectoral competition that I call the politics of institutional transfer, their focus is decidedly on the process of negotiating the formal design of the institutions. Their key claim is that in sectors with highly incremental decision-making processes and multiple veto points, the western German status quo necessarily became the design by default for eastern Germany. Even in the extremely "embedded" case of industrial relations, however, pursuing the issue of institutional transfer past the initial "setup point" reveals a variety of important changes that leave the claim of structural continuity open to question.

The third approach is also based on a wealth of empirical research about the variations across policy sectors and casts transfer as an ideal type. Gerhard Lehmbruch reserves the concept to describe only those sectors—such as health care—where West German regulatory "governance" was extended to eastern Germany. Lehmbruch separates this "transfer" process from three other modalities of institutional change: first, the "indigenous" innovation in the GDR between the fall of the Berlin Wall and the signing of the unity treaty, which established the basic political institutions of parliament, federalism, and local government; second, those sectors where eastern German interests have successfully resisted or modified transfer attempts; and third, the institutional "borrowing" processes that have occurred in Eastern and Central Europe.[11]

In my view there are good reasons to adopt a broader notion that locates uses of institutional transfer *within* each of Lehmbruch's three other modalities. First, it is implausible to argue that some *policy areas* are strictly shaped by exogenous processes (transfer) while others are shaped only by endogenous

---

9. The concept of institutional transfer would hold no real comparative promise because, if transfer is just a technique of governance, then comparativists should study the governments that use it rather than the "tool" itself.

10. Tobias Robischon, Andreas Stucke, Jürgen Wasem, and Hans-Georg Wolf, "Die politische Logik der deutschen Vereinigung und der Institutionentransfer," *Politische Vierteljahresschrift* 36 (1995): 423–59.

11. Gerhard Lehmbruch, "Die ostdeutsche Transformation als Strategie des Institutionentransfers: Überprüfung und Antikritik," in *Institutionenbildung in Ostdeutschland: Zwischen externer Steuerung und Eigendynamik*, ed. Andreas Eisen and Hellmut Wollmann (Opladen: Leske + Budrich, 1996).

ones (innovation). Rather, in any given sector one finds a mix of exogenous and endogenous changes.[12] Second, although Lehmbruch is correct that between January and July 1990, GDR decision makers had recourse to "older German traditions" in redesigning institutions (and thus had no need for transfer), it is empirically difficult to show that they were not simultaneously influenced by contemporary West German structures. Much evidence suggests that they were, such as the fact that large numbers of elites—including Volkskammer members—favored reunification at the earliest possible date. In short, those racing to use institutional transfer in East Germany hardly needed to wait for the GEMSU starting gun.[13] Third, the comparative perspective reveals many processes in eastern Germany to be extreme variants of other cases of imitation in post-Communist states. Lehmbruch himself shows that institutional transfer represented a mechanism that Chancellor Helmut Kohl could use to suspend and circumvent the usual processes of protracted political negotiation familiar to students of the Federal Republic. Under great electoral pressure, Kohl opted for the fastest and simplest route to reunification.[14] As noted in Chapter 2, such "problem simplification," especially under the short time horizons of elected officials, is precisely what students of policy borrowing have long seen as a prominent motive for institutional transfer, including cases in Eastern and Central Europe.[15]

Whether transfer is seen as a tool for colonizers, for institutional setup, or for extending West German governance, all three approaches mistake one possibility for the universe of possibilities. Rather than a tool of exogenous change to be sharply contrasted with endogenous change, imitation (even under the extreme duress of an occupation army) can be seen to benefit from a foundation of indigenous tradition. Analysts must indeed keep these indigenous and external sources distinct—and for this, case studies are the only possibility—while asking whether the distinct forces come together at some point to make something quite different. Chapter 3 demonstrated that the new hybrid institutions created in postwar industrial relations depended upon Allied support for German pioneers of minority traditions such as industrial unionism or antitrust policy. The question now at hand is, what happens when non-state actors are extraordinarily weak—perhaps too weak to

12. Indeed, as Lehmbruch himself recognizes, easterners may reshape these institutional practices through a combination of routines familiar from the GDR period or, more often, those that arise out of the desperate economic and social problems of the region. See his "Institutionen, Interessen und sektorale Variationen in der Transformationsdynamik der politischen Ökonomie Ostdeutschlands," *Journal für Sozialforschung* 34 (1994): 34–38.

13. The next chapter shows that GDR educational elites had begun looking to West German school models well before reunification came to the top of the agenda.

14. Gerhard Lehmbruch, "Die improvisierte Vereinigung: Die dritte Deutsche Republik," *Leviathan* 18 (1990): 463.

15. Robert Cox, "Creating Welfare States in Czechoslovakia and Hungary: Why Policymakers Borrow Ideas from the West," *Government and Policy* 11 (1993): 349–64.

pull in outside institutions?[16] After all, it is precisely after policy failures that elites are most inclined to attempt institutional transfer, and there are good reasons to suppose that policy failures might correlate with the weakness or disorganization of social groups.[17] Are policy domains or regions without competent indigenous actors doomed to failure?

THE ORGANIZATION SET AS COMPENSATION?

If institutional transfer during reunification seems disadvantaged by the weakness of eastern German civil society, might this weakness not be compensated for by other apparent advantages of reunification? From a theoretical perspective the most important potential advantage is that West German institutions have been transferred as a remarkably complete package. Recall that many students of policy borrowing have bemoaned the poor fit of isolated institutions borrowed from foreign climes.[18] This case is well suited to investigating the thesis that institutional transfer attempts are especially vulnerable to the organization-set problem. Emphasizing interinstitutional linkages, this perspective sees the outputs of one institution as the inputs of another.

Surely, it is hard to think of another case where institutions have been transferred in a package so completely as after reunification. And many astute observers of German industrial relations seem to suggest that the institutionalized package functions in eastern Germany as what might be called a redundant system, where weakness in one place is quickly compensated for by strength in another. The key theme is that the transfer of both *rights* and *norms* embedded in West German institutions can act as a compensatory stabilizing mechanism for a range of inevitable problems during the period of "transition."[19] It is argued that even with high unemployment, the legal basis of codetermination and regionwide collective bargaining agreements and the employer commitment to extending that system to eastern Germany will likely protect labor there from an erosion of the institutional prerogatives it has heretofore enjoyed.[20] Thus, the "institutionalization" of the

---

16. A good review of civil society in Eastern Germany is Susanne Benzler, "Chancen der Zivilgesellschaft in den neuen Bundesländern," in *Deutschland-Ost vor Ort: Anfänge der lokalen Politik in den neuen Bundesländern*, ed. Benzler, Udo Bullmann, and Dieter Eißel (Opladen, Germany: Leske + Budrich, 1995).

17. Joshua Cohen and Joel Rogers, "Secondary Associations and Democratic Governance," *Politics and Society* 20 (1992): 393–472.

18. Dennis Muniak, "Policies That Don't Fit," *Policy Studies Journal* 14 (1985): 1–19.

19. See, e.g., Ulrich Jürgens, Larissa Klinzing, and Lowell Turner, "The Transformation of Industrial Relations in Eastern Germany," *International Labor Review* (1993): 229–44; Stephen Silvia, "'Holding the Shop Together': Old and New Challenges to the German System of Industrial Relations in the Mid-1990s" (ZSF working paper 83, Berlin, July 1993).

20. Jürgens, Klinzing, and Turner, "Transformation," 3.

broader West German industrial relations system will likely prevent the development of a substantially new and weaker form of labor participation in eastern Germany. This argument also stresses the norms of negotiated adjustment and the ideology of management-labor cooperation in certain industrial sectors.[21] The finding is that West German managers have learned to cooperate with unions, and the implication is that these processes, whether institutionalized or informal, can be largely carried over into eastern Germany. The 1991 decision to equalize wages in the metal sector—a decision that spread quickly to other sectors—is taken as evidence of this cooperation. Further, the successful defense of this pact by IG Metall, the metalworkers' union, is seen as evidence that unions are doing well in eastern Germany.[22]

It remains rightly obligatory for anyone writing about eastern Germany to say that it is still too early to predict the region's economic development, let alone the character of organizations that ultimately will emerge there. Further, the optimist-pessimist debate about eastern German industrial relations begins to sound like the discussion about whether the glass is half empty or half full.[23] It is clear that western German unions and employer associations have done yeoman's work in establishing certain familiar organizations and routines in an economically volatile region. Were institutional transfer a merely formal setting-up process, then one could point to the existence in eastern Germany of industrial unions, employer associations, labor courts, and works councils and declare the transfer, at least, a "success."

Yet these organizations and routines have often foundered in eastern Germany. How should one evaluate their shortcomings? First, it is necessary to be clear about the difference in aspirations of policy elites in the two periods. Where the post–World War II Allies effectively shifted German industrial relations, they did so on the rather vague basis of "functional" models, which left many crucial details to the Germans themselves. West German aspirations for a wholesale, exact transfer of western industrial relations to the East have been more ambitious in scope.[24]

But respect for the magnitude of the endeavor must not obscure the ways that institutional transfer has generated barriers to its own effectiveness. My premise regarding the transfer of industrial relations is simple: where opti-

21. Kirsten Wever, *Negotiating Competitiveness: Employment Relations and Organizational Innovation in Germany and the United States* (Boston: Harvard Business School, 1995), 161–75.

22. Lowell Turner, "Unifying Germany: Crisis, Conflict, and Social Partnership in the East," in *Negotiating the New Germany*, ed. Turner (Ithaca, N.Y.: ILR Press, 1997): 114–21.

23. For recent summaries, see Carola Frege, "Workplace Relations in Eastern Germany after 1989: A Critical Review of the Debate," *German Politics and Society* 15 (1997): 65–93; Richard Hyman, "Institutional Transfer: Industrial Relations in Eastern Germany," *Work, Employment and Society* 10 (1996): 601–39.

24. I do not imply (or believe) that West Germany somehow cared more than did the Allies about the success of their endeavor and *for this reason* took a more comprehensive approach to institutional reform. The Allies had made heavy sacrifices of blood and wealth to stop the Nazis.

mists focus on institutionalization and stress as further assets an ideology of partnership and cooperation between capital and labor, I focus on the need for market power to enforce and define those institutional guarantees and to keep that ideology ahead of other common and less generous notions about unions that circulate among West German managers.[25] The large drops in employment have badly weakened labor's position. With underemployment officially fluctuating well above 30% in eastern Germany, the regional contract system is badly strained, and even the constitutional obligation to equalize living conditions across regions increasingly appears unreachable.[26] In short, although labor market weakness does not explain all the unions' problems in eastern Germany, it stands out as the most significant contextual difference that has bedeviled efforts to make western structures function in the East. Rather than seeing this labor market weakness as an exogenous shock resulting purely from the rottenness of Communist firms or the mendacity of capitalist employers, this chapter shows that the West German industrial relations model also functioned as a surprisingly aggressive predator in the new environment of eastern Germany. As it devoured weak firms, the model undercut some of the key conditions for its own regeneration. The point is significant because when talking about institutional design, one must consider very basic points about economic variables as well as strictly "institutional" factors.[27]

With reference to the organization-set hypothesis, the case of the exact transfer of industrial relations institutions suggests *not* that linkages to other institutions are missing—for they have been transferred as well, along with a great many organizational norms and routines—but that since the context is different, linkages transferred intact can be quickly weakened or even broken. Thus the missing political dimension in the organization-set hypothesis becomes evident. Economic institutions often represent political compromises which must be held in place by competent actors. Some of these actors may have alternative conceptions of how institutions should be designed but are often prevented by other actors from acting on their conceptions. This limitation does not rule out the possibility of amicable, cooperative, or positive-sum interactions between, for example, unions and employers, but it does make that cooperation context-dependent. Moreover, as the case re-

25. Ironically, although American management inspired many Germans seeking to promote acceptance of unions after World War II, it is now ritually invoked by those who see German unions as too powerful.

26. The Basic Law includes two different injunctions to equalize living standards across the FRG: article 106, paragraph 3(2), and article 72, paragraph 2.

27. In a simple analogy to another widely advertised "model," it would make little sense to imitate Sweden's active labor market policy without also taking into account its ability (prior to EU membership) to devalue its currency and thus cheapen its exports and provide jobs for those who have been retrained.

veals, linkages between institutions and *their own members* are as problematic as those among institutions.

"Exact Transfer" in Design and Practice

As skillfully as Chancellor Kohl managed the prospects of reunification on the international level, he sought to build a consensus for it at the domestic level in both East and West Germany. Against the backdrop of a national election campaign, Germans were promised that no one would be worse off and that sacrifice would be unnecessary.[28] Kohl's unlikely claim about the painless reconstruction of an entire society received a certain surface plausibility from the assertion that the blueprint for East Germany was ready-made.[29] The resources would come from private investors seeking to profit from the many business opportunities in eastern Germany. Investment would stream in because West Germany would function as the institutional blueprint. The twin pillars of this logic were mutually reinforcing: investors would be primarily from West Germany, and they would be drawn by the reassurance of familiar institutions while helping to build these institutions further through the acts of investing and doing business in the region. The state would ensure the legal foundation, and western German actors would teach the eastern Germans to animate the institutions and sustain them over time.

From the start, therefore, expectations about the extent of institutional transfer were much higher than the hopes for functional equivalents had been in the postwar era. Given the GDR's sudden collapse, of course, the shadow of West Germany would have loomed over any process of institutional reconstruction in eastern Germany. Nevertheless, one must appreciate the ambition of the actual conception: the West was held up as the model not only in a legal-institutional sense but also for sectoral and firm organization and for interest representation and political participation. In the terms introduced in Chapter 2, it was to be an extreme case of exact transfer, wholesale transfer, *and* continuous interaction.[30]

The actual process of exact transfer has had three important consequences. First, it obscured deep disagreements among West Germans about what their "system" is. These disagreements could be masked effectively in the euphoria of the moment and by the prerogative captured by the state to design the re-

---

28. The memoir of Horst Telchik, a member of the chancellor's staff, shows that electoral considerations colored every important decision in the reunification process: *329 Tage: Innenansichten der Einigung* (Berlin: Siedler, 1991).

29. The claim that it had been done before was also prominent. In October 1990 the conservative mass daily *Bild* ran a week-long series on "economic miracles."

30. As such, it was thus quite different from the functional equivalent, piecemeal, and time-limited transfer after World War II.

unification treaties. But conflict was bound to reemerge in more sober moments. Any moratorium on aggressive competition between western German interests in eastern Germany weakened rapidly. For example, Martin Richter's study of the private energy sector demonstrates that West German interests secured, at the expense of local government authorities, significantly more lucrative institutional prerogatives in eastern Germany than they had enjoyed in the West.[31] Such examples reinforce the point that scholars of imitation should anticipate competition over institutional designs and that reintegrating their accounts of the creation and the maintenance of institutions may shed new light on apparently technical setup processes.

The second result was that exact transfer brought to firms in a decidedly aging command economy an institutional system geared to a very modern capitalist one. This "mismatch" was no mistake; indeed, it was part of the design: the new institutions would regulate and shape market competition to force a shift in the boundaries of firms toward much smaller units of production. These restructured units could then, in combination with other firms in both western and eastern Germany, exploit the substantial home and East European markets that GDR firms had traditionally served. When, unexpectedly, the East European market collapsed, however, western German producers proved fully capable of supplying additional eastern German demand from western production.

What remained of the original plan was a modified version of the harsh environment the West German institutional landscape had created to discipline firms and encourage steady increases in productivity. Eastern German firms, though, were disciplined right out of business. In briefest form, this harsh environment is a function of free trade, tight money, high wages, and weak industrial policy. It is normally tempered by some active labor market policies, subsidies in some sectors, and unions that allow changes in technology and work organization. In eastern Germany the key modification has been the especially heavy subsidization of *new* investment and the massive retraining of workers.[32] But alongside subsidized investment, the conventional system of high wage floors was maintained. The resulting labor costs contributed to an impressive number of firm failures and a staggering loss of employment in those firms that have managed to survive. The "disciplining effects" of the German model of industrial relations became a kind of sword of Damocles hanging over the industrial remnants of eastern Germany. The leading edge of the blade has been the system of regional collective bargaining agreements

31. Martin Richter, "Sektorale Transformationsprozesse der ostdeutschen Ökonomie am Beispiel des Umbaus von Strom- und Gaswirtschaft" (manuscript, University of Konstanz, 1995). See also Robischon, et al., "Die politische Logik."

32. Investors in eastern Germany often find well over half their investment costs covered by the state; Lichtblau, *Von der Transfer- in die Marktwirtschaft*, 78–94.

between the employer associations and the trade unions, best illustrated by the case of the metalworking sector, which has generally functioned as a "pilot" sector according to which others have oriented their agreements.

The third way that the process of reunification has hampered the reconstruction of eastern Germany involves its effect on interest formation and representation. Put bluntly, East Germans were "recruited" to join interest groups whose structure, goals, and leadership were based in the West. GDR unions were dissolved and the fledgling employer associations integrated into the West German ones. Of course, no reunification process could have ignored pre-existing concentrations of power in West German interest groups and parties. To repeat: the claim is *not* that the West Germans "colonized" East Germany and thus muzzled a "revolutionary" civil society; indeed, against the backdrop of deindustrialization, West German unions sometimes tried hard to politicize East Germans, many of whom would otherwise have been even more passive. The point is precisely that under the current system it has been unclear to eastern Germans when, where, or how they should take an active role on their own behalf. Sixteen million East Germans with a major industrial economy represented a great deal of potential political influence, but the *actual* reunification process has had the effect of significantly dampening that potential.

The contrast here with the occupation cases is especially striking: in the last episode of widespread institution building in Germany, the U.S. and British occupation forces consciously sought to build up certain indigenous actors. They did so because they knew they would be leaving but wanted their basic designs and policies to endure. West German actors, in part because they knew they were staying, took a different approach and recruited East German members in ways that tended to minimize their voice within existing institutions. In short, then, institutional transfer took place against the backdrop of political competition (for advantageous labor law), firm competition (for market shares), and organizational competition (for membership). This ubiquitous competition serves as a reminder that the world does not stop while technocrats restructure it.

Three assumptions underpin what follows. First, I assume that a period of stress is a good time to observe the basic contours of an institutional complex, because strengths and weaknesses that are obscured in times of prosperity come into sharper focus then. Second, I assume that reunification is a time of substantial stress on German institutions, that the subsequent mood in Germany is not simply a reflection of angst but that the system really is in crisis—a crisis reflected in unemployment that approaches five million. Finally, for purposes of simplification, I take unions and employer associations as the central areas of inquiry. I discuss the privatization agency called the Treuhandanstalt (or, commonly, Treuhand) and the role of the federal and state governments only as they absorb functions normally reserved for the social partners under the West German model or as they spin off those functions to the social partners.[33]

THE MODEL THAT WAS SUPPOSED TO BE TRANSFERRED

The basics of German wage bargaining, works councils, and industrial policy that were introduced in Chapter 3 are elaborated only briefly here. The resulting picture is necessarily highly stylized and cannot portray many important features of German industrial relations.[34] One of the central tenets guiding the postwar reconstruction of West Germany was that state power should be balanced by a strong civil society.[35] As part of this division of labor, wage negotiations are the preserve of the social partners. In simplified form, they work as follows: each industrial union negotiates, in a series of regional agreements, wage and benefits packages with the corresponding employer association. These agreements then acquire force of law for all shops in that region and industry except for firms that choose not to join the employer association; they can usually negotiate their wage contracts directly with the union (as does Volkswagen, for example). In addition to regional industry wage agreements, the individual firms' works councils—nonunion elected bodies that represent all the firm's employees—can negotiate with management for, among other things, additional bonuses and benefits. Throughout the 1970s and 1980s this provision has been an increasingly important source of flexibility in setting wage and employment terms in individual plants. Since firms are legally prohibited from undercutting the negotiated wage floors, the result is a system of "economic hygiene" in which weak firms fail.

With respect to regional and industrial policy, the German model has become increasingly liberal. In the first postwar decades the state targeted promotion of certain favored sectors and drew intermittently on a palette of regional policies, especially for the Ruhr. Although these policies never helped move firms into new markets, they did stretch out sectoral declines and ease the transition of workers to new sectors. But during the 1980s, policies became less generous. The older corporatist mode of dealing with problem

33. Data sources include three rounds of interviews among trade union and employer association officials between 1993 and 1996, plus government documents and secondary sources. I thank Martin Behrens for access to two further interviews that he conducted. For accounts of the other issues, see Wolfgang Seibel, "Innovation, Imitation und Persistenz" (paper presented to KSPW Conference, April 1995, Berlin); Roland Czada, "Schleichweg in die 'Dritte Republik,'" *Politische Vierteljahresschrift* 35 (1994): 245–70.

34. For purposes of simplification, I treat the German industrial relations system as uniform and thus ignore variation across regions in West Germany. For a much fuller account, see Volker Berghahn and Detlef Karsten, *Industrial Relations in West Germany* (Oxford: Berg, 1987). A useful update is in Turner, *Fighting for Partnership*, 28–34.

35. Peter Katzenstein, *Policy and Politics in West Germany: The Growth of a Semi-Sovereign State* (Philadelphia: Temple University Press, 1987).

areas gave way, as a more reluctant federal state deferred to the agenda of managers in the industrial adjustment process.[36]

Five areas of change in this stylized model are of interest here, divided roughly into "actors" and "tasks." Two areas involve the constitution of the central actors, through links, first, between individual firms and employer associations, and second, between workers and works councils and unions. The third and fourth areas have to do with the way these actors have sought, in eastern Germany, to shape the system of wage bargaining and the development of industrial and regional policy. The fifth area concerns the broad shifts in the balance between state and social actors which have resulted from the changes in the first four areas.

Again, rather than engage in an extended discussion of the West German industrial relations model, I highlight the way reunification has exacerbated traditional tensions and created new ones. The claim is not that the developments one sees in eastern Germany are, in every case, unprecedented in the West. In fact, most, though not all, of the tensions apparent in the East are familiar to students of German industrial relations. What seems different is both the extent of these tensions and the range and simultaneity of unusual developments. To understand the tensions, one must examine the original process through which unions and employer associations were constructed in eastern Germany.

UNIONS: EXTREME FLUCTUATIONS

As reunification became a certainty in the wake of the March 1990 elections, West German unions soon decided that rather than maintain a reformed version of the Communist Party's labor organization, the Freier Deutscher Gewerkschaftsbund (FDGB), individual western industrial unions would recruit members from their counterpart industrial unions in the East. As western unions extended their domain into the East, the individual GDR industrial unions would be dissolved along with their federation. Although some western union leaders—including many in the largest union, IG Metall—had real misgivings about such a takeover, this development can be traced to a combination of concerns about the very low legitimacy of the FDGB and its member unions among East German workers at that time, and to the obvious attraction of substantial membership increases for their own unions.[37]

The individual West German unions took a range of different approaches

36. Jutta Helm, "Structural Change in the Ruhr Valley," *The Federal Republic of Germany at Forty*, ed. Peter Merkl (New York: New York University Press, 1989).

37. See Michael Fichter, "A House Divided: German Unification and Organized Labour," *German Politics and Society* 2 (1993): 21–39.

to transferring their organizations eastward.[38] The chemical workers' union, IG Chemie, integrated a reformed East German union leadership into its own organization. The huge metalworkers' union, IG Metall, relied much more heavily on transferring personnel from western locals to leading eastern locals and on generally extending the domain of existing western regional units to include eastern German territory. Only in the case of Saxony was a purely eastern German IG Metall regional allowed to form. As one of their final organizational acts, the GDR unions called upon their members to join the corresponding western unions. Although unions in West Germany had rarely fought substantial battles over which union was entitled to organize which firms, the opportunities for substantial membership growth among the thousands of suddenly unorganized firms in the East led to several nasty "border wars."[39]

The early enthusiasm of East German workers for membership in the western unions was dampened considerably, however, by heavy job losses. After increasing substantially in 1990 and 1991 to the point where densities reached 50% of the working population (as against just over 30% in West Germany), membership soon fell off rapidly. During 1992, for example, the DGB unions lost 766,000 members (18.4%) in eastern Germany but only 19,000 (0.2%) in western Germany.[40] Another 500,000 left in 1993, and membership declined further in 1994 and 1995 so that between 1991 and 1995 the eastern unions lost 43% of their members.[41] Further, although official densities in the East remain roughly comparable to those in the West, the common reality is that over half of union members are unemployed. These members draw heavily on union services, especially in legal representation, while paying dues of only a few marks per month.[42] Figure 4 shows the differential rate of membership losses in selected unions. Public-sector unions such as the police (GdP), teachers (GEW), and administrative personnel (ÖTV) have lost members at much lower rates than have industrial unions such as metalworking (IGM), textiles (GTB) and leatherworking (GL). Banking (HBV), the only private-sector service occupation shown, has also suffered very significant losses.

38. Ibid., 21–25.
39. Hanjo Gergs, Rudi Schmidt, and Rainer Trinczek, "Die Claims der Einzelgewerkschaften sind umstritten," *WSI–Mitteilungen* 3 (1992): 149–57.
40. *Die Welt*, June 11, 1993.
41. The decline was from 4,157,826 members to 2,360,378. Michael Fichter, "Trade Union Members: A Vanishing Species in Post-Unification Germany?" *German Studies Review* 20 (1997): 90. During this same period, membership in western Germany fell only 8%, from 7,642,587 to 6,994,292.
42. The evidence here is confirmed from several different union locals. For example, DGB officials in Leipzig informally estimate that employed members constitute about 40% of total union membership there (interviews: 1995). For union work with the unemployed, see Petra Karrasch, "Gewerkschaftliche und gewerkschaftsnahe Politikformen in und mit der Kommune," in Benzler, Bullmann, and Eißel, *Deutschland-Ost vor Ort*.

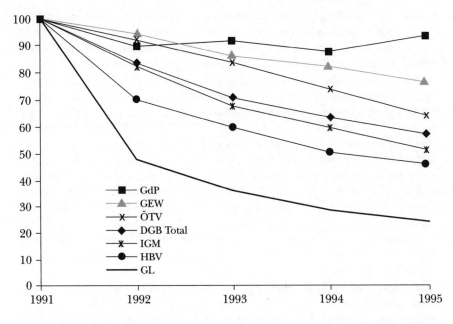

Figure 4. DGB membership trends in selected unions in eastern Germany, 1991–95 (1991 = 100)

Source: Reprinted by permission from Michael Fichter, "Trade Union Members: A Vanishing Species in Post-Unification Germany?" *German Studies Review* 20, no. 1 (1997): 90.

What do such losses say about institutional transfer? The organization-set argument implies that transfer fails because some crucial supportive structure is missing, but these trends imply that there may also be a problem between unions and members. What potential for voice has there been in DGB unions for former FDGB members? Early on, it was unclear what impact the new eastern constituency would have on the combined union movement in Germany. Some speculated that rank-and-file support for the CDU meant that the unions would move away from the SPD toward political neutralism.[43] Others argued that the presence of former FDGB functionaries in the new works councils might push the unions leftward. But both speculations have so far proved irrelevant because the eastern Germans have had relatively little say in broader union policies.[44]

For an understanding of this lack of voice, it helps to recall the techniques

43. Klaus Armingeon, "Gewerkschaftliche Politik im Prozeß der deutschen Vereinigung," *Die Politik der deutschen Einheit: Probleme, Strategien, Kontroversen,* ed. Ulrike Liebert and Wolfgang Merkel (Opladen, Germany: Leske + Budrich, 1991).

44. Interviews: Chemnitz, 1993; Frankfurt, 1993.

that accompanied exact transfer for integrating eastern German members. West German unionists were aware of the possibility that the new members might imbalance them as actors. For example, IG Metall leaders worried about a rekindling of their union's old internal divide between progressives—who had successfully pushed a "modernizing" agenda on technology, women, and the environment—and "traditionalists," who pursued a classic materialist agenda. The union countered this possibility by extending the boundaries of *existing* western-based districts into the new eastern states. This meant that existing districts would exercise control of personnel in eastern Germany and would be in a position to shape eastern German demands. In Saxony, the district with the most innovative policies to date and the only purely eastern district allowed to form, union leaders maintain that this organizational independence has been a crucial factor in keeping the district's focus on the "peculiar problems of eastern Germany."[45] With a thin civil society in the East, western unions stepped in to support and promote the new institutions. Yet in so doing, they sought also to manage their own long-standing organizational dilemmas.

In the case of works councils, too, the unions have been forced to rethink their strategies in the East. The challenge of linking union locals (*Verwaltungsstellen*) to the works councils of individual firms and production plants remains vexing for German labor, even after a century of effort and experience; West German unions long chafed at their inability to bring the works councils under strict formal control. Yet Kathleen Thelen has shown that concerted union efforts to integrate the strategies of unions and works councils have allowed German labor to speak with a reasonably unified yet flexible voice. Crucially, council influence cannot be reduced to formal structures, however important those structures may be. In Thelen's words, "The political strength and savvy of works councils determine how the law operates."[46] In postwar West Germany, unions feared that works councils would form "productivity coalitions" with managers and promote the interests of the internal labor market over union aims of increasing employment and advancing general labor market ambitions. But instead, synergies developed between national- and plant-level labor representation. Unions lobbied the state and bargained over wages with employer associations, while councils sought to tailor those broader bargains to the possibilities of individual firms and plants.[47]

45. Interviews: Chemnitz, 1993. In at least one case, however, IG Metall found its problem-solving capacity *enhanced* by a district that combined East and West: the "coastal" district's shipbuilding sector could be better coordinated in union strategy. See Martin Behrens, *Die Gewerkschaften in den neuen Bundesländern am Beispiel der IG Metall* (Düsseldorf: Hans Böckler Stiftung, 1995).

46. Kathleen Thelen, *Union of Parts: Labor Politics in Postwar Germany* (Ithaca: Cornell University Press, 1992), 149.

47. Works councils had other functions in such areas as personnel and work organization policies. The major recent studies of West German works councils are Heinrich Kotthoff's

Several problems have strained works council–union relations in the East, however.[48] First, of course, cohesion has been challenged by the losses in labor's leverage due to high unemployment. Beyond the familiar dilemma of whether to promote the interests of current workers or of those on the external labor market, eastern works councils had to participate in massive layoffs of their firms' workers. Tensions were highest in cases where new works councilors strongly agreed that the firms needed a more rational employment structure and were subsequently accused by workers of too easily accepting each new round of employment cuts. (In subsequent years, other axes of tension have been council approval of difficult shift-work arrangements and, especially, wage concessions.) Works councilors in this situation often saw union pressures for maintaining employment as incompatible with firm survival and kept unions at arm's length except for the services they could provide.[49]

The pragmatic goals of avoiding low-wage competition and organizing new eastern members often took priority over building ties to works councils. In 1991, as noted, unions and employers signed industry-level agreements to equalize wages rapidly to western levels. This pact clearly served the established unions' interests in avoiding low-wage competition inside their own country. The equalization schedules also met with broad approval from the employed members of the eastern population, who gained symbolic acceptance as equals as well as material benefits from the deal.[50] With the potentially contentious issue of wages seemingly behind them, individual unions focused enormous efforts on providing services to individual workers. This activity dovetailed nicely with most East Germans' visions of the function of a union, since the FDGB, as a kind of transmission belt of the Communist Party, had been primarily responsible for distributing a wide range of services to individual members.

Yet not all the fragility of the link with works councils can be attributed to union neglect, for eastern works councils use the de jure limits of the law to avoid involvement in political fights they believe would harm their firms. Interestingly, in one region of Saxony the works council that had done the most to mobilize political opposition to the privatization policies leading to job losses in its firm was the first to declare the 1993 metal strike useless and to

Betriebsräte und betriebliche Herrschaft (Frankfurt: Campus, 1981) and *Betriebsräte und Bürgerstatus* (Mehring: Rainer Hampp, 1994).

48. The best summary of these trends is Jürgen Kädtler, Gisela Kottwitz, and Rainer Weinert, *Betriebsräte in Ostdeutschland: Institutionenbildung und Handlungskonstellationen, 1989–1994* (Opladen, Germany: Westdeutscher, 1997).

49. Turner, *Fighting for Partnership*, 48–68, emphasizes these union services, especially in large metalworking firms around Berlin.

50. Jonathan Zatlin has rooted this sensitivity at least in part in eastern Germans' feelings that western Germans owe them; see his "Hard Currency and Soft Revolutionaries: The Economics of Entitlement and the Debate on German Monetary Union," *German Politics and Society* 33 (1994): 57–84.

refuse to participate. Thus, where political power has been mobilized, it is also guarded against "appropriation" by the union for a broader agenda. The qualified victory in the metal strike of 1993 did reinvigorate some union–works council linkages, but it remains unclear whether this foundation can be further built upon in this sector, let alone other sectors.

There are at least two prominent obstacles. First, after eight years, privatization-induced layoffs no longer function as a common target of protest in bringing union and works council together.[51] Second, in West Germany the strong division of labor between council and union was built around distribution of the fruits of highly profitable firms in an expanding economy. Works councils of highly profitable firms could extract cash bonuses that represented wage gains above the collectively bargained rate. Labor sparred with capital using a well-coordinated one-two combination. But in the East, union efforts to equalize wages with those in the West have driven unit labor costs significantly higher than in the West.[52] In the face of this difference, eastern German employers often threaten to move production to lower-cost sites unless they are allowed to pay wages substantially below the scale negotiated by the unions. To do so, they need the blessing of the works council, since employees of the firm could take an informal agreement to court. This practice was documented in a substantial minority of eastern firms—especially in new start-ups or in buy-outs by eastern German employers.[53] Since then, anecdotal evidence suggests that the practice has become very common: members of some employer associations indicated in interviews that subcontract wages were virtually universal in their districts; officials at Deutsches Institut für Wirtschaftsforschung (DIW), a major economic research institute, suggest that over half of all metal firms pay wages below the legal minimums.[54] Not all below-contract wages are paid illegally; since the 1993 strike, it has been possible for metalworking firms to receive a "hardship" exception from the union, and there are similar provisions in other sectors. One study of thirty-eight firms in the metal, chemical, and construction industries found that of the subset of 25 firms that did not conform to contract provisions in wages or

51. Jürgen Kädtler and Giesela Kottwitz, "Industrielle Beziehungen in Ostdeutschland: Durch Kooperation zum Gegensatz von Kapital und Arbeit," *Industrielle Beziehungen*, 1 (1994): 1–26.

52. Estimates on this point vary by sector and by estimator, but range from 20 to 50% higher in the East than in the West: Lichtblau, *Von der Transfer- in die Markwirtschaft*, 29; interview: Erfurt, 1998. Of course, investors in eastern Germany are compensated by very high investment subsidies.

53. A study by the Institut für Wirtschaftsforschung Halle found that 12% of a 1992 sample and 24% of a 1993 sample admitted to paying lower than legal wages. Wilfried Ettl and André Heikenroth, suggesting that methodological problems probably led to underreporting, cited other studies showing that 35% of industrial firms pay subcontract wages; see their "Strukturwandel, Verbandsabstinenz, Tarifflucht," *Industrielle Beziehungen* 3 (1996): 139–42, 149.

54. Interviews: Cologne, 1995. DIW data from "Gesamtwirtschaftliche und unternehmerische Anpassungsfortschritte in Ostdeutschland," *DIW Wochenbericht* 15 (1994): tables 1–2.

hours, 44% had worked out union approval, while 56% had not.[55] It is likely in the latter kinds of cases that union-council tensions are most pronounced.

But where Thelen emphasized the ways in which labor often used its mobilization potential to gain substantially *more* material and procedural benefits than prescribed by law, labor in eastern Germany often gets substantially *less* and in many cases allows managers to set aside provisions of the law in order to increase the firm's chances for survival.[56] As time passes, these differences between eastern and western Germany appear more than just transitional. Indeed, the firms most likely to break contract wages illicitly are disproportionately economically healthy rather than weak, which cast doubt on the notion that such deviations reflect temporary payments problems rather than ambivalence about the utility of regional wage bargaining.[57]

In short, the unions can perhaps best accommodate works councils by tolerating the widespread illegal practices in which the councils are complicit. Along with evidence of membership declines, this dilemma suggests that even the transfer of a complete organization set has left unions needing to innovate in order to preserve their traditional prerogatives. For the employer associations, the dilemma is even more severe.

EMPLOYER ASSOCIATIONS: MEMBERSHIP PROBLEMS AS EXISTENTIAL DILEMMA

As with the trade unions, reunification caught the West German employer associations in the midst of a series of internal debates.[58] Thus, although West German industrial relations practices functioned as a blueprint, each major actor in the system was caught up in internal disputes about its own organization. Since reunification, whereas trade unions faced a loss of labor market power in eastern Germany, the employer associations have been in a fight for their very existence. In membership terms, unions started strong and then faded; the associations started weak and then stagnated.

At the time of reunification the central tension among West German employers was a long-simmering dispute between small and large producers.

---

55. Ingrid Artus and Gabriele Sterkel, "Brüchige Tarifrealität: Ergebnisse einer empirischen Studie zur Tarifgestaltungspraxis in Betrieben der ostdeutschen Metall-, Bau-, und Chemie-industrie," *WSI Mitteilungen* 7 (1998): 431–41.

56. Jürgen Kädtler and Giesela Kottwitz, "Wie kommt der Interessengegensatz in den Betrieb zurück?" *Sozialist* 1 (1993): 19–25.

57. Artus and Sterkel, "Brüchige Tarifrealität," 439.

58. Good treatments of these developments, from which the next paragraph borrows, are found in Fred Henneberger, "Transferstart: Organisationsdynamik und Strukturkonservatismus westdeutscher Unternehmerverbände," *Politische Vierteljahresschrift* 34 (1993): 640–73; and Walther Müller-Jentsch, "Das (Des) Interesse der Arbeitgeber am Tarifvertragssystem," *WSI-Mitteilungen* 46 (1993): 496–502.

Again, the very large metalworking sector serves as a convenient illustration of a broader trend.[59] In that sector, traditionally used by the unions to lead the annual collective bargaining rounds, large manufacturers such as Daimler-Benz and Bosch were routinely accused by smaller, often less modern, metalworking firms of buying labor's cooperation at a premium price. Accordingly, during the 1980s the agenda of smaller West German employers centered on achieving a more flexible collective bargaining system, one that used wage "ranges" instead of fixed percentage increases, "menus" of benefits rather than fixed packages, and the abolition of the laws that extend regional collective bargaining agreements to all firms in the industry. Notwithstanding these tensions over strategy, with reunification the associations were used as a blueprint for the East.

The mechanism by which employer associations were transferred to eastern Germany was, however, somewhat different from that of the unions. Whereas West German unions were active in encouraging reform processes in GDR unions in the first months after the fall of the Berlin Wall, most employer associations were not interested in helping the GDR reform itself. The few pioneers who began organizing firm managers—often to resolve production problems in an increasingly chaotic eastern economy—initially did so without much help from westerners. As in the immediate post–World War II period the employer associations were restarted on a regional level. Managers in the socialist economy had always relied heavily on their individual industrial ministries for advice and coordination. Thus, the West German concept of associations of employers originally appealed to many East German managers as a continued source of assistance. In some sectors the newly formed associations were greeted eagerly by firms in transition toward market conditions; clearly, many managers expected them to become conduits for the funds and expertise needed to transform their companies. Only in this very limited sense was there a process of pulling in structures modeled on West German ones. Given the pervasive uncertainty about firm structure, ownership, capitalization, debt, personnel, and markets, the situation could hardly have been otherwise. In short, it was clear that West German structures presupposed a certain configuration of actors and interests that did not yet exist in the East.

When it became clear that the associations would not be the primary channel for investment and training subsidies, interest in them among firms declined considerably.[60] As one official put it, "The managers were disappointed to learn that we could not cover their wage overruns."[61] On the other

---

59. Similar divides can be seen in the chemicals sector; see Steve Silvia, "German Unification and Emerging Divisions within the German Employers' Associations," *Comparative Politics* 29 (1997): 194–99.
60. Interviews: Berlin and Erfurt, 1993.
61. Interview: Schwerin, 1993.

hand, the enthusiasm of the West German associations for the East German regional associations was growing. With reunification imminent, these regional associations began receiving substantial support in the form of material and personnel from the West German associations. On March 9, 1990, the peak associations of the employers and unions (BdA and DGB) agreed to help extend West German–style bargaining to the East. Thereafter, unions in some areas actually helped spur the creation of employer associations in order to find familiar bargaining partners![62]

Over the course of 1990 virtually all the GDR associations were merged into West German associations.[63] The key West German actors were the *Land*-level sectoral employer associations (*Landesfachverbände*), each of which coordinated the transfer of the wage bargaining from its state. Here again, distinct features that blur from a distance into one "model" betray the competitive potential in the apparently technocratic process of transfer. Since the new *Länder* would be taking over the form of collective bargaining agreements in their "partner" states, there was competition among West German states for eastern German partners. For example, the Bavarian employer association actually refused a proposed partnership with Thuringia in order to block a planned partnership between Saxony and Baden-Württemberg. Baden-Württemberg has often been IG Metall's "pilot" district, and other employer associations worried that the regulations there were too inflexible. In the end, Bavaria took Saxony; Hessen was matched to Thuringia; and Baden-Württemberg received no official partner state.[64]

Another significant development of these partnerships was the acceleration of a West German trend toward combining the functions of economic associations (lobbying) and employer associations (wage bargaining). As noted in Chapter 3, the U.S. occupation was unable to alter this "traditional" division of labor, but a number of West German *Länder* later moved toward an "integrated" model, and because of the structure of partnerships, four of the five new *Länder* also have the integrated model (only Saxony has the divided form).[65]

Episodes of misunderstanding, competition, and even reform are far from the only challenges faced in the process of transfer. Like the unions, employer associations seeking to promote relatively homogeneous wage conditions for firms with quite disparate interests have had severe headaches with firm-level actors. Even among those eastern employers who initially imagined the associations would be useful, subsequent developments left most man-

---

62. This occurred in both the metal and chemical sectors. Interviews: Frankfurt, 1993; Göttingen, 1995.
63. The (relatively insignificant) exception is the *Unternehmenverband der DDR*, which had an active group in Saxony until well into the 1990s. Interview: Cologne, 1995.
64. Interview: Cologne, 1994.
65. Interview: Konstanz, 1995.

agers less enthusiastic. Those who did not join early have not joined at all. In one sample from all across eastern Germany, 98% of the organized firms had joined the associations in either 1990 (66%), 1991 (16%) or 1992 (15%); only 2% joined as recently as 1993 or 1994. In the same sample, not a single one of the start-ups had bothered to join an association at all.[66] Here is the existential dilemma of the associations, for without dues they cannot survive.

Employers in the East have rejected membership in the regional associations at much higher levels than those in the West, where membership has also been on the decline.[67] Recall that one of the central pillars of German industrial relations is the regional nature of collective bargaining agreements.[68] Individual firms in West Germany generally had strong incentives to join the employer associations, not only because they provided services—including funds during lockouts and strikes—but also because firms that dealt on an individual basis with the unions usually paid much higher wage bills. But by the same logic, labor's current bargaining weakness in eastern Germany allows firms to negotiate deals that fall below the regional agreements.[69] In the western metalworking sector, despite the tensions between large and small firms, 50 to 65% of the firms employing more than 70% of the labor force were organized in the nominally voluntary associations, and even higher numbers were covered by the binding "extension" of contract wages.[70] In eastern Germany, however, a far lower percentage of firms are members of the associations. The 1994 DIW study found that only 36% of industrial firms were organized—and that number, subsequent interviews with regional associations suggest, is inflated.[71] Even in the construction sector, where business boomed until 1996 and labor markets have been much tighter than in other sectors, only about half the workers are in firms organized by the employer association. A 1997 Federal Labor Office survey of 3,500 eastern German firms in all branches found that in only one sector—mining and energy—were 50% of firms covered by regional contracts; the overall average was 26%—compared with 49% in West Germany. Even more striking, the survey found that the few large eastern firms (above 500 employees) were slightly *more* likely to be covered than equivalent West German firms. But in firms with 100 to 500 employees there are sharp differences, and below 100 employees there are, on this dimension, simply two different po-

---

66. Ettl and Heikenroth, "Strukturwandel," 144.

67. Federal Labor Office, "Flächentarifvertrag im Wester Sehr viel weiter verbreitet als im Osten," *IAB Kurzbericht* 19 (1998): 1.

68. Works councils can bargain up from these floors for special bonuses in individual firms, but their contracts do not have the same legal status as collective bargaining agreements.

69. Firms that leave the employers' associations can, after waiting until the current regional agreements have expired, individually bargain with the unions or workers.

70. *Allgemeinverbindlichkeitserklärung*; see Silvia, "German Unification," 192.

71. Interviews: Dresden, 1994; Erfurt, 1995.

litical economies in East and West.[72] Here is a perfect microcosm of the optimist-pessimist debate: whether one thinks the transfer has worked or not depends a lot on which part of the economy one concentrates on.

Collective bargaining coverage would have been worse had not the state, in the form of the Treuhand, initially put substantial pressure on its managers to join the associations. As soon as firms were privatized, however, their willingness to stay in the associations dropped sharply.[73] The heavy reliance on state backing for the traditional associations suggests that there may be little depth of commitment to the associations on the part of the eastern German firms that *have* joined, and there are some data to support this speculation. In one state association's 1995 internal study of industrial firms currently belonging to the associations, more than one-fourth said they contemplated leaving. In the craft sector the numbers were only slightly more positive for the associations: 43% of firms were members, and not quite 25% contemplated departure.[74] Associations have managed to retain a high percentage of firms that initially joined—in part because organized firms can still pay subcontract wages—but have been much less successful in attracting new start-ups.

Of course, since the employer associations depend heavily on their role in negotiating collective bargaining agreements, they remain, even in the East, fully committed to extending the western model and have gone to extraordinary lengths to overcome the resistance of employers in eastern Germany. In Thuringia, "shell" employer associations have been constructed: these have no wage-bargaining function at all but are supposed to entice firms to maintain some connection to the employer associations. A firm can, with the approval of its "normal" association, remain in this halfway house for up to two years.[75] The example confirms not only the kinds of temporary adaptations of which German industrial relations have been capable in the East but also the extent to which those adaptations are not alternatives so much as ways of buying time. There is hope that if the economy comes around, the old system might yet be stabilized. If producers find they can live outside the traditional model and avoid the regulations, however, hopes will dim that the employer associations can retain their importance in wage bargaining.

To this point, my argument has suggested that even the extraordinarily comprehensive transfer of West German structures has not been able to meet all the challenges of transferring industrial relations to a new setting. Further, it is too simple to say that the West German model has been disadvantaged by unexpectedly difficult labor market conditions; in fact, the model has itself

72. Federal Labor Office, "Flächentarifvertrag," 1–4.
73. From over 90%, membership dropped to 33–46%, depending on the form of privatization: DIW, "Gesamtwirtschaftliche," table 2.
74. Interviews based on survey results from Thuringia, 1995.
75. Interviews: Erfurt, 1995.

contributed to those conditions by the harsh environment to which it exposes firms. In a very real sense it has undercut the conditions for its own maintenance. Finally, and contrary to the expectations of the organization-set hypothesis, the chief problems have been not necessarily between organizations—after all, in some cases unions actually encouraged the establishment of employer associations—but rather between the organizations and their own members. How have such hamstrung organizations coped with key tasks of economic regulation? The following section explores this question both in the core domain of wage bargaining and in the traditionally secondary issue of industrial and regional policy.[76]

CONTESTED GROUND: SOCIOECONOMIC FUNCTIONS IN TRANSITION

Wage Bargaining

It is clear that even when employer associations can convince firms to join, neither the unions nor the associations can compel firms to pay the collectively bargained contract rate. The fear of high wage obligations has kept many firms out of the associations and strained union ties with works councils. Looking at the constitution of these actors allows one to say more about their interactions. What original choices of the social partners contributed to the current mess in the East? What do their subsequent responses reveal about the exact transfer process more generally?

The broad outlines are clear. The ruling CDU-FDP state officials in Bonn and the social partners originally envisioned that wages and investment would be organically linked in the process of helping the eastern economy converge with western Germany's; they justified large nominal and real wage increases on the assumption that West German investment in the East would create jobs at productivity levels that would soon justify wages equal to those in the West. In 1991 a series of wage agreements negotiated in the various sectors called for the step-by-step equalization of wages—the so-called *Stufentarifverträge*—between the two parts of Germany, to take place by the mid-1990s (the anticipated year varied by industry). The unions were interested in avoiding the development of a low-wage region in the East, which might pull investment and jobs away from the West, and they expected the attainment of immediate wage increases to benefit them in membership recruitment. The idea of a high-wage region in the East had the strong initial support of the trade unions.

Two further influences on the wage deals of 1991 were the actions of both

---

76. As noted earlier, industrial and regional policies have been of moderate size in western Germany and have clearly never held a dominant position in union priorities.

individual eastern employers (*not* the associations; the first wage deals in 1990 occurred before the employer associations were established) and of the state. GDR firm managers, looking to the possibility that in the near future they themselves would become employees, and confident of the state's deep pockets, negotiated a series of generous increases with the plant-level unions. The first regional agreements signed by the employer associations then guaranteed that no layoffs could occur until 1991. Only then was the state, which in early 1991 still owned the vast majority of eastern German firms, forced to reckon with the consequences of layoffs from the privatization policies. Wildcat and organized strikes, demonstrations, and plant occupations quickly convinced the government to buy union acceptance of privatization with a policy of rapid wage equalization.[77] It was clear to unions that very large layoffs would be inevitable, but under this bargain the disagreeable necessity would be balanced by significant wage gains for those who did find work and benefits payments to those who could not. Further, the state clearly worried about the migration of easterners into West Germany and hoped to stem the flow by raising expectations for high-paying jobs in the East.

The western employer associations were also interested in pursuing rapid wage equalization and, in the metal sector, pushed hard for the first of the equalization plans.[78] The weak eastern associations were highly dependent on the advice of western employers in their wage negotiations. The western associations were motivated by a web of calculation and miscalculation. They were concerned, especially in manufacturing sectors where productivity could hardly be expected to reach that of western Germany quickly, that service sector firms paying high wages would pull away the employment base.[79] From this perspective, higher wages—even if not justified by the current productivity levels of eastern Germans—would help secure a skilled workforce for future production.

Concerns about labor market competition dovetailed with concerns about product market competition and pointed toward a high-wage solution. For many West German industrial interests, high wages could potentially form a kind of protection against possible eastern competition. Existing West German firms, especially in sectors already suffering from unused capacity, were not keen to see the maintenance or extension of competitors in eastern Germany. When pressured by the state or the threat of foreign investment to acquire firms there, western firms sometimes simply acquired eastern capacity

77. See Wolfgang Seibel, "The Privatization of the East German Economy: Unintended Consequences of Political Action and Political Coping" (manuscript, University of Konstanz, 1995), 25–28.

78. Helmut Wiesenthal, Wilfried Ettl, and Christiane Bialas, "Interessenverbände im Transformationsprozeß" (working paper, Max-Planck-Gesellschaft Berlin, October 1992), 25.

79. See the statements by *Gesamtmetall* officials quoted in IG Metall, *Wir verteidigen unseren Tarifvertrag*, strike documentation (Frankfurt: IG Metall, 1993), 4; interviews: Cologne, 1995.

and then closed it down.[80] In this context, the push for higher wages made firm survival very difficult, drastically reduced capacity, and shifted the burden of adjustment from industrial policy to active labor market policy. Anecdotal evidence of investment and plant closings based on such intrasectoral competition abounds, but I am aware of no documentary evidence that the associations themselves were involved in any conspiracy to limit competition through high wages.[81] In fact, the most careful analysis of the metal sector suggests that with the wage deals of 1991 the discourse inside the associations reflected western calculations that eastern German firms would be able to compete in East European markets.[82] Yet if "miscalculation" is the sounder conclusion for this sector than "mendacity," the two are not mutually exclusive. Doubtless, the collective miscalculation among western German managers and associations endured as long as it did because, if they turned out to be wrong, most costs would be borne in the East (in jobs lost or forgone) and not in the West.

But the agreements for equalizing wages soon came under fire. Production and employment plummeted as market guarantees for eastern German production ended, and the employers soon began to claim that both existing and new investment was incompatible with a high-wage region in eastern Germany. Eastern employers argued that their wage bills made most firms economically unviable. Throughout 1992, Gesamtmetall, the metal sector's employer association, pressured IG Metall to revise the contracts that called for an increase in eastern workers' base pay from 71% to 82% of that of western metalworkers.[83] The union, however, argued that without markets, wage cuts would make little difference to firm survival, and it rejected the call for new negotiations as an attempt to impose the costs of reunification on the workers alone.[84] The employers, union leaders said, had predicated their investment in eastern Germany on all manner of state subsidies and then tried to argue that wages should be calculated on a "market" basis.

In February 1993, Gesamtmetall unilaterally canceled the contracts and instituted a 9% wage increase instead of the agreed-upon 26%. This was the

---

80. Western employers also worried about the fiscal costs to the state of managing a large industrial agglomeration under the Treuhand.

81. The motives of western firms in investing were hardly uniform. They could buy eastern firms in order to gain a foothold in eastern markets (as often happened in construction, retail sales, and food processing); control sectoral overproduction (potassium mining); prevent foreign (often non-EU) competitors from gaining an EU-based foothold (chemicals, railcar manufacturing); purchase complements to their own production palettes (machinery, autos); or even shift the higher costs of western German production to the East (shipbuilding).

82. Ulrike Berger, "Engagement und Interessen der Wirtschaftsverbände in der Transformation der ostdeutschen Wirtschaft," in Wiesenthal, *Einheit als Interessenpolitik*, 100–110.

83. The 71% base represented only 56% of actual wages and benefits, since it was calculated on the basis of western German *minimum* standards in the sector; see Silvia, "German Unification," 21.

84. Helmut Schauer, "Was ist das noch für ein Tarifvertrag, den Sie uns bieten?" *Frankfurter Rundschau*, May 3, 1993, 13.

first time in the history of the Federal Republic that employers had taken such a step.[85] From April 26 to 28, 85% of the union's eastern membership approved the proposed strikes, and in May they struck a growing number of plants for almost two weeks.[86] IG Metall portrayed the strike as political, concerned with protecting the integrity of regional wage agreements without which the union foresaw no possibility of mobilizing enough power to keep eastern Germany from becoming a low-wage region. The union argued further that given the massive layoffs that had already occurred, striking could hardly be more detrimental to future employment prospects than not striking had so far been. Leaders also reminded eastern workers that if unemployment came, it would be better to be laid off at a higher wage than a lower one, since unemployment benefits were based on the last monthly wage.[87] Martin Behrens has persuasively maintained that the union's most convincing argument for hesitant members was that the cancellation represented a breach of trust: eastern German workers had quietly accepted unprecedented layoffs; they struck only when management reneged on promises to end them.[88] Thus, the union was able to paint the strike as an appropriate response to employer betrayal. By implication, eastern workers are unlikely to show this level of solidarity on a routine basis.[89]

After negotiations, the cancellation of the contracts was rescinded, and some modest wage concessions were made by the union. On May 17–18, 1993, 77% of the union members voted to approve the settlement.[90] The revised contracts called for wage equalization in the metalworking sector by 1996. More important, they also included a "hardship" clause under which firms could petition a joint board of union and employers' representatives to be allowed to pay wages below the floor set in the regional agreement. Approval of such a hardship petition was predicated on a firm's demonstration that it could remain in business only if wages were lowered and that all other measures had been taken. Initially, the union was very resistant to granting hardship approval, however. Of the first forty-five applications, for example, only fifteen were approved. But in subsequent years, with employment

85. It was not the last. In the spring of 1997 the construction employers also canceled a valid wage agreement. *Die Zeit* 37 (September 6, 1996).

86. Strikes occurred only in some of the eastern states. For more details, see IG Metall, *Wir verteidigen unseren Tarifvertrag*; and Turner, "Unifying Germany," 114–23.

87. One saw this logic repeated in a subsequent deal in which Volkswagen workers agreed to a thirty-hour work week in exchange for lower pay: the cuts were made exclusively in fringe benefits and bonus pay, so base wage rates for insurance and pension purposes would remain at the previous levels.

88. Behrens, *Die Gewerkschaften*, 31–46.

89. For example, eastern IG Metall secretaries noted in interviews (Chemnitz, 1998) that the intense conflict over employer cancellation of some sick-pay provisions led to immediate membership increases in the West but did not do so in the East. On the more general causes of worker resignation in the metalworking sector, see Andreas Hinz, "Arbeitswelt im Umbruch: Vom Sozialistischen Gang zur westdeutschen Klassenlotterie" (Ph.D. diss., University of Göttingen, 1996).

90. IG Metall, *Wir verteidigen unseren Tarifvertrag*.

growth low, hardship clauses have become widely used. They are a compromise in the face of employer demands for "opening clauses" that would give *works councils* the legal right to approve below-contract wages. Opening clauses are at the top of the agenda of small employers in western Germany, and the employer associations aggressively sought them in the East. At one point in the strike, Norbert Blüm, the CDU minister of labor, threatened the unions with a legislated "emergency opening clause" if no agreement was reached.[91]

The formal proposal to allow works councils to negotiate subcontract wage and benefit packages has generally been resisted by German unions in both East and West, but the de facto situation in many eastern firms belies the formal prohibition on opening clauses.[92] As shown above, labor market conditions have posed a stiff challenge to union–works council cooperation in eastern Germany. The implications of this strained division of labor are quite significant. Unions not only typically provide works councils with training, legal, and technical support but also deal with a range of conflicts over wages and benefits that are, by definition, removed from the firm itself. Although there may be a short-run convergence of interests between managers and "their" works councils in promoting the individual firm, they may quickly find that where their interests diverge more widely, the resulting disputes threaten to wreck all they have built.[93] This scenario has already been played out in western Germany: in the March 1995 metal sector strike in Bavaria, firms that had good relations with works councils were deeply angered at other employers' determination to force a showdown with IG Metall. The bitter strike resulted in the suspension of efforts in several firms to hammer out new agreements on work time.[94] The arm's-length relationship hurts the unions as well, since works councils have traditionally been a crucial agent of union membership recruitment inside firms. Although the steep membership declines outlined earlier have diverse causes, the unions clearly must depend on the councils if recruitment is to bring the numbers back up again.[95]

91. Reinhard Bispinck, *WSI-Tarifarchiv* (1992): 122–33; IG Metall officials later expressed consternation that their hard line on hardship clauses in eastern Germany was used by the employer associations as evidence that the union would take similar positions in the proposed "opening clauses" in western Germany. The crucial difference between the hardship clauses and the proposed opening clauses is that the former are negotiated by the unions, not by the works councils. One thus sees both the concern of unions for maintaining regional wage agreements and the way in which experiments in eastern Germany feed back into the western German debates. Interviews: Berlin, Erfurt, Leipzig, 1995.

92. The main exception is that opening clauses are now widely used in the chemical sector. Increasingly, there are reports of western firms too paying subcontract rates, presumably with the support or tolerance of their works councils. Interview: Cologne, 1995.

93. Only recently has IG Metall encouraged its works councilors to speak of "my firm" rather than "the firm in which I work" (interviews: Nuremberg, 1995).

94. Interviews, Nuremberg and Cologne, 1995.

95. Unions have very few stewards in eastern German firms.

In short, the transfer of western German wage bargaining has kept eastern German firms under intense cost pressures. It has led to de facto flight from the associations, which, in the firms' eyes, do not represent their interest in wages that more closely approximate relative productivity (eastern German unit wage costs were 159% of western ones in 1991 and in 1997 were still at 125%).[96] The resulting unemployment has cost trade unions dearly in terms of employed membership. The two social partners, which represent ever smaller shares of capital and labor in eastern Germany, have had considerable difficulty defending the integrity of their core mission: setting wages.

If exact transfer has necessitated experimentation even where the German model seemed most institutionalized, it has also done so in industrial policy where the social partners had less experience.

Industrial Policy

The promise of wage equalization made rapid privatization politically *sustainable* by achieving union support. But it also made privatization less *achievable* because wage costs made investment in the East less attractive than Bonn had anticipated. Even greatly depressed Treuhand asset prices did not lure investors in the hoped-for numbers.[97] The state, it became clear, would have to help promote investment. What role could the unions assume in such an effort? Could innovation in industrial policy compensate for problems that accompanied the imitation of the western wage-bargaining system?

German unions have acted defensively in wage bargaining in eastern Germany, hoping to preserve the essential pillars of a system that brought them prosperity and autonomy in the West. In industrial policy, however, the unions had much less to preserve and have tried to innovate aggressively, expanding old policies and developing new ones in a desperate effort to sustain an employment base in the East. Yet as noted earlier, West German regional policy and industrial policy instruments have traditionally been modest. At its most successful, German industrial policy during periods of economic growth has required national-level political bargains over subsidy levels, complemented by both EU-level bargains over the pace of adjustment and firm-level bargains with works councils over the development of social plans for layoffs.[98] These policies have arguably made some steel firms more profitable and leaner, but they have been substantially less successful in coal. And in

96. Bach et al., "Labour Market Trends," table 2.

97. As Gerlinde Sinn and Hans-Werner Sinn have argued, selling everything at once also pushed down prices; see their *Jumpstart: The Economic Reunification of Germany* (Cambridge: MIT Press, 1992).

98. Josef Esser and Wolfgang Fach, "Crisis Management 'Made in Germany': The Steel Industry," in *Industry and Politics in West Germany: Toward the Third Republic*, ed. Peter Katzenstein (Ithaca: Cornell University Press, 1989): 247–48.

neither sector have firms been able to diversify out of their original industries. Thus, although the West German model has some impressive private coordination capacity in the more modern parts of the economy, the state-society bargains around older sectors have helped firms shed labor but have not led to new markets.

None of this seems to provide an auspicious basis for an eastern German industrial policy. Social actors were weakly constituted, and firm boundaries were yet unclear, so there was only weak pressure from eastern Germany to force any early state attention to regional policies. Given existing sectoral overcapacity, corporate interests in the West were generally aligned toward preventing the growth of a large state-subsidized economy in the East, yet only a few had strong incentives for new investment there. Once state subsidies for building infrastructure indicated that former East German markets could be served from West German production, and after currency developments ended the advantageous position of East German firms in East European markets, the preferred strategy of western firms was to acquire the best industrial and real estate assets at modest prices and then favor state subsidization of individual worker training over the subsidization of existing firms. This strategy was intended to allow the reconstitution of East Germany's economic life to be guided by private investment.[99] In eastern Germany the western German trend of the 1980s toward more firm-led industrial policies was combined with massive state support of individual training. Privatized firms shed labor at a tremendous rate throughout 1991 and 1992, whereas the Treuhand firms (those the agency had not yet been able to sell) were restructured very little, as the organization's leadership maintained that "privatization is the best method of restructuring."[100]

The unions were fairly quiet during this process, focusing on membership recruitment, promoting the absorption of individual workers into the secondary labor market and retraining, publicizing Treuhand layoffs, and hoping that new investment would come before deindustrialization was complete. Rhetorically, some industrial unions advocated holding actions to save the "industrial cores" as the centerpiece of industrial and regional policy in eastern Germany. In the early period after reunification the unions issued many such calls for coherent regional and industrial policies; however, they

99. The precondition of this strategy was the acceptance by the eastern German population of positions in training and the secondary labor market, instead of jobs in the primary labor market. On union strategies toward the secondary labor market, see Mathias Knuth, "ABS-Gesellschaften: Agenturen des sozial begleiteten externen Strukturwandels," in *Zwischen Krise und Solidarität: Perspektiven gewerkschaftlicher Sozialpolitik,* ed. Horst Schmitthenner (Hamburg: VSA, 1992).

100. This is not to say that the Treuhand undertook no restructuring at all. For a discussion of its most innovative aspects, see Horst Kern and Charles Sabel, "Zwischen Baum und Borke," *SOFI Mitteilungen,* 1992.

appeared to devote few organizational or political resources to developing them.[101]

As job losses continued virtually unabated and new investment remained low, the unions began to develop and push a more activist policy on the Treuhand and state governments. As firm failures continued throughout 1991 and 1992, IG Metall—a union slower to make its peace with capitalism and thus embrace industrial policy than IG Chemie, IG Bau, Stein und Erden, and IG Bergbau und Energie[102]—began to grope toward a more activist policy. It was motivated by the recognition that actions to maintain employment were the only way to preserve labor's power at both the political and firm levels. Although early developments had brought the unions many new members, it became clear that job losses ultimately meant membership losses and political weakness. Not only were unions' market and political positions weak, but time was clearly also working against them. So in 1992, IG Metall moved to counterattack before it was too late.

A disappointing first step was the IG Metall involvement in the ATLAS program in Saxony. ATLAS was an amalgamation of nonprivatized Treuhand firms about which the Saxon Ministry of Economics could make proposals to the Treuhand, subject to input from labor and the employers. ATLAS was a disappointment primarily because there was no real decision-making competence, and the *Land* Saxony, the Treuhand, and IG Metall all maneuvered to shift the burdens and the blame.[103] Another step began in early summer 1992, when the Aufbauwerk Sachsen—a council of IG Metall, the employer association, and the DGB—was erected with the help of the *Land* government of Saxony. Again, the joint goal was to pressure the Treuhand into a specific policy to save the industrial core of the region. But it was soon apparent that the sectoral employer association opposed the holding plan because it favored the creation of smaller firms, and a stalemate quickly ensued. In response, in January 1993, IG Metall proposed an industrial holding company that would remove the key remaining firms from Treuhand control and restructure them under the joint auspices of the social partners.[104] The *Land* government showed an initial interest in the plan, but then the dispute over wages and the resulting strike shifted attention away from industrial policy for several months.

---

101. Karrasch, "Gewerkschaftliche."

102. These three unions have since merged.

103. Horst Kern, "Intelligente Regulierung: Gewerkschaftliche Beiträge in Ost und West zur Erneurung des deustchen Produktionsmodells," *Sozialen Welt* 1 (1994): 11–13; Lichtblau, *Von der Transfer- in die Marktwirtschaft*, 110–12. Mecklenburg-Vorpommern developed a similar program—the ANKER program—designed to save its "industrial cores," even though they were much smaller than the key firms in Saxony.

104. Kern, "Intelligente Regulierung," 18.

In the immediate wake of the strike, IG Metall gained in confidence and stature in eastern Germany, and this change helped complete a rethinking of its previously skeptical attitude toward industrial policy.[105] Officials now routinely asserted that the union could and must push specific proposals for saving and restructuring existing firms, and the union began trying to develop the organizational skills needed to participate in discussions about specific restructuring plans for troubled firms. Given the general weakness of the SPD in eastern Germany, the lack of funds at the *Land* level, and employers' worries about sectoral overcapacity, the unions decided to step up calls for regional and industrial policies. Although they faced major barriers because of their own weak power position, they had clear incentives to promote employment before they were weakened further.

In this context, several developments are noteworthy—developments that reflect organized labor's combination of innovative ideas and political weakness in eastern Germany. IG Metall officials in Saxony began by pushing for the construction of umbrella organizations for sectoral restructuring. Instead of *Land* and Treuhand officials making restructuring and management decisions, unions supported a proposal that private managers be allowed to recombine pieces of still unprivatized firms (including parts of the moribund ATLAS program) into more productive units. The original proposal was for a small number of separate so-called Management KGs linked together in one regional organization.[106] Management KGs had been initially unpopular in eastern Germany purportedly because they reminded the stronger firms of their own disadvantageous positions under the industrial combine structure in the GDR. But those firms still unprivatized as the Treuhand closed its doors at the end of 1994 were in a weak position to avoid incorporation, and ultimately several KGs were constructed, including ones formed around the machinery-building plants in Chemnitz and the auto subcontractors in the so-called *Sachsenring*.

The Chemnitz example illuminates both the possibilities and the limits of union involvement in regional and industrial policy. In response to huge job losses in Saxony's machinery-building region and to the bitter fights inside the public administration about appropriate responses, IG Metall in 1992 pressured the employer association to form a sectoral "interest association" called the Interessenverband Chemnitzer Maschinenbau.[107] The ICM was unlike anything previously seen in western Germany. The initial intent was to

---

105. Interview: Frankfurt, 1993.

106. KG: *Kommanditgesellschaft*. This legal form is distinct from the standard limited liability and public corporate forms usually encountered in western Germany.

107. Katharina Bluhm, "Regionale Unterstützungsnetzwerke in der ostdeutschen Industrie," in Wiesenthal, *Einheit als Interessenpolitik*; Evelyn Preusche, "Hilfe zur Selbsthilfe," *WISOC Informationsblatt* 21 (1993).

bring together the union and the employers, the chamber of commerce, the city government, the technical university, and the trade college as a way to coordinate employment-promotion measures. Contentious wage and work-time issues were consciously left out of the mandate, as was vocational training. The textile machinery sector was originally excluded, but the unions later won its admission in order to make the interest association a regional instead of a merely sectoral body.

The ICM had some immediate success in making joint purchases, thus saving on input costs for the predominantly small and medium-sized local firms. On the other hand, joint research and development moved slowly, as did joint marketing. For IG Metall the market advantages of joint action were a complement to the political advantages of tying smaller firms together into a larger community of interests. "As individual firms, ours are simply too small to command political attention," remarked the leader of the local, who added, "we have to stay together."[108] By 1998, however, the lobby and coordination functions the union valued in the ICM had taken a back seat to using the association to capture subidies (especially from the EU) for the healthier member firms. Meanwhile, many smaller firms—in 1998 the ICM had fifty-six firms—were not members of the employer associations and, while avoiding contract wages, were using the ICM to provide services. Finally, in 1998, when the union leadership proved unable to reverse these trends in the direction of a "subsidy mafia," it renounced its membership.[109]

Yet the tensions that the unions must overcome are not just with their more opportunistic partners among the employers but also with the Social Democrats, traditionally the party closest to the unions. The city's original CDU administration took a consistently neoliberal approach to employment policy and used subsidies to promote new start-ups rather than maintain existing firms. In response, the unions attempted to mobilize politically. But since works councils were and are loath to engage in extra-firm "politics," the usual linkages between parties, unions, and works councilors—which are often embodied in single *individuals* who wear many different hats—have been very difficult to reproduce in eastern Germany. Instead, the unions as *organizations* are forced to wear different hats. In Chemnitz they have been active in promoting particular infrastructure developments to the municipal administration, and they actively sought private investors for local firms. They even mounted an explicit political challenge at the municipal level: accusing the SPD of failing to counter the city administration's policies, IG Metall and the DGB in Chemnitz organized a party list to run in the 1994 municipal elections. The platform of this "leftist electoral compact" (*linker Wählerbündnis*)

108. Interview: Chemnitz, 1993.
109. IG Metall subsequently founded a Regional Agency for Chemnitz Machinery, which tries to push forward the union's view of the ICM's original purpose.

was the protection of the remaining firms and their employees.[110] To this end the unions, through the ICM, proposed a number of organizational, capital acquisition, and marketing strategies. The DGB regional offices in Dresden were skeptical of this move but did not forbid their DGB local's involvement. Ultimately, however, the SPD offered the union candidates spaces on the party's election list (including the number one position) in exchange for dropping the separate list.

The prospect of unions acting as parties involved in making industrial policy is a clear departure from West German patterns.[111] Yet although much remains to be done, the outlines of a different kind of union activity are visible in Chemnitz. Unions understand that the magnitude of the challenges in the East precludes the development of any one magic bullet, and some unions are trying, as the Saxon experience shows, to integrate themselves into a larger number of decision points across the institutional landscape.[112] Whether this presence is achieved over the medium term will in large part depend on their strategy and vision. But whether it endures over the long term will also be a function of their ability to mobilize members.

Conclusion: The Politics of Imitation

In retrospect, "No experiments!" was an unrealistic slogan. Even when transfer is done exactly, it can have unintended effects that require subsequent adaptation. In policy domains with histories of failure, efforts to transfer best practices begin a process that goes beyond merely setting up institutions; its outcomes must be surveyed over time. But how can one know whether the aforementioned changes in the German model are transitional or permanent? Such analytical ambiguity mirrors the region's political uncertainty. There seem to me three plausible perspectives on the future of efforts to build effective industrial relations institutions in eastern Germany. Although parts of each vision are implicit in much research on eastern Germany, these three stylized perspectives should not be taken as the coherent statements of any particular actors or analysts. I have been partial to each of them at one time or another.

110. *Chemnitzer Freie Presse*, November 6–7, 1993.

111. Officials at DGB headquarters in Düsseldorf were downright dismissive of the effort, invoking the "obvious" division of labor between parties and unions. Experiments in the East often provoke consternation and formal prohibition from western headquarters. Interview: Düsseldorf, 1994.

112. IG Metall has begun similar initiatives in its coastal district but has been substantially less effective in its Hanover and Frankfurt districts. Each of these three districts includes both western and eastern territories.

The first proposes that in order to catch up to the West's level of economic development, eastern Germany needs institutions different from those of western Germany but only for a temporary period. From this perspective, remaining differences between the two regions are transitional; they spring from objective economic differences whose narrowing will also allow institutional convergence over the ensuing decade or so. As evidence, one can point to several special measures that have already been phased out and also to a number of quite efficient eastern German firms—including the Opel Eisenach plant visited by President Bill Clinton in 1998—which stand as markers for an imminent increase in western German investment. Nothing in the logic of this vision rules out institutional experiments in eastern Germany, but it does imply that these experiments will not be "institutionalized" in law or become part of the key social actors' conceptions of normality. Such tacit prohibitions against institutionalization would be important in Germany, where actors' conceptions of who they are derive in important ways from what they legally can do.

A second vision is agnostic about the medium-term equalization of the economies of eastern and western Germany but insists that the core of the German model depends on a degree of institutional homogeneity that is threatened by experimentation in the East. In this view, strength allows unions to be flexible in Germany, and solidarity provides that strength. Differences in collective bargaining agreements across regions and sectors or between smaller and larger firms must be minimized in order to maintain incentives for firms to remain in high-value-added product markets that can deliver profits both to sustain investment and to benefit all of the employed. It is better, from this perspective, to accept the growth of compensatory welfare measures than to promote more investment in eastern Germany by relaxing labor market rules. Nothing in this vision rules out the possibility that a combination of investment subsidies, welfare payments, and patience may ultimately produce in the East an economic structure approximating that in the West. The key point, however, is that even if this best-case scenario does not occur, the hard-won accomplishments of the West German industrial relations model will not have been risked on the hope that a different model might have functioned as well in the West but even better in the East.

A third vision sees exact transfer not just as generous cooperation but also as hidden competition. Eastern Germany's economic misery has been a function not only of the evident weaknesses of firms, workers, and managers inherited from the GDR but *also* of a less noticed competition with the western German economy. To suggest that a hidden competition has run parallel to the public morality tale about the generosity of the West Germans need not imply a conspiracy theory about western managers. It is true that the legal constitution of individual eastern business sectors was driven heavily by western commercial interests and that investment flows left substantial eastern capacity vulnerable to western competitors who bought capacity and then shut it down.[113]

But of course the unions also saw wage equalization as a mechanism to prevent the development of a lower-wage sector in the East that could drag down wages in the West—even though high wages would clearly damage employment in the East. Further, the state's policy of restitution of property instead of compensation made investment much more difficult for everyone, while the Treuhand's fire sale approach depressed asset prices and left easterners owning few viable firms.[114] In short, the kind of competitive, calculating, self-regarding strategic logic that one expects of experienced interest associations and state actors was evident in many aspects of the reunification process. In all of this, easterners were in positions of extraordinary weakness, a weakness masked by incorporation into interest groups dominated by West Germans. While the GDR existed, the possibility of "exit" to the FRG atrophied the "voice" of the East Germans.[115] But in the united Germany, easterners have found that western willingness to speak for them carries its own set of costs.[116]

This third vision holds that eastern Germany must begin building a different kind of economy from that in western Germany. Whether those differences are in work organization, capital markets, regional policy, corporate organization, or industrial relations, the reforms must be tied to more promising product market strategies, since institutional changes must promote more successful commercial activity than do current arrangements. Most important, new arrangements will need to dampen the direct competitive pressures between western and eastern capitalism. Just as a Fordist America helped rebuild Germany by purchasing its capital equipment, a united German economy must become more complementary across the East-West divide. Because a strategy of complementarity would require new markets, industrial and regional policies other than those developed in the Ruhr will be needed, and this chapter has shown that some initial steps have already been taken. Further, ideas such as local content preferences for eastern German domestic production might be the equivalent of the undervalued currency that West Germany long enjoyed in building its export markets.

---

113. The most publicized case was in potassium production: eastern German miners went on a hunger strike to protest the closing of their mine while western ones remained open. But even in construction, long eastern Germany's fastest-growing sector, the western German construction industry (which did not have overcapacity at the time of reunification) has acquired a very large number of eastern German firms as wholly owned subcontractors, and East-West tensions have arisen there as the industry has finally slowed. See *Die Zeit* 37 (September 6, 1996).

114. Wendy Carlin and Colin Mayer, "Structure and Ownership of East German Enterprises" (paper prepared for Economics of Transition Conference, January 1995, Tokyo).

115. Albert Hirschman, "Abwanderung, Widerspruch und das Schicksal der DDR," *Leviathan* 20 (1992): 330–58.

116. See Joyce Marie Mushaben, "Auferstanden aus Ruinen: Social Capital and Democratic Identity in the New Länder," *German Politics and Society* 15 (1997): 79–101.

The first of these three different visions of an appropriate link between western institutions and the eastern future counsels patience for the east; the second emphasizes the need to consolidate, reinforce, and defend western structures against corrosive forces accelerated by eastern problems. Yet each in its own way does take leave of the illusion that western institutions and money can bear the full weight of the necessary changes. The dreams about the future of economic development in eastern Germany which made possible the attempt at exact transfer of industrial relations institutions have been shattered. As arrangements in the East feed back into pressure for changes in the West, the implication is that a process of important changes is beginning in both the eastern and western production models. If one of the two more or less static visions dominates through intent or default, Germany may find itself periodically confronting the same dilemmas for years to come, but without the measure of social health and material wealth it now enjoys. In such a context, says the third perspective, the institutional arrangements chosen might well reflect a very different set of ideas about how the burdens of production and adjustment should be distributed.

Shifting from politics to theory, I believe that transfer is less threatened by incomplete institutional packages than by the difficulty of recreating basic balances of social power which defend structures against other institutional options. As unions and employers scrambled to build organizations in eastern Germany, they constructed themselves in ways that maximized West German influence. This occurred both in the constitution of actors themselves (the incorporation of the FDGB unions) and the policies they pursued (employers' support for wage equalization). As the very weak indigenous civil society was circumvented, it atrophied further. As a result, no matter whether there were indigenous GDR actors (as in the unions) or largely were not (as in the employer associations), control has been securely in the hands of western Germans. Finally, as institutional structures and actual wage levels have been strictly oriented to those in western Germany, flexibility (in the sense highlighted in this book) has meant merely special provisions that buy time for eastern Germany to adapt to the western structures.

If this characterization is correct, two questions follow. First, are German unions returning to the "state fixation" that Andrei Markovits (echoing sentiments often expressed by U.S. occupation officials) has identified as one of their characteristic historical features?[117] Certainly, the unions in eastern Germany get much better deals through the state than they can hope for in direct negotiations with employers. It is hard to see what alternative to state fixation might exist for the unions. Of their members' three core interests— better compensation, better work conditions, and having a job in the first

117. Andrei Markovits, *The Politics of the West German Trade Unions* (New York: Cambridge University Press, 1986), 129–32.

place—only the former two are the subject of well-institutionalized negotiations.[118] Record levels of unemployment make it seem less likely than it once was that unions can maintain accustomed standards of living, let alone fulfill expectations about real wage growth, through their labor market power alone. Certainly, the threat to withhold labor is less impressive when more than four million Germans are officially without work.

The second question flows from the first. If unions depend heavily on the government, does this change the nature of a German state that has been called "semisovereign?"[119] This question cannot, of course, be answered only on the basis of policy areas touched by trade unions, but it deserves consideration in further research. Evidence from various policy domains suggests that the state has taken on extraordinary new financial commitments in eastern Germany.[120] Will the state come to play a larger role in determining wages in eastern Germany, even if that role is quite unlike the forced arbitration of Weimar? Unions have welcomed state intervention to extend collective agreements to all firms—even those not organized in the associations.[121] Yet the state has also recently changed the law on employment promotion to stipulate that the so-called employment companies supported by labor market funds can pay only 80% of the contract rate. Although unions have felt compelled to accept this change, they have denounced it as a de facto breach of principle: the autonomy of the social partners to set wages free of state interference. For a semisovereign state used to offloading potentially divisive economic issues on responsible corporatist bargaining partners, this may be a disconcerting responsibility indeed. It is already an expensive one.

118. And the *Bündnis für Arbeit* struggles demonstrate that neither employer associations nor the state can easily commit individual employers to the creation of jobs; see Stephen Silvia, "The Alliance for Jobs: Social Democracy's Post-Keynesian/Process-Oriented Employment Creation Strategy," *German Politics and Society* 50 (1999): 84–93.

119. Katzenstein, *Policy and Politics in West Germany*.

120. This has happened even in domains where Germany has long been considered a model for others to emulate. As I argue in Chapter 6, state-financed training has filled the gap in the dual system of vocational training as employers retreat from the firm-financed system.

121. In 1994 there were ninety-two extensions of collective agreements which involved all or part of eastern Germany; see Reinhard Bispinck, *Tarifpolitisches Taschenbuch, 1995–96* (Cologne: Bund-Verlag, 1995), 53–54.

CHAPTER SIX

Experimentation and Aggregation: Education in the East

The borrower is servant to the lender.

—PROVERBS 22:7

In March 1999 a Hanover criminologist, Professor Christian Pfeiffer, claimed in a radio interview that East German schools' reliance on what he called "group education" had "suppressed individualism and creativity and made children and youth subservient (into *Untertanen*) and best able to function only in groups."[1] He reminded listeners not only that violence against foreigners was four times as common in eastern as in western Germany but that 55% of those acts were group attacks, as opposed to only 20% in the West. And given eastern Germany's far smaller number of foreign residents, Pfeiffer suggested that group attacks should actually be seen as twenty-five times more likely in the East. His characterization of GDR education was not entirely new.[2] Nevertheless, the reaction from eastern Germans was breathtaking. Pfeiffer debated the topic in sold-out lecture halls in several eastern cities, and newspapers such as the *Magdeburger Volksstimme* recorded their highest number of letters to the editor since reunification. In the end, the debates were less notable for their substance than for the fury with which eastern Germans responded to this westerner's attack on the day-care centers and schools of their former state.

To understand the roots of their rage, one must go back to the transfer of institutions of secondary education to eastern Germany since 1990. That story contains three themes crucial to an understanding of institutional

1. *Frankfurter Allgemeine Zeitung*, March 12, 1999. *Die Zeit*, July 15, 1999.
2. See Karl-Günter Schirrmeister, *Erziehung zum Hass: Geistige Militarisierung in der DDR* (Stuttgart: Bonn Aktuell, 1987); Hans-Joachim Maaz, *Der Gefühlsstau: Ein Psychogramm der DDR* (Berlin: Argon, 1990).

transfer during reunification. First, transfer often involves shifts in authority, and this chapter describes two different examples: for secondary schools, responsibility was shifted from the GDR regime to the newly constituted state governments in eastern Germany; for vocational training, by contrast, central state competence was shifted to private actors, and their associations, which conduct and oversee such training in western Germany. Second, the case of education helps emphasize that models are abstractions and that they conceal geographic variation. Different eastern states drew on different aspects of the West German school models, and different eastern localities had very different experiences with the same vocational training structures. Third, the chapter provides data about the difficult legitimation of the transferred institutions. Although this account does not attempt to explain the differences in youth violence, it does highlight reasons for the eastern Germans' bitter reaction to Pfeiffer's charges.[3]

School reform also complements the book's other cases. Comparison with eastern German industrial relations after reunification reveals two common themes: labor market differences have made it easier for employers to withdraw from West German practices, whereas unions and the state have desperately sought compensation through experimentation. Whether these experiments are acceptable to West Germans raises the issue of the aggregation of interstate difference. Comparison with educational institutions after 1945 allows me to continue the theme of "democratizing" schools while adding coverage of training for future employment. Finally, comparison with postwar industrial relations reprises the theme of hybridity, as pieces of the old and the new recombine in a politicized environment.

Schools in the Two Germanys

Education is a state prerogative in Germany, and adaptive institutional changes in education reflected this location of policy competence. Most important, institutional designs were deferred until after the constitution of the new state governments, an event simultaneous with reunification on October 3, 1990. Formal reunification also coincided with the beginning of the school year, and so only tentative reforms occurred initially. Temporary institutional changes were delayed until the 1991–92 school year; permanent changes were to be in place by 1993. Thus, some flexibility resulted from the combination of German federalism, which allowed a *range* of choices, and the decision to start with *provisional* structural changes. On the other hand,

---

3. For an excellent recent account of the pedagogy in eastern German schools, see Rosalind Pritchard, *Reconstructing Education: East German Schools and Universities after Unification* (New York: Berghahn Books, 1999).

the absence of indigenous organized interests in educational policy—so unlike the postwar period—meant that school reform laws quickly became a playground for western German associations seeking to establish purer versions of their favored institutions.[4]

In this case, the institutional transfer perspective has two important advantages. First, it demonstrates a paradox: although federalism allowed some deviation from West German models, that same federalism may limit flexibility just when suffering eastern German regions most need it. Eastern German states find that they are most often "servant to the lender" not when they borrow but when they experiment. Second, it comes close to the developments in Eastern Europe since 1989. There new state actors have drawn on different "foreign" approaches and modified them as time has passed. Education was the most "voluntarist" case of imitation that one could find in German reunification.

GDR School Structures

Above all, school reform meant changing two GDR structures—the tengrade polytechnical secondary school (POS) and the extended secondary school (EOS) that led to a university entrance certificate[5]—into the West German–style elementary schools plus secondary *Hauptschulen, Realschulen, Gesamtschulen* (comprehensives), and *Gymnasien*. GDR schools represented a curious mix of German and Soviet-style structures, all formally subjugated to the control of the Communist Party. Their most striking aspect from a western perspective was the common school structure.[6]

The Soviet occupation forces and the German Communists and Social Democrats laid the foundations for common schools early, but the actual implementation of their plans—against the background of the prevailing track-based school system—was a long and arduous process. The first major step was taken in 1946 with the introduction of eight-year mandatory common schools—two years longer than those the Americans had sought in their zone. In 1959 the eight-year school was de jure expanded to ten years, a change not realized in practice until the mid-1960s. During this period, "polytechnic education"—a core course for all youth, comprising manual

4. Other public institutions were transferred with efforts to "improve" on West German structures; Stephanie Reulen, "Die Entwicklung landesspezifischer Strategien am Beispiel der Kreisgebeits- und Gemeindereform in Sachsen und Brandenburg" (Master's thesis, University of Konstanz, 1994).

5. The ten-grade POS included consecutive elementary, intermediate, and secondary levels; the EOS gave about 10% of each youth cohort a two-year university preparation course. Virtually all youth who did not attend the EOS entered the GDR version of dual vocational apprenticeship.

6. Dietmar Waterkamp, "Schule in der DDR: Eine Bilanz," in *Jahrbuch der Schulentwicklung* 6, ed. Hans-Günther Rolff et al. (Weinheim: Juventa, 1990).

Table 6. Educational achievements of fathers of GDR postsecondary students, 1982

	Education of fathers of beginning students (%)	Education of all men ages 40–50 (%)	Ratio of columns 1 and 2[a]
University	39	11	3.5
Technical school	22	14	1.6
Master	13	10	1.3
Skilled worker	25	53	0.5
Unskilled worker	1	12	0.1
Totals	100	100	1.0

Source: Reprinted by permission from Dietmar Waterkamp, "Schule in der DDR: Eine Bilanz," in *Jahrbuch der Schulentwicklung,* ed. Hans-Günther Rolff et al. (Weinheim: Juventa, 1990), 6:110.
[a]Equivalent ratios for mothers were 5.0, 2.5, 2.0, 0.9, 0.3, 1.0.

training, technical drawing, the tending of school gardens, and theory of "socialist production"—was added in order to compensate for shortened apprenticeships. The final major step in the construction of common schooling was the dismantling in 1983 of a de facto differentiation between the ninth and tenth grades of the POS—a measure that helped the better pupils prepare for entrance into the EOS. The Party also standardized content and pedagogy for both POS and EOS pupils. In contrast to schools under West German federalism, all east German schools were tightly bound to centrally produced curricula.

GDR leaders claimed that common schooling increased the mobility of underprivileged classes, but this was only partially accurate. Whereas in the 1950s the percentage of workers' children in the EOS and postsecondary education approached their percentage in the East German population, a certain self-reproduction of the new elites soon occurred.[7] By 1982 the youth entering universities and other post-secondary education were once again the children of parents who had also had access to higher education. Thus, as Table 6 demonstrates, children of both skilled and, especially, unskilled workers reached the universities in proportions noticeably smaller than their percentage of the total population. This trend accelerated over the decade so that by 1989 more than half of GDR university students had at least one parent who had also attended the university; the corresponding figure for the FRG was about one-third.[8]

7. See also Thomas Baylis, *Communist Elites and Industrial Society: The Technical Intelligentsia of East German Politics* (Berkeley: University of California Press, 1968).
8. Elisabeth Krekel-Eiben and Joachim Ulrich, "Berufschancen von Jugendlichen in den neuen Bundsländern," *Aus Politik und Zeitgeschichte* B19 (May 7, 1993): 14.

FRG School Structures

The West German schools that served as models for eastern Germany have changed in important ways since the battles outlined in Chapter 4, although the distinctive three-track system remains. At least three changes in West German schools since the 1950s have direct relevance to the investigation of institutional transfer: the establishment of some mechanisms for reconciling interstate educational differences and providing for the mutual recognition of certificates, the large expansion of schools beginning in the early 1960s, and the modified successes of the common school agenda.[9]

The Basic Law originally provided for no federal competence over schools, reserving this capacity strictly to the *Länder*. Nevertheless, the states have the responsibility of making school certificates compatible so that pupils can effectively live and work anywhere in the FRG. The key institution for interstate educational policy is the Standing Conference of the State Ministers of Education and Cultural Affairs (KMK), established in 1948. Although the KMK is unremarkable in its formal powers (it can only recommend legal changes to the individual states, and even its recommendations must be unanimous), the states have used the forum in preparing major harmonizations of the German education system in Düsseldorf (1955) and Hamburg (1964). In fact, the KMK has come to play a key role in the East.

The second change, the striking expansion of education, is manifest in the increasing numbers of pupils who stay in school for higher certificates. In the early 1960s, Georg Picht's dire warnings of an impending "educational disaster" painted the German education system as a premodern outlier among industrial nations. Picht compared Germany unfavorably with France, which, despite its smaller population, qualified almost three times the number of pupils for university entrance. Subsequently a remarkable shift occurred among the three tracks, and the vector (if not the magnitude) of that shift continued from the 1960s throughout the 1980s and into the 1990s. Whereas during the occupation the lowest track enrolled over 80% of pupils, Table 7 shows that a system emerged in which attendance was almost equally divided among the three tracks.

Third, beginning in 1969, the KMK allowed the establishment of comprehensive schools, generally for grades five through ten. The driving forces behind the comprehensives were the SPD and the trade unions. The CDU was willing to consider experiments with different school structures, but the CDU state governments strongly resisted SPD attempts to push comprehensive schools beyond the experimental stage. Consequently, in the 1970s a series

9. Comprehensive studies in English of West German education include the Max Planck Institute for Human Development and Education, ed., *Between Elite and Mass Education: Education in the Federal Republic of Germany* (Albany: State University of New York Press, 1983); and Christoph Führ, *Schools and Institutions of Higher Education in the Federal Republic of Germany* (Bonn: Internationes, 1989).

Table 7. Distribution of FRG eighth gradeers across school types, 1960–86

Type of school	1960	1970	1980	1986	Change since 1960 (in %)
Hauptschule	70.2%	55.0%	40.5%	38.0%	−45.9
Realschule	13.2	21.9	28.2	29.2	+121.2
Gymnasium	16.6	23.1	27.3	27.6	+66.3
Integrated comprehensive	0	0	4.0	5.2	
Totals	100%	100%	100%	100%	

Source: Reprinted by permission from Christoph Führ, *Schools and Institutions of Higher Education in the Federal Republic of Germany* (Bonn: Internationes, 1989), 2.

of political battles was fought inside the KMK over mutual recognition of the comprehensive school certificates and over the decision of several SPD-governed states to elevate comprehensives to the same status as other schools—a step which, the CDU argued, violated the 1964 Hamburg Agreement. The formal experimental stage ended in 1982, but the comprehensives have remained a source of controversy, as changes of state government often lead to rapid shifts in policies toward them. The political fury had abated somewhat by the late 1980s, but reunification brought a new opportunity to play out old arguments about educational opportunity in Germany. As indicated in Table 7, comprehensives have enrolled a comparatively small number of German pupils.

Educational Reunification in the Eastern *Länder*

From the fall of the wall in November 1989 until the elections in March 1990, a variety of proposals to reform GDR education were floated in both parts of Germany.[10] The vast majority of these focused on internal reform, especially pedagogical changes and teacher education. In opinion polls the teachers also emphasized internal reforms, with only about 20% agreeing that the established common schools required fundamental structural reform.[11] But with the growing realization that reunification was on the horizon, strategy in Bonn and Berlin shifted toward providing a new institutional framework. In May 1990 negotiations began between the national governments of the FRG and the GDR and quickly produced a consensus at minis-

10. For a collection of reform proposals, see Otto Lange, ed., "Aufbruch und Besinnung im Bildungswesen der DDR" (working paper, University of Oldenburg, 1990).
11. Horst Weishaupt and Peter Zedler, "Aspekte der Schulentwicklung in den neuen Ländern," in *Jahrbuch der Schulentwicklung* 8, ed. Hans-Günther Rolff et al. (Weinheim: Juventa, 1994), 415–16.

terial level to adopt the broad structures of West German education.[12] Even though the GDR had initially stated its intention to keep a few minor points that reflected GDR "traditions and conditions," the ultimate legal framework produced by the Joint Education Commission GDR-FRG in July 1990 called for the complete acceptance of the Hamburg Agreement of 1964 and a range of related measures decided by the KMK in the intervening period. The East German delegates reported that there was no West German pressure for the broad takeover and described their motivation as the hope of avoiding a "two-class educational system" in a united Germany.

The commission's recommendations were then codified in the unity treaty of August 1990, which provided a set of temporary measures for the school year beginning that fall. The elementary schools were reduced immediately to four years, and the upper level of the *Gymnasium* replaced the EOS. The secondary school part of the POS, however, generally remained in place throughout the first year, though with no effort to prejudice *Länder* decisions on the actual organization of the schools. The states were to have reform laws in place by June 30, 1991, in time to take effect for the 1991–92 school year.[13]

Thus, the very newness of the eastern *Länder* and their ministries meant that only after that first school year was thorough reform attempted.[14] The unusual and diverse outcomes of subsequent school reform laws in the six eastern states reflected western German party preferences overlaid on particular eastern German party constellations. The influence of western school models came primarily through party actors seeking to influence eastern German decisions about structural reform, especially within the formal partnerships that emerged between western and eastern German *Länder*.[15] Whereas the politics of transfer in the industrial relations case revolved around deviations from national laws and socially negotiated patterns, the politics in the school case revolved around which state models to emulate and how fully to emulate them.[16]

The dominance of party struggle was clearest where party control was clearest. In Saxony the CDU's absolute majority adopted a school reform law in July 1991 which had been revised seven times since the previous October as a result of struggles over comprehensive schools. In the end, notwith-

12. See ibid., 417–19.

13. In Saxony they were to begin with the 1992–93 school year.

14. The material on legislative reform is based on articles from regional and national newspapers and on Wolfgang Schmidt, "Die Neustrukturierung der allgemeinbildenden Schulen in den neuen Bundesländern," *Aus Politik und Zeitgeschichte* B37–38 (1991).

15. Secondary sources of pressure for particular institutional changes were West German associations of teachers, the teachers' union (GEW), and the associations for the promotion of comprehensive schools.

16. West German pedagogy also functioned as a model from which reformers could pick and choose; see A. Hoffmann and Jutta Chalupsky, "Zwischen Apathie und Aufbrucheuphorie," *Pädagogik und Schule in Ost und West* 2 (1991): 114.

standing the support for comprehensives of about one-third of the Saxonian parents polled, the CDU excluded them, arguing that a combined middle school would provide a form of comprehensive school and thus mitigate the need for that now common western German form. In Saxony, therefore, party policies narrowed the school options available to parents.

On the left, the initial effort of West Berlin's ruling SPD–Alternative List coalition during 1990 was to establish *only* comprehensives in East Berlin and, indeed, to use the reunification of the city to draw up a new citywide school reform.[17] But the December 1990 elections brought a coalition of SPD and CDU, which forged an agreement to retain for the whole city the "multiplicity" of schools found in West Berlin. The number of parents hoping to send their children to *Gymnasien* turned out to be substantially larger than planned, however, while the number for comprehensives, *Hauptschulen*, and *Realschulen* was substantially smaller. Thus, the original SPD–Alternative List plan—to open about 135 comprehensives, 25 *Gymnasien*, and no new *Hauptschulen* or *Realschulen*—was changed twice, once to accommodate CDU preferences and again to accommodate parental preferences. In the end, 54 comprehensives, 46 *Gymnasien*, 24 *Realschulen*, and 8 *Hauptschulen* were opened in the first year of reformed schools. The West Berlin model was therefore extended fairly unreformed.

With the end of the left government in Berlin, Brandenburg became the hope of the left for school reform. The SPD–Alliance '90/Greens–FDP coalition passed a provisional reform in April 1991 which called for a six-year elementary followed by a secondary system of 392 comprehensives, 79 *Gymnasien*, and 68 *Realschulen*, the last a concession to the FDP coalition partners. The Brandenburg *Gymnasien* run through the thirteenth school year (which makes them like those in western German states but unlike the twelve-year *Gymnasien* established by the other eastern German states), and there is also ten-year compulsory schooling—even though the Brandenburg CDU fought unsuccessfully for a twelve-year *Abitur* (university entrance certificate) and only nine years of compulsory schooling.

Brandenburg's Ministry of Culture also decided against the wholesale dismissal of teachers. Arguing that it was immoral to connect judgments about political suitability with an organizational need to cut teaching staffs, the ministry offered teachers reduced salary in exchange for reduced hours and thus avoided mass layoffs.[18] In order to break up "old connections" it did, however, move teachers around very significantly (and in some cases inadvertently undercut the initiatives of citizens who, in 1990, had hand-picked

17. The plan envisioned the preservation of, for example, the hot school lunch system in East Berlin and its extension to West Berlin—a cause of disagreement intimately connected with debates about the proper length of the school day, which remains very short in the FRG.
18. *Frankfurter Rundschau*, September 5, 1991.

teams to run particular new schools).[19] Indeed, the hope that activist groups would step forward and become engaged in building a new kind of school system in Brandenburg has gone largely unfulfilled.

In Saxony-Anhalt the CDU-FDP established a four-year elementary school, after which pupils either moved on to a *Gymnasium* or attended a middle school that had an orientation stage during fifth and sixth grades and was followed by separate *Hauptschule* and *Realschule* classes under the same roof. But after the election of an SPD–Green–Alliance '90 minority government in 1994, the ministry expanded the orientation level to include pupils who would otherwise have begun the *Gymnasium* with the fifth grade. The bitter denunciation of this proposal in conservative circles included the charge that the plan was an import from western German *Länder* ruled by the SPD and the claim that the KMK had accepted the eastern German de facto two-track system only because CDU governments had guaranteed that adequate differentiation would be maintained. In the new government's approach, educational conservatives saw an attempt to reduce the *Gymnasium* to a "rump *Gymnasium*" of only six years in length.[20]

Thuringia also was ruled in 1991 by a CDU-FDP coalition, and its reform was remarkably similar to Saxony-Anhalt's. In its initial law, which covered the 1991–93 school years, a four-year elementary was to be followed by an orientation level inside a combined middle school in addition to the *Gymnasium*.[21] Proponents of comprehensives were able to achieve permission for them only as "exceptions," and only six had been allowed by 1997. Mecklenburg-Vorpommern was also ruled by a CDU-FDP coalition, which agreed in April 1991 to a new school structure that took over the full range of western German school types and, alone among the eastern German *Länder*, actually envisioned independent *Hauptschulen* and *Realschulen*. The SPD, unable to achieve a general allowance for comprehensives, then used its power base in cities such as Rostock to push on the ministry a handful of special applications for comprehensives.[22]

In short, which West German model was chosen depended upon who was choosing (and who was advising the choosers). Party constellations clearly drove the educational landscape in the new *Länder*. Shifting coalitions, as in Berlin during 1990 and in Saxony-Anhalt in 1994, had a major effect on reforms. Public interest was fairly low in 1990 and 1991; with relatively high numbers of people agreeing, at that early point, that West German structures

19. *Frankfurter Rundschau*, January 9, 1992.
20. *Frankfurter Allgemeine Zeitung*, September 8, 1994.
21. Thus, the Saxonian *Mittelschule*, the Saxony-Anhalt *Sekundärschule*, and the Thuringian *Regelschule* all include both *Hauptschule* and *Realschule* tracks and offer grades five to nine or ten, depending on the certificate sought.
22. *Frankfurter Allgemeine Zeitung*, March 21, 1991. After the SPD joined the government, the number of comprehensives rose to nineteen (by 1997).

were preferable to East German ones, public hearings on reform proposals revealed little controversy, leaving the impression that school reform was the purview of elite party politics. Yet eastern party preferences for school structure closely followed the preferences of the western parties; in essence, each eastern state's Ministry of Culture initially sought a "purer" variant of the system traditionally favored by its party. That is, CDU-led governments in Mecklenburg-Vorpommern, Saxony-Anhalt, Saxony, and Thuringia all endeavored to eliminate the possibility of comprehensives as an official school form, whereas the ministries in SPD-governed Berlin and Brandenburg tried to exclude the *Hauptschule* and *Realschule* options and to establish comprehensives and *Gymnasien* only. In the end, however, dominant coalitions did not simply run roughshod over opposition parties. The original reform plans in each state were revised further during debates in 1991 so that opponents were sometimes able to include more options: the *Hauptschule* and *Realschule* in Berlin and Brandenburg; comprehensives—as "exceptions"—in Saxony-Anhalt and Mecklenburg-Vorpommern.

Towns without Schools, Schools without Pupils

As is so often true in cases of institutional transfer, the authors of these initial laws could not have forecast the acceptability of the structures they created. With so little time and so little public input, this is hardly surprising. Further, demands for flexibility are placed on transferred institutions not just by inherited culture, norms, or traditions but also by new problems. And since institutional transfer often happens in the wake of institutional failure, new organizational designs usually confront unforeseen difficulties. This was clear in the case of industrial relations, where strict adherence to standard West German–style wage deals threatened to drive most eastern firms bankrupt. Demographic developments in eastern Germany will also tax any amount of built-in flexibility in educational structures. As in the case of industrial relations, transferred institutions face difficult tests. Also as in industrial relations, the new institutions will have to reconcile competition between the two parts of Germany in order to endure in the long term.

Migration and fertility patterns greatly reduced the number of young people in eastern Germany. More than one million people have migrated from eastern to western Germany since reunification, and the fertility decline has been breathtaking. Live births dropped 60%, from 182,000 to 72,000, between 1989 and 1993 before settling at the much lower levels (see Figure 5). This demographic shift is having a major effect on eastern German elementary schools. Secondary schools still often struggle with high numbers of pupils as a consequence of strong birth years in the mid-1980s and of the failure of many youth to find apprenticeships. But as the smaller cohort moves through the system, it is leading to three forms of school consolidation: a much tighter integration of the *Hauptschule* and *Realschule* tracks (within the

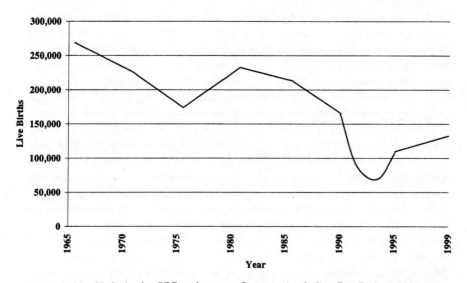

Figure 5. Live births in the GDR and eastern Germany (excluding East Berlin), 1965–99.

Source: Adapted from Horst Weishaupt and Peter Zedler, "Aspekte der Schulentwicklung in den neuen Ländern," in *Jahrbuch der Schulentwicklung 8,* ed. Hans-Günther Rolff et al. (Weinheim: Juventa, 1994), 411; *Statistisches Jahrbuch für die Bundesrepublik Deutschland,* 1997–2000.

three states that have combined middle schools), the creation of multi-year classrooms, and the closing of many schools entirely. The Brandenburg Education Ministry estimates that the number of pupils in grades seven to ten will fall from the 149,000 of 1994 to 83,000 in 2004. In Saxony-Anhalt the pupil cohort will fall from 385,000 in 1998 to 190,000 in 2008. In Mecklenburg-Vorpommern the situation is even more dire: from 28,000 first graders in 1993, fewer than 9,000 are predicted for 2001.[23]

With declining cohorts, it has also become necessary to bus children to distant schools and allow a smaller pupil-teacher ratio by keeping on most of the teachers despite falling numbers of pupils.[24] Because *Gymnasien* tend to have three to four different classes per age cohort, while the middle schools and the elementary schools have at best two and often only one, the effects of the demographic drops are hitting the latter two types of schools particularly hard.[25] For example, twenty-two Berlin elementary schools have had to merge

23. Interview: Berlin, 1999.
24. Hermann Budde and Klaus Klemm, "Äußere Schulentwicklung in den neuen Bundesländern: Perspektiven und Gefährdungen," in *Jahrbuch der Schulentwicklung 7,* ed. Hans-Günther Rolff et al. (Weinheim: Juventa, 1992), 147. In Berlin, the teachers' union agreed to a 40% cut in hours in 1999 as a means of avoiding layoffs of elementary school teachers.
25. Weishaupt and Zedler, "Aspekte der Schulentwicklung," 411.

grades one and two for the 2000 school year, and 120 of 626 Berlin elementaries are slated for closure between 2000 and 2004.[26] If standard western German rules, which generally require a minimum of fourteen pupils per elementary grade, are applied, then fully half the Thuringian elementary schools that were open in 1995 will eventually fall below the numbers needed to stay open; even relaxing the rules substantially to require only ten pupils per grade would still put every third elementary school in danger of closure.[27]

The most recent data confirm the thinning out of many eastern German schools. In elementaries, class sizes in all eastern states except Brandenburg average one to four fewer pupils than those in western *Länder*. In the three eastern states that have *Hauptschulen*, the pattern is similar, with most classes having about eleven pupils, compared with fourteen to sixteen in western Germany.[28] Case studies in several eastern German regions suggested that up to 60% of the *Realschulen* might disappear by 2000, and the numbers of *Gymnasien* could drop by up to half in some regions, as these schools shrink considerably in size in virtually all regions.[29] The most recent comprehensive data, unfortunately, cover only the years through 1994. By then, *Realschulen* in eastern Germany had already dropped from 1,715 to 917, though the number of Gymnasien had actually increased slightly, from 627 to 648.[30]

Eastern German cities are substantially more and rural regions substantially less densely populated than is the case in western Germany—a consequence of city planning in the GDR with its focus on urban life and the strict limitation of suburbs. Urban areas may be able to reshuffle teachers, buildings, and pupils in manageable ways, but in the 135 of 216 counties in eastern Germany which are predominantly rural, the prospects for such adjustment are slim. Many schools that remain open there are at the lower limit of regulations about class size, despite drawing from perhaps ten to fifteen different villages. In Brandenburg, rural development problems threaten the existence of many of the small comprehensive schools; in other *Länder*, policymakers must either accept a further fusion of *Hauptschulen* and *Realschulen* or pay the additional costs of running smaller schools in the hope that future economic and demographic developments will justify the investment.

Ministry of Culture officials in the various states often maintain that precisely in a period of demographic drops, it is essential for each region to in-

26. *Berliner Zeitung*, June 11, 1999.

27. Manfred Kuthe, "Ungleichheiten im Thüringer Schulwesen" (manuscript, Institut für Allgemeine Erziehungswissenschaft und Empirische Bildungsforschung, Erfurt, 1995), 19.

28. Bundesministerium für Bildung und Forschung (BMB+F), *Grund- und Strukturdaten, 1998/99* (Magdeburg, Germany: Garloff, 1998), sec. 2, "Schüler je Lehrer" (table).

29. J. Baumbach, E. Holldack, and K. Klemm, *Demographische Perspektiven, regionale Schulentwicklung und schulrechtliche Rahmenbedingungen in Mecklenburg-Vorpommern* (Düsseldorf: Hans-Böckler-Stiftung, 1994), 53.

30. BMB+F, *Grund- und Strukturdaten*, sec. 2, "Allgemeinbildende Schulen nach Schularten" (table).

vest heavily in the education of the fewer youth they have left. The problem is that such investments must be funded by transfers from western Germany at a time when those states face *rising* numbers of students and stagnant funding: education spending as a percentage of GDP in western Germany was 4.1% in 1990 (in 1975 it was 5.5%) and represented 13.4% of total government spending (1975; 15.8%).[31] The acquiescence of the KMK to such transfers is far from assured. Thus, as in industrial relations, old-fashioned distributive conflicts, largely defined away in an institutional transfer process designed to help eastern Germany catch up, have reappeared in ways that compromise the institutions now in place. Should eastern Germans come to see themselves as disadvantaged by "technical" rules designed in western Germany, the legitimacy of the transferred institutions might decline.

The Legitimation of Transferred Institutions

I argued in Chapter 1 that as a consequence of the weakness of eastern civil society and the demonstrated weight of western German actors in choosing structures for the East, transferred institutions would have to be self-legitimating. Few indigenous actors were available to gather reliable information, make binding promises, vouch for the moral acceptability of strange new structures, or motivate their members to cooperate with others or even sacrifice their own short-term interests for longer-term ones. The presence of indigenous elites hardly guarantees legitimation. In the post–World War II case, educational elites flatly rejected American institutional proposals that a significant proportion of the population saw as acceptable. In post-reunification industrial relations, too, legitimation has been problematic, since many workers have voted with their feet and left the unions, while large numbers of firms have refused to join the employer associations in the first place. Given the demonstrated weight of western party preferences, what legitimacy have school structures in the East achieved?

Opinion poll data suggest a qualified acceptance of the new schools in eastern Germany. For example, in a 1993 poll of parents, pupils, and teachers in Thuringia, all groups said they had more advantages than disadvantages from the new schools.[32] Around 55% of teachers saw advantages for themselves; not quite 20% saw disadvantages. The equivalent figures among parents were 45% and less than 20%; for pupils, just under 40% and about 25%. On the other hand, even though eastern Germans tend to rate the new schools as acceptable, they rate some of them *lower* than the corresponding GDR schools. Thus, as Table 8 shows, the new elementary schools are rated as "good" or "very good" somewhat less often, depending on the category,

31. Budde and Klemm, "Äußere Schulentwicklung," 158.
32. Weishaupt and Zedler, "Aspekte der Schulentwicklung," 422. In the disaggregated data, however, one group, *Hauptschule* pupils, actually said they were worse off.

Table 8. Thuringian teachers, pupils, and parents rating new and old schools either "good" or "very good," 1993

School type	% Teachers			% Pupils		% Parents			
	elem	mid	Gymn	mid	Gymn	elem	mid	Gymn	IFS[a]
Elementary (new)	82	77	65	69	78	84	84	75	60
Middle (new)	54	54	34	60	52	62	69	55	36
Gymnasium (new)	65	47	72	45	81	75	71	78	73
Comprehensive (new)	70	57	54	48	57	72	66	62	48
GDR POS grades 1–4	79	82	85	68	77	84	83	85	71[b]
GDR POS grades 5–10	50	47	41	62	69	71	76	70	71[b]
GDR EOS grades 10–12	55	54	55	56	72	66	67	67	70
Sample size	536	514	268	3,252	3,540	1,097	1,320	2,388	607

Source: Reprinted by permission from Horst Weishaupt and Peter Zedler, "Aspekte der Schulentwicklung in den neuen Ländern," in *Jahrbuch der Schulentwicklung* 8, ed. Hans-Günther Rolff et al. (Weinheim: Juventa, 1994), 420.
[a]Data taken from an *Institut für Schulentwicklungsforschung* (IFS) poll of parents.
[b]The IFS poll did not differentiate between POS grade levels.

than the first four classes of the old POS, and the POS grades five to ten usually received higher marks than the new middle school. Only the new *Gymnasien* were rated more highly by virtually all groups than their GDR counterparts, the EOS.

How stable are positive evaluations of the new schools? Opinions on the quality of new and old schools have swung substantially since 1990. In 1995 a representative poll of one thousand eastern German adults, commissioned by the news weekly *Der Spiegel*, confirmed a widespread appreciation in eastern Germany for certain aspects of GDR life. Only 15% of those polled agreed with the statement that they "wished there had never been a reunification" of the two countries, but whereas in 1990 GDR citizens rated the GDR as superior to the FRG in only three of nine areas (see Table 9), eastern German citizens in 1995 rated the GDR as having been superior in seven of the nine. Changes in the relative evaluation of GDR vocational training and schools are striking. Where 36% of eastern Germans in 1990 held that West German schools and vocational training were superior (28 and 33%, respectively, thought the GDR superior), in 1995 the numbers had radically shifted so that around two-thirds said GDR schools and training were superior, and those who rated FRG education superior dropped to 11 and 12%.

184

Table 9. Eastern Germans' assessment of relative merit of FRG and GDR subsystems, 1990, 1995

	1990 responses (N = 1,000)		1995 responses (N = 1,000)	
Criterion	% FRG superior	% GDR superior	% FRG superior	% GDR superior
Standard of living	91	2	85	8
Protection against crime	13	62	4	88
Equality for women	10	67	3	87
Science and technology	87	2	63	6
Social security	16	65	3	92
Schools	36	28	11	64
Vocational training	36	33	12	70
Health system	65	18	23	57
Housing	34	27	21	53

Source: Adapted from *Der Spiegel* 27 (1995): 43.

What is unclear from such data, of course, is whether the relative evaluation changed because eastern German assessments of FRG education got worse or because retrospective evaluation of GDR education was more positive. There is some clear evidence for the latter trend in polls taken by the Institut für Schulentwicklungsforschung (IFS) in 1991 and 1993, each based on representative samples of just under one thousand respondents. Responses to one question in particular give a sense of the magnitude of the shift toward more positive evaluations of GDR education. The question read, "The school system in the former GDR is now in transition. Which opinion of the three listed below most closely reflects your own?" The three choices were (1) the educational and school system in the former GDR was an effective system, and nothing should have been changed; (2) a reform of education can only succeed when both the form and the content of schools are changed; (3) it was right to end the Party-dominated pedagogy of the GDR, but it would have been better to retain the key structural features of the GDR system (comprehensive schools close to home, the EOS and apprenticeship system, and the possibility of dual qualifications). In 1991, 5% would have favored no changes; 38%, the decision for both internal and structural changes; 57%, internal reforms only. In 1993, the proportion of respondents who would have favored no changes jumped to 20%; those approving the total changes dropped by half, to only 19%; and 61% felt that internal reforms with structural continuity would have been preferable.[33]

33. Rolff et al., *Jahrbuch der Schulentwicklung* 8 (1994), 28.

If western structures have not been self-legitimating, one can ask which improvements eastern Germans most desire. Do they want the schools to teach different things than western Germans want for their children? Do they expect different things from the schools? From the available data, the answer to the first question is "no"; the answer to the second is "yes." In a 1992 poll, given lists of personal qualities that they might wish their children to develop, eastern and western German parents consistently chose the same characteristics with about the same frequency (in both parts of Germany, the leading answers were honesty, capacity for judgment, and a sense of responsibility). Polls of pupils in both parts of Germany also revealed virtually no difference in the things they expected to learn in school.[34] Yet when asked about which *functions* they expected the schools to perform better, western German parents emphasized better teaching of general education, whereas eastern Germans focused on the need to teach working together and discipline.[35] The poll also revealed a continuing interest in increased opportunities for full-day schooling or for vastly improved after-school activities.

It seems reasonable to infer from these findings that the GDR experience with local schools, after-school activities, and day care continues to inform eastern German perception of what makes for good schools. As the American experience suggests, however, it is possible to overload schools with functions, including those tied to social welfare, until they can no longer concentrate on pedagogical tasks.[36] Western German schools, in part because they are half-day schools, tend to stick strictly to passing on knowledge and intellectual skills. Imparting "social competency" is a task seen as belonging primarily to the realms of family and church. Thus, the West German model sets real limits on the desire of many eastern Germans to reintegrate some familiar functions into their schools.

As outlined in Chapter 1, self-legitimation can come through effectiveness, fairness, or familiarity.[37] The most effective of the schools is widely seen to be the *Gymnasium*; the result has been a run on higher education and determined flight from the *Hauptschule*. This picture of uneven effectiveness is reinforced by uneven fairness. Localities fortunate enough to maintain a critical mass of pupils may well enjoy low pupil-teacher ratios that please parents, pupils, and teachers; unfortunately, many other localities have faced school closures, and much different urban-rural demographics in eastern and western Germany will continue to bedevil efforts for fair access to close and competent schools. And although there is little doubt that eastern Germans are becoming familiar with the new institutions, that familiarity is leading to

34. *Max-Planck-Gesellschaft Spiegel*, April 1993, 11.
35. Weishaupt and Zedler, "Aspekte der Schulentwicklung," 426.
36. Hal Hansen, "Caps and Gowns: Historical Reflections on the Institutions That Shaped Learning for and at Work in Germany and the United States, 1800–1929" (Ph.D. diss., University of Wisconsin, 1996).
37. See the section headed "Legitimation" in Chapter 1.

some contempt and some very striking retrospective acceptance of the old GDR schools. Thus self-legitimation has been incomplete through all three posited routes.

The legitimation of transferred institutions involves meeting particular expectations, some of which in this case stem from the particular functions of GDR schools. Yet the decline in satisfaction with FRG schools and the increase in retrospective esteem for GDR schools also mirrors more general assessments of reunification.[38] Disenchantment with the difficulties of reunification appears to have fed back into assessments of individual policy areas. As indicated earlier, acceptance may be built mostly upon a lack of alternatives.

Federalism Giveth and Federalism Taketh Away

Both the magnitude and mechanism of change in eastern German schools since 1990 are striking. Although education policy has been notoriously resistant to attempts at institutional transfer, eastern German states relied heavily on West German models to reshape the structures of their schools. Generally they asked only one major concession: that the independent *Hauptschule* not be a part of the design. Acquiring a ninth-grade certificate had been the equivalent of dropping-out in the GDR, and with the end of state-controlled access to channels of education, most eastern Germans were looking for higher, not lower, certificates. The western German states, through their representatives in the KMK, ultimately agreed, in part because the three states seeking to build "middle schools" were all ruled by the CDU. This political alignment increased the confidence of CDU officials in the West that the intent of the middle schools was not to undermine the track-based system but to give it a chance by making a credible guarantee that youth who wanted to move upward could do so, often within the same building.

How effective have the plans been? First, there have been no major discontinuities in school structures since 1991, even though the provisional nature of the reforms would have made large changes possible. Thus, in no state has the transfer simply failed, been rejected and replaced. At some fundamental level the exact transfer mechanism appears to have made a remarkable institutional transformation imaginable, and thus possible, by providing some clear indicators of the necessary tasks. Only when the definition of these tasks seemed to be political rather than technical was the process slowed. For a variety of reasons outlined earlier, eastern German states planned some deviations from the West German models, and so far, neither Brandenburg nor the three states with middle schools have been forced off their separate paths. Further, a 1996 KMK plan to force a reconciliation of

---

38. To attribute this all to crude nostalgia is too simplistic: eastern Germans are still eminently capable of differentiating the elements of the old schools which they admire from those which they continue to reject.

the twelve- versus thirteen-year *Abitur* was put off until after 2000. In the meantime, this eastern peculiarity has been dying by attrition. Saxony quickly passed its twelve-year *Abitur* into permanent statute, indicating that it has no intention of changing, and Thuringia also intends to stay at twelve. Officials in Mecklenburg-Vorpommern muse about moving to thirteen but have so far taken no real steps to do so. Meanwhile, officials in Brandenburg acknowledge that their thirteen-year *Abitur* is probably dependent upon a continued SPD absolute majority. If Brandenburg's policy changes, the thirteen-year *Abitur* would exist only in Saxony-Anhalt and East Berlin—probably an insufficient basis for a long-term minority tradition in the East. As in the case of industrial relations, exact transfer has actually led to significant experimentation.

Yet if the magnitude of transfer's effect must be seen as very high, one must also interrogate its durability. The new structures will soon confront a massive demographic challenge at a time when their acceptance by the population has already declined. Ironically, the same federalist system that provided a variety of institutional forms for eastern German states to consider (and material assistance in setting up their new systems) also acts as a brake on further development there. This is so because cooperative federalism in Germany is also conflictual federalism, in that distributional issues are a permanent feature of inter-*Länder* discussion. In order to meet the demographic shift in a way that maintains distinct tracks, takes account of the desire of eastern Germans for local schools, and leaves open the possibility that economic recovery may eventually occur, eastern *Länder* need special provisions and transfer payments from western *Länder*. But with western educational spending profoundly strained, it is not obvious that the allowance or the funds will be forthcoming.

Recall that building institutions through transfer can involve constituting actors as well. As in the postwar case—in keeping with federalist traditions that were interrupted by the Nazis, overturned by the Communists, and supported by the Americans—education control was vested in the *Länder* even before their reconstitution as actors. In both cases, allowing for variation in educational systems was held to be part of the democratic development of state governments. Of course, in the postwar case only some social groups were mobilized over education, while others were conspicuously neglected. In the reunification case it has been even more difficult to engage a poorly organized civil society on issues of educational reform. This has been especially troubling in a state such as Brandenburg, where the school reform laws presuppose an engaged public willing to fill out the framework given by the state with schools whose characters fit local desires.

Additionally, whereas states such as Bremen once worried that American common school designs would leave their education system incompatible with those in other German states, institutional transfer since 1990 has nominally guaranteed mutual recognition. This guarantee made transfer more palatable, but the federalist blessing carried its own curse. Whereas *Länder* differences in the post–World War II period were reconciled slowly over the course of the 1950s, culminating in the Hamburg Agreement of 1964, the eastern German states were immediately confronted with limits on the structures they could develop and the standard operating procedures they could implement. The KMK has made clear that there will be little tolerance for lower pupil-teacher ratios than those existing in western Germany—not even if somewhat more integrated classes in the East might require smaller class sizes.

There are real limits, then, to the claim that institution building in eastern Germany has been democracy in practice. To put it metaphorically, although the East Germans were allowed to order their own meal, the menu was limited, substitutions were not welcome, and the chefs were easily insulted if the specials were ignored.

Vocational Training since 1990

In vocational training, competence was shifted from the centralized GDR state to the complex division of labor between state and society that prevailed in the West German dual system. That system is itself facing a dramatic challenge, however, so its transfer to eastern Germany has been attempted under the shadow of serious ongoing concerns. Massive levels of government funding, the presence of the same complementary institutional supports, and the concerted efforts of the country's major social partners notwithstanding, dual training arrangements are experiencing significant difficulty taking root in the East. Further, problems with vocational training in eastern Germany are helping to accelerate pressures for changing the system in all of Germany.

Transfer has been challenged by the underlying weaknesses of the eastern German sociopolitical infrastructure (chambers of industry and commerce, local unions, business organizations, etc.) on which the dual system rests. Yet despite the weaknesses of social actors in the East, some localities have managed the problems much better than others. To illustrate, I compare two cities in Saxony. One city, Leipzig, was able to overcome or at least compensate for economic and institutional deficiencies and establish dual training, since it possessed a network of secondary associations and interest groups capable of coordinating efforts, pooling resources, and sharing information. In the other, Chemnitz, which possessed more limited sociopolitical resources, the new institutions are still struggling to develop.[39]

39. This section draws on research conducted by Richard Locke and Wade Jacoby, published in "The Dilemmas of Diffusion," *Politics and Society* 25 (1997): 34–65.

The West German Dual System

Approximately 70% of German youth sixteen to nineteen years of age participate in the so-called dual system of vocational training, typically seen as an effective way of combining work and learning. Because it matches youth to prospective occupations and firms, it is also seen as an efficient allocative mechanism, critical in smoothing the school-to-work transition and in reducing youth unemployment. And because the system provides German firms with highly skilled workers, it is often seen as facilitating firm-level adjustment and the introduction of new technologies.[40] In fact, an abundance of material on various aspects of the German system of training has been published, much of it with an eye to replicating these practices in other national settings.[41]

Three key features characterize the system: (1) the role of the social partners in developing the content and regulating the implementation of training programs; (2) the shared investment made by private employers, the government, and individual apprentices during the training process; and (3) the role of the local chambers of industry and commerce (or craft chambers) in certifying the quality of the portable skills gained through training.

In Germany's dual system of training, for one or two days a week apprentices attend a public vocational school, where they are taught general subjects such as mathematics, history, and languages as well as the underlying "theoretical principles" associated with their future occupation. The remainder of the week is spent working at a firm, where apprentices acquire practical skills by taking part in the ongoing production process. The required general school training is funded by the state governments; the costs of in-firm training are covered by the firms. The apprenticeship is based on a training contract between the individual apprentice and the employer. As part of their contribution, the trainees accept wages that are one-quarter to one-half the skilled wage rate during their three years of apprenticeship.

Firms can choose whether or not to engage in such training, and only about 20 percent of West German firms have done so any one time. A web of laws and regulations sets the standards to be met by training firms, develops and periodically revises the curriculum offered in the schools, and institutionalizes the participation of the unions and business organizations. According to federal law, all youth under eighteen are eligible to be trained in any one of 374 (as of 1991) official occupations. The content of the training programs is determined at the federal level, while unions, employer associa-

---

40. A useful summary is Richard Koch and Jochen Reuling, eds., *Modernisierung, Regulierung und Anpassungsfähigkeit des Berufsausbildungssystems der Bundesrepublik Deutschland* (Bonn: BiBB, 1994).

41. On the most recent attempts in the United States to replicate German training, see Heinrich von Pierer, "Brückenschlag über den Atlantik: Lehrlingsausbildung in der USA," *Amerika in Uns*, ed. Beate Lindemann (Mainz: Hase & Koehler, 1995).

tions, state governments, and the federal government (through the Federal Institute for Vocational Training—BiBB) negotiate the curriculum and the occupations available for apprenticeship. At the plant level, certified trainers are employed by the firms and monitored by the works councils. National standards are maintained through a set of exams administered locally by the chambers and covering both the theoretical and practical aspects of training. Apprentices who pass these exams receive a certificate that is recognized all over Germany, so certification and quality control of training programs promote the portability of worker skills.

Central to the functioning of the system are supporting institutions and secondary associations, especially the local chambers of industry and commerce (or craft chambers).[42] Aside from examining apprentices and determining the eligibility of firms to train them, the local chambers provide an array of services to assist firms in developing or improving their training. Chamber representatives also meet with union leaders, local school administrators, and officials from the local office of the government employment agency to coordinate activities and ensure both that there are sufficient numbers of apprenticeship slots for each year's youth cohort and that the training meets established standards. In short, the system depends on both a dynamic private sector and an articulated network of other organizations and associations in order to function properly.

Yet the dual system faces a number of problems.[43] A complicated discussion has long been under way in Germany about the sources of its difficulties, but it is sufficient for my purposes to identify a "demand" issue on the part of youth and a "supply" issue on the part of firms. The demand issue is best encapsulated in the increasing trend of German youth toward the *Gymnasium*, as noted earlier in this chapter. Whereas only some 16% of West German pupils attended *Gymnasien* in 1960, the figure had essentially doubled by the end of the 1980s; thus, the traditional clientele of the vocational system—especially from the *Hauptschulen*—has long been shrinking.

The supply of apprenticeships in firms is also problematic. A long-term concern has been the importance of training in the smaller, more artisanal firms in which the German dual system originated during the late nineteenth century. Traditionally, craft training accounted for about one-third of all apprenticeships, but the quality of training and likelihood for long-term employment in such firms have generally been lower than in industry or the public sector. In recent years, however, it has become relatively more important because of large reductions in the number of industrial and public-

42. Wolfgang Streeck et al., *The Role of the Social Partners in Vocational Training and Further Training in the Federal Republic* (Berlin: CEDEFOP, 1987).

43. A useful overview of these problems is Antonius Lipsmeier, "Das duale System der Berufsausbildung: Zur Reformbedürftigkeit und Reformfähigkeit eines Qualifizierungskonzeptes," in *Kasseler berufspädagogischer Impulse*, ed. Martin Kipp, Gere Neumann, and Günther Spreth (Frankfurt: Gesellschaft zur Förderung arbeitsorientierter Forschung und Bildung, 1994).

sector apprenticeship slots. The most striking case is that of the metalworking sector, where the number of new apprenticeships in metal and electrical occupations fell from 80,000 in 1987 to 57,500 in 1991 and 41,000 in 1994.[44] Additionally, some argue a need to adjust the occupation-centered focus of the current system so that it can respond to (rather than hinder) the efforts of firms to restructure along new and more flexible lines.[45]

These problems were well known among specialists in the field in 1990 yet found no expression in official efforts to extend West German training to eastern Germany. The transfer process itself has further exposed major problems inherent in West German training arrangements. Nevertheless, the reservoir of the system's societal legitimacy has proved itself virtually bottomless, even when the large sums committed to perpetuating it threaten to undercut the essential logic of private financing. As a result, the crisis of the system has only recently become an important political issue.

Vocational Training in the GDR

The central feature of the East German system was state authority over vocational training. The GDR developed a hybrid form of training that was essentially a compromise between traditional German dual apprenticeship arrangements and the Soviet practice of unified firm-based training. Most East German youth entered vocational schools after successful completion of the ten-grade POS. Apprenticeships usually lasted two years and, as in West Germany, were regulated by training contracts between individual youth and training firms. Also as in West Germany, a constitutional clause assured free choice of occupation, but GDR citizens had a constitutional duty to finish at least a partial apprenticeship.[46] Because these two principles often conflicted, central planning did restrict the range of vocational choices available to East German youth: by the late 1980s only about 50% of apprentices were being trained in their first-choice occupation or a related field.

As in the FRG, apprentices spent time both attending school and working in firms. GDR vocational schools were of two principal kinds. In 1982 those operated by firms enrolled about 68% of GDR apprentices, and those run by local communities taught 32%. The community schools primarily serviced small firms, especially in sectors that could not afford their own training facilities.[47] Over the course of the 1980s, however, training became increasingly

---

44. See Martin Baethge et al., "Die Zukunft des Facharbeiters" (manuscript, Soziologisches Forschungsinstitut Göttingen, 1995), 2.

45. Ulrich Beck, *Risikogesellschaft: Auf dem Weg in eine andere Moderne* (Frankfurt: Suhrkamp, 1986).

46. Hartmut Zimmerman et al., *DDR Handbuch*, 3d ed. (Cologne: Wissenschaft und Politik, 1985), 330.

47. Ibid., 333.

concentrated in the firm-based schools, so that by 1989 about 80% of all vocational training was located exclusively within large companies.[48]

Participating firms in East Germany were generally much larger, trained many more apprentices, and were far more concentrated in industry than was the case in West Germany. Small firms engaged in craft and artisanal work were increasingly denied access to apprentices: in 1950, 80% of East German apprentices were trained in small firms; by 1989, only 3%.[49] In the Federal Republic, by comparison, 35% of all apprentices in 1989 were being trained in small craft enterprises. Moreover, at the end of the 1980s, 80% of GDR apprentices but only about 52% of West German youth were training in industrial firms, and 20% of apprentices in the GDR were trained in service occupations versus 48% in the FRG.[50]

Curricular changes were a major focus of training policies during the 1980s, and as in the FRG, GDR reforms brought a dramatic decline in the number of vocations offered: from 922 in 1957 to 318 in 1984.[51] The training continued to include both general knowledge and more specialized applications linked to a particular occupation. Despite curricular reforms, however, the prohibitive costs of technologically sophisticated equipment, especially following the microelectronics revolution, clearly affected the content of GDR training. Moreover, throughout the 1970s and 1980s, spending for vocational training represented a declining share of East German GDP.[52] Consequently, only about 20% of the apprenticeships (by official Party estimates) actually saw curricular change that reflected the "scientific-technological revolution" represented by microelectronics.[53] In the metalworking industry, for example, apprenticeships offering training in computer numerically controlled (CNC) machinery and hydraulics were virtually nonexistent.

Table 10 summarizes the key differences between the FRG and GDR systems—differences that would come to play a significant role in shaping the process of institutional transfer and reform in the years immediately following reunification of the two Germanys.

48. See Ulrich Degen, Günther Walden, and Klaus Becker, *Berufsbildung in den neuen Bundesländern* (Berlin: BiBB, 1995).

49. Ibid., 16.

50. Ibid., 36.

51. The latter number includes all the subspecialties in twenty-eight broad occupational groups. Zimmerman, *DDR Handbuch*, 330.

52. Dieter Burkhardt, "Aspekte zur Finanzierung und Förderung der Berufsausbildung in den neuen Bundesländern," *Gewerkschaftliche Bildungspolitik*, January 1990, 9.

53. Oskar Anweiler, ed., *Vergleich von Bildung und Erziehung in der Bundesrepublik Deutschland und in der Deutschen Demokratischen Republik* (Bonn: BiBB, 1990).

Table 10. Differences between West and East German vocational training before 1990

	FRG	GDR
Role of social partners	Actively involved in curriculum development, training, certification, and quality control	No appreciable role
Distribution of training by sector	52% industry; 48% services	80% industry; 20% services
Distribution of training by firm size	35% small firms; 65% medium and large firms	3% small firms; 97% large firms
Locus of training	Split between publicly funded schools and private firms	Primarily within conglomerate-based schools
Focus of training	Providing firms with skilled labor and youth with portable skills	Economic development; channeling youth into "targeted" industries
Freedom of choice	Firms choose whether or not to train; youth can choose occupations but firms accept them on basis of performance	Firms had no choice; youth could choose occupations only within highly structured state targets

EMULATING THE WEST: THE REDESIGN
OF EASTERN VOCATIONAL TRAINING

Following monetary union in July 1990, the East German parliament adopted the West German vocational training law (*Berufsbildungsgesetz*, or BBiG), craft regulations (*Handwerksordnung*, or HwO), and the provisions for training in the professions and in agriculture. The BBiG provides the legal framework governing training in industry and commerce, and the HwO regulates training in the artisanal and craft occupations (which include most construction trades, baking, auto mechanics, and the skilled trades). Also, the BiBB took over much of the personnel from the GDR's *Zentralinstitut für Berufsbildung* (Central Institute for Vocational Education) and extended its responsibilities to eastern Germany.

Following reunification, the remaking of vocational training in the image of the West continued. There was no effort to accommodate particular GDR techniques in order to address problems that had long vexed the FRG system. For example, the close cooperation between East German vocational school teachers and in-firm trainers was seen by West Germans as an outgrowth of centralized planning and thus incompatible with West German–style training. In reality, however, closer cooperation had long been a desired goal in the FRG, but because so much training took place in small firms, coordination with the schools was very difficult to achieve. Likewise, the East German practice of allowing some youth to integrate academic and vocational credentials in one apprenticeship, a step that West German employers' associations had begun to demand publicly by 1995, was opposed in 1990 by the West German chambers of commerce and damned as a political tool for privileging an SED elite. West German training authorities did initially agree to recognize some thirty East German vocational profiles, although in most cases this process stalled before official regulations were ever written.[54] In short, the overwhelming thrust of efforts to reform East German vocational training was toward reproducing West German structures and practices as closely as possible. East German practices were deemed unacceptable solutions to long-standing West German weaknesses.

With reunification on October 3, 1990, authority for the vocational schools was transferred to the newly established state and municipal governments. Physical facilities located inside the large East German conglomerates were given over to local authorities. The municipalities also began transferring their role in overseeing in-firm training to the craft chambers and the chambers of industry and commerce.[55] Craft chambers had existed during the GDR period but oversaw only the training of master craftsmen; the chambers of industry and commerce had been completely dismantled by the GDR regime. An enormous cooperative effort on the part of West German chambers, however, along with substantial investment subsidies from the federal government, led to the relatively rapid establishment of formal competence by the new chambers.[56]

The FRG and GDR regimes negotiated special provisions for recognizing GDR certificates as prerequisites for further training in the West.[57] Youth already in training at the time of reunification could choose to continue under the GDR curriculum or switch to a new curriculum adopted from the West.[58] Ad hoc programs were designed to ease the transition toward a West German–style dual system to build training capacity in eastern Germany and to train youth for whom traditional in-firm training was not yet available. These measures included bundling European Community, federal, and state moneys to provide incentives for firms to maintain and refurbish their training facilities. Federal spending on physical infrastructure totaled 450 million DM from 1990 to 1994.[59] In addition, various programs were developed to encourage more firms to train youth. A high priority was assigned to training in

54. Interview: Berlin, 1993. See also Carsten Johnson, "Die Rolle intermediärer Organisationen beim Wandel des Berufsbildungssystems," in *Einheit als Interessenpolitik*, ed. Helmut Wiesenthal (Frankfurt: Campus, 1995), 133.

55. I translate *Handwerkskammern* as "craft chambers" and the IHK (Industrie- und Handelskammer) as "chambers of industry and commerce."

56. Johnson, "Die Rolle," 137–39.

57. See IG Metall, *Informationen zum jetzt geltenden Recht der beruflichen Bildung in den neuen Bundesländern* (Frankfurt: IG Metall Department of Vocational Training, 1991).

58. Several of my interview partners suggested that youth overwhelmingly chose to switch to the West German curriculum offered for their occupation.

59. Degen, Walden, and Becker, *Berufsbildung*, 136.

the craft and professional areas (tax advisers, legal assistants, medical technicians). Each state developed programs that provided 4,000 to 10,000 DM to small firms (under twenty-five employees) for each new apprenticeship they offered. Industrial and commercial firms received relatively less public funding: just over 10% of public subsidies in Saxony between 1991 and 1994, with the rest going to craft, artisanal, and white-collar employers.[60]

DEVELOPMENTS SINCE REUNIFICATION

Institutional transfer, economic crisis, and ad hoc policies have fundamentally shifted the structure of vocational training in eastern Germany. The sheer volume of change since reunification is striking. A massive reduction of industrial training in large firms has been accompanied by vigorous efforts to promote training both among small and medium-sized firms and in the administrative and service occupations of the public sector. Whereas in 1989 only 3% of the GDR youth cohort were being trained in craft firms and over 80% in industrial firms, by 1993, 49% of the youth in the new federal states were being trained for careers in industry and commerce, 38% in crafts, 5% in professional occupations, and 2% in agriculture. When one disregards extra-firm training, the shifts appear even more stark: 50% in crafts, 30% in industry and commerce, 11% in the public sector, and 5% in the professions.[61]

Carsten Johnson has attributed the increase in craft-based training to three factors. First, there was pent-up demand from the GDR period for craft and artisanal work, demand that had never been accommodated because of the shortage of craftsmen. Second, a boom in the craft economy endured until about 1996, especially in the construction trades, because the rebuilding of eastern German cities, housing stock, commercial properties, and transportation networks resulted in a demand for skilled labor. Third, both federal and state government programs favored the creation of new apprenticeships in the smallest firms.[62]

Along with the substantial shift away from industrial training and toward crafts came a significant number of new non-firm-based apprenticeships. The original reunification statutes envisioned both the use of the standard West German provisions for training educationally disadvantaged youth at "extra-firm" sites and the creation of a special program to promote extra-firm training through the 1992–93 school year. Policymakers' original hopes that

60. Interview: Leipzig, 1995.
61. Karen Schober, "Der schwierige Weg zum dualen System," *Materialien aus der Arbeitsmarkt- und Berufsforschung* 3 (1994): 5.
62. Johnson, "Die Rolle," 138.

Table 11. Composition of apprenticeships in eastern Germany, 1990–96

	1990–91	1991–92	1992–93	1993–94	1994–95	1995–96
Total applicants	145,700	138,300	145,600	171,100	191,692	208,700
Total apprenticeships	99,700	95,800	97,200	114,600	114,079	119,000
Extra-firm slots	37,000	20,700	13,200	27,100	21,057	20,800
Firm-based slots	62,700	75,100	84,000	87,500	93,022	98,200
Ratio of firm-based slots to applicants	.43	.54	.58	.51	.49	.47
New applicants		95,130	98,951	117,872	122,646	125,028

Sources: Reprinted with permission from Karen Schober, "Der schwierige Weg zum dualen System," *Materialen aus der Arbeitsmarkt—und Berufsforschung* 3 (1994): 4; *Berufsbildungsbericht,* various years.

substantial extra-firm training would be limited to the first three years were soon shattered, however. It did decline from 37,000 slots in 1990 to 20,700 in 1991 and only 13,200 in 1992. But as these special provisions neared their expiration dates, it became clear that extra-firm training was still needed, especially to cope with the larger cohorts resulting from both strong birth rates in the mid-1970s and the appearance of youth who had earlier stayed in nonvocational school, in part because of a lack of training opportunities.

Each spring since then newspaper headlines have trumpeted the huge gaps between the number of youth seeking apprenticeships and the number of apprenticeships advertised by firms at the local labor offices. As the figures in Table 11 demonstrate, extra-firm training made a substantial contribution to total training in each of the first six years of unification. Further, despite the declining birth rate, the demographic figures show that youth cohorts, after rising from an average of about 175,000 per year during the first four years of unification, have run at an annual average of 210,000 through 2000.[63] In other words, state efforts to retreat from financing the nonschool portion of vocational training are colliding head-on with firms' recalcitrance and with demographic developments that exacerbate the shortfall of apprenticeships. Thus, notwithstanding the substantial efforts of political and social actors, dual firm-based vocational training has not yet been securely established in eastern Germany—at least, not in ways that reconcile firms' financing of their own labor market needs with the aspirations of eastern German youth.

It appears that eastern Germany now suffers from particularly acute versions of ills that had previously plagued the West German training system. Firms increasingly view training as a cost to be controlled; young people increasingly see higher education as necessary insurance against unpredictable labor markets. The fundamental dilemma is that policies designed to make

63. Ibid., 142.

training more attractive for firms almost invariably make it less attractive to eastern German youth. To the extent that the federal and state governments try to transcend this dilemma with financial incentives, they run the risk of being forced to assume permanent financial responsibility for a sizable portion of vocational training. Whether or not this responsibility proves permanent depends, in turn, on how firms react when the smaller youth cohort reaches the age of apprenticeship beginning in about 2005.

Compounding the challenge to the dual system that arises from the expiration of special transitional programs and a growth in demand for apprenticeships is the danger that eastern firms are becomming collectively unenthusiastic about training. Systematic data are hard to find, but eastern chambers of commerce routinely cite figures suggesting that only 5–10% of their member firms are engaged in vocational training.[64] More worrisome still, those that currently do participate are often ambivalent about continuing. A 1994 survey of 1,575 eastern German firms that offered apprenticeships revealed that far more were planning to reduce their training efforts over the next three years than to expand them.[65] And a study of approximately one hundred eastern German firms that did not train youth revealed varied reasons, claiming that they did not do so because of the time and resources required, the lack of need for new apprentices, the lack of training personnel, or the uncertainty of their future (even though 55 percent called their economic health "very good" or "excellent").[66]

Confronted with this reluctance, the state stepped in, but the heavy reliance on public funding has since become a contentious issue. In order to prevent a "training catastrophe" in eastern Germany, the government has heavily subsidized apprenticeships in many firms and has also established many extra-firm training slots. Whereas public funding for extra-firm training in the old federal states amounted to a mere seven thousand spaces annually, various reports from the East suggest that 60 to 80% of all apprenticeships in the new federal states are either partially or fully government funded.[67] Many eastern firms have come to expect financial assistance from the state, and it appears that without such financing there might well be a substantial drop in the provision of vocational training.

64. Interviews: Chemnitz, Erfurt, 1995; statements of IHK officials at the Second South Thuringian Workshop on Vocational Training, 1994.

65. Ulrich Degen and Günther Walden, "Situation, Organisation und Gestaltung der betrieblichen Berufsausbildung in den neuen Bundesländern," *Informationen für die Beratungs- und Vermittlungsdienst des IAB* 23 (June 8, 1994): 2063–64.

66. Ulrich Degen, "Was könnte die nicht-ausbildenden Betriebe in den neuen Ländern zur Ausbildung motivieren?" *BWP Nachrichten* 22 (1993): 30–31.

67. *Frankfurter Rundschau*, February 18, 1995, reported 60%, but in a *Landtag* speech in Potsdam on March 23, 1995, Brandenburg's minister of labor, Regina Hildebrandt, claimed that the figure was about 80%.

Even in Saxony, the most prosperous of the new federal states, Ministry of Economics and Labor officials claim that 47% of all training slots receive partial or complete funding from the government. In short, labor market developments in eastern Germany have stubbornly refused to conform to the western German practice of private-sector funding for apprenticeship training. Although German policymakers envisioned a rapid phasing-out of state subsidies for both in-firm and extra-firm training, the need for such funding has remained steady. For the 1994–95 school year, for example, approximately 35,000 in-firm slots were subsidized by the federal and state governments at a total cost of 400–500 million DM.[68]

I have suggested that West Germany's duel system was more fragile than was widely understood in 1989. In the East it has had to struggle with more severe versions of problems that still plague it in the West. Yet not all eastern localities have responded in the same way. I argue that the capacity of local actors to engage in a variety of information-gathering, persuasion, and monitoring tasks—tasks integral to the dual system—and to make optimal use of various public and private resources available to promote training in eastern Germany is, in turn, dependent on the underlying structure of associationalism and intergroup relations of their localities. In some, sociopolitical relations are structured in a way that promotes the sharing of information and the pooling of scarce resources; in others, local actors are divided and suspicious of one another, making collective endeavors difficult to imagine, let alone implement.

I develop this argument through case studies of the Saxonian cities of Chemnitz and Leipzig. Saxony represents a "best case" scenario for transfer because the dual system is dependent upon a healthy underlying economy, and Saxony is the state with the highest levels of absolute and per capita economic activity in eastern Germany. Leipzig and Chemnitz, although both suffering from severe post-reunification deindustrialization, did not experience the reduction of industrial employment to the truly insignificant levels found in many other parts of eastern Germany. The two cities were hardly socioeconomic peas in a pod in 1989, but several commonalities in industrial structure, demographics, and institutional supports allow me to explore through them the importance of local sociopolitical relations for institutional transfer.[69] The logic of comparison is to see whether exceptional local

---

68. *Frankfurter Rundschau*, January 9, 1995.

69. Before reunification, Leipzig was larger and less industrial than Chemnitz, but both cities have since suffered population losses and rapid deindustrialization. In 1993, labor participation rates in both cities were comparable: 59% in Chemnitz; 54% in Leipzig, according to *Statistisches Jahrbuch der deutschen Gemeinden* (Cologne: Deutscher Städtetag, 1993), 153; the demographic profiles of the workforces of both cities were almost identical; and the composition of the two local economies in terms of employment were roughly similar as well, as shown in the accompanying table. Although the official unemployment rate in Leipzig (12.4%) was lower than in Chemnitz

outcomes (in Leipzig) can be distinguished from more ordinary ones (in Chemnitz) and explained by underlying sociopolitical relations.

Struggling to Change: A Tale of Two Saxonian Cities

In Leipzig and Chemnitz, as in other parts of eastern Germany, efforts to establish dual vocational training have encountered serious difficulties. Private firms are reluctant to invest scarce resources in training youth, while youth are wary of committing themselves to a three-year apprenticeship program that may not result in stable employment. Notwithstanding these shared difficulties, differences in training outcomes have emerged in the two cities—divergent outcomes that illuminate the important role of sociopolitical relations in facilitating institutional development and performance.

Three rough indicators allow an assessment of efforts to establish dual training in the east.[70] One measure is the *absolute number* of youth who find apprenticeships. In absolute terms, the Leipzig labor office district offers more apprenticeships than any other in eastern Germany. Moreover, the number of available firm-based apprenticeships grew from 4,044 in 1991 to 6,364 in 1993 and rose again to 7,482 in 1994. By contrast, total supply in Chemnitz remained almost stagnant: 4,020 in 1991, 4,035 in 1993, climbing slightly to 4,564 in 1994. Thus, whereas total supply in Leipzig increased 85% over the period for which full data are available, supply in Chemnitz grew only 13.5%.[71]

A second indicator is the *range* of available apprenticeships. Of the fifty occupations listed in the Federal Labor Office statistics for 1992 and 1993, Leipzig offered (after controlling for the size of the districts) substantially more opportunities than Chemnitz in fourteen occupations, while Chemnitz offered more advantageous conditions in only four.[72] BiBB data confirm the picture of an almost across-the-board advantage in the availability of training opportunities in Leipzig: of the thirteen occupational categories listed,

---

(15.7%), official underemployment in the two cities was comparable, at about 33%; see *IAB Werkstattbericht* 13 (15 March 1995): 11. The latter figure includes unemployment plus a range of so-called second labor market programs and also early retirement.

	Indust.	Crafts	Const.	Transp.	Trade	Other	E,C,H[a]	Total
Leipzig	34%	4%	8%	9%	13%	6%	26%	100%
Chemnitz	42%	3%	7%	8%	11%	7%	22%	100%

[a]Education, culture, and health.

70. The *official* ratio of supply (of apprenticeship slots) to demand (by youth for these places) in each local labor office district is virtually always reported to be about 1 to 1. But this statistical artifact both inflates the number of adequate training slots and camouflages regional differences. See Locke and Jacoby, "The Dilemmas of Diffusion," 49–50.

71. Data provided by the state labor office (Landesarbeitsamt Sachsen).

72. *Ausbildungsstellenmarkt* (Nuremberg: Bundesanstalt für Arbeit, 1995).

Chemnitz offered a better supply-demand ratio in only two, while Leipzig led in all other occupational groups. Overall, Leipzig's performance was the best of all the districts in eastern Germany; that of Chemnitz was slightly above the average.[73]

A third measure of how well West German–style training practices are performing is the relative reliance on extra-firm training to accommodate demand not met by firms. In-firm training is widely seen as superior to extra-firm training: for youth, because it links them to potential employers; for employers, because it permits them to recruit, screen, and train future employees; and for the government, because it splits the costs of training with the private sector. But with firms resisting the calls for apprenticeships, extra-firm training in eastern Germany has exploded in recent years. Although fears abound of youth being trained as florists, auto mechanics, and hair stylists in numbers that the local labor markets will clearly be unable to absorb, even the trade unions (which bitterly denounce what they perceive as employer efforts to shift the costs of skill formation from the private to the public sector) have generally supported extra-firm training on the grounds that "some training is better than none at all."

Leipzig was, at one point, head and shoulders above other labor market districts in eastern Germany in the percentage of total training slots that were firm-based: 98% in 1992. The corresponding figure for Chemnitz was 88% and the East German average was 81%.[74] Although its distinctiveness vis-à-vis Chemnitz on this dimension disappeared in subsequent years, Leipzig has relied less than other eastern districts on extra-firm training at a time when it has dramatically *increased* the number of apprenticeships available. Most other districts, including Chemnitz, have built up much more slowly (see Table 12). Measured along these three dimensions, the differences in vocational training outcomes in Chemnitz and Leipzig are striking. How can these differences be explained, especially since both cities are embedded in the same institutional and cultural environment?

Given the importance of economic activity for the functioning of dual training and the fact that eastern Germany has experienced a severe economic crisis since unification, one's first instinct is to attribute the two cities' differences in performance to differences in either their overall levels of economic activity or the composition of their local economies. Certainly economic differences do exist. Most important, new investment in Leipzig's banking and services sector has made the city somewhat less dependent on industry than Chemnitz, and the unemployment rate in Chemnitz tends to be about 3% higher than in Leipzig.[75]

---

73. BiBB, *Erhebung* (Bonn: BiBB, 1994), table 1/1.
74. BiBB, *Berufsbildungsbericht* (Bad Honnef, Germany: Bock, 1993), 46.
75. See the long-term trend in *IAB Werkstattbericht* 13 (March 15, 1995): 11.

Table 12. In-firm training slots as percentage of total supply, 1992–94

	1992	1993	1994	Total supply growth 1992–94	In-firm supply growth 1992–94
Leipzig	98%	90%	87%	59%	41%
Chemnitz	88%	90%	88%	1%	2%
East German average	81%			6%	16%

Sources: Adapted from *Berufsbildungsbericht* (1993): 46; author's calculations; Carsten Johnson, "Die Rolle intermediärer Organsationen biem Wandel des Berufsbildungssystems," in *Einheit als Interessenpolitik,* ed. Helmut Wiesenthal (Frankfurt: Campus, 1995), 143.

Table 13. Available apprenticeship slots by sector, 1992–93

	Leipzig		Chemnitz	
Major sector	1992 (%)	1993 (%)	1992 (%)	1993 (%)
Industry and commerce	52	47	57	49
Crafts	33	42	28	39
Administrative and office work	03	04	03	05
Agriculture	02	05	02	03

Source: Author's calculations based on Federal Labor Office statistics.

Yet these economic differences do not translate directly into different opportunity structures for vocational training. For example, if one uses unemployment rates as rough indicators of the *level* of economic activity, it is not clear how a 3.3% difference between Leipzig and Chemnitz would by itself translate into a 72% difference in the growth of training opportunities. Moreover, a quick look at the breakdown in Table 13 of apprenticeship slots in the two cities reveals that notwithstanding underlying structural differences in their local economies, the *composition* of their training opportunities is basically the same. Further, even though Chemnitz is now somewhat more industrial, Leipzig added about six hundred industrial apprenticeships in those years, while Chemnitz lost about the same number. In other words, differences in their underlying economic profiles do not translate into starkly different opportunity structures for youth in search of training. Thus, economic vitality or structure, although certainly important in accounting for the divergent patterns observed between these two cities, cannot alone explain the differences. And given that Leipzig and Chemnitz are located in the same state and are thus eligible for the same programs and funds, policy differences between the two cities are also controlled for.

A third possible explanation centers on the underlying sociopolitical relations of the two localities. Vibrant and well-developed networks of secondary associations are important for both economic development and institutional performance. Do localities with more developed and effective political and economic institutions possess greater numbers of associations than settings with less effective institutions? Not in this case. A quick glance at the associational patterns of the two cities reveals some remarkable similarities rather than differences. Since 1990, 2,455 organizations and associations have registered in Leipzig, 1,700 in Chemnitz. After controlling for population, one sees that Chemnitz does not suffer, relative to Leipzig, from a paucity of associational life.

Richard Locke has argued that at least as important as the actual number of associations are the qualitative features and patterns of interaction among the different groups in civil society.[76] Groups linked through multiple horizontal ties are more likely to share information, pool scarce resources, and engage in collective efforts than groups whose relations are more polarized or hierarchical. Given the recent establishment of such associations in eastern Germany and their lack of organizational resources, one would expect that alternative modes of interaction (cooperative versus competitive) and divergent patterns of local interest representation and aggregation would have a tremendous impact on local patterns of political and economic behavior. In training, cooperation and coordination among local associations are key in ensuring sufficient numbers of apprenticeship slots for each year's youth cohort and training that meets national standards. The reluctance of eastern firms to train and the diffidence with which youth view this system make cooperation among local groups all the more important.

My interviews with key actors in both cities revealed that it was precisely along this dimension that Leipzig and Chemnitz appeared most different. Although secondary associations and interest groups in both localities were struggling simply to establish themselves, let alone build a dual training system, those in Leipzig transcended both their own organizational concerns and the minimalist institutional roles assigned to them; they began cooperating with one another in new and important ways that had a direct consequence for the development of vocational training. In contrast, local groups in Chemnitz, though diligent in performing the institutional duties required of them, did little to extend their roles or to cooperate with one another in order to facilitate the development of training institutions. A review of these alternative patterns of interaction reveals how they contributed to the divergent training outcomes manifest in the two cities.[77]

76. Richard Locke, *Remaking the Italian Economy* (Ithaca: Cornell University Press, 1995), 23–27.
77. For the significant nineteenth-century variation in localities' institutional networks in vocational training, see Hansen, "Caps and Gowns," 4.1–4.60.

Cooperation and Polarization in Saxony

Of the many labor market districts I investigated, Leipzig took the most comprehensive approach toward convincing youth to consider training positions and encouraging firms to offer them. In every German labor office district a "vocational advising committee" discusses supply and demand for apprenticeships, but this organization has few formal means of dealing with the most pressing problems (such as creating in-firm training slots) in eastern Germany. In Leipzig, however, local actors have experimented with new forms of cooperation aimed at addressing these problems. For instance, the periodic meetings of the local vocational advising committee are augmented by a biweekly meeting of a "Coordination Round" that includes regular members of the committee but also more "practitioners." Together, members of this Coordination Round seek to encourage local firms to train by engaging each year in five intensive weeks of firm and school visits. Labor office officials and training specialists from the respective chambers visit local firms together, armed with information about state subsidies, sermons about the need for sound long-term personnel policies, and lists of local youth appropriate for each firm. They also visit local schools in order to stimulate demand among youth for the training opportunities available. According to a member of the Leipzig labor office, "The motivation for the Coordination Round was that we were tired of wasteful duplication of efforts to match youth to apprenticeships they found desirable. For us in the labor office, the advantage is that we can visit firms with the training experts of the chambers—the people who really know the firms and their personnel plans."[78]

The Coordination Round's membership comprises representatives of the labor office advising staff, the chambers of industry and commerce, the crafts chamber, and the office of schools. The participation of school representatives is interesting in two ways. First, their inclusion is an attempt to recapture one of the strengths of the former GDR training system: close communication between teachers and firm-based trainers. Although it is much more difficult to sustain in a network of smaller training sites than in a large industrial conglomerate with its own vocational school, virtually all vocational training personnel who worked under the GDR regret the incapacity of the West German system for such communication and hope to restore it. Second, and perhaps more important, the school officials in Leipzig are able to use their ties to the Ministry of Culture to fund worthy local projects.

Local actors have also countered the messages youth receive from parents and the media suggesting that industrial work has no future in Leipzig. Since 1992 the chamber of industry and commerce has held an annual one-day event to which they invite all the young people who have sought an apprenticeship through the local labor office but have yet to find one. Firms that

78. Interview: Leipzig, 1995.

have available slots are also invited to introduce their companies. The chamber hopes to promote the mind-set among employers that they need to engage in public self-promotion as part of a long-term strategy for reproducing their own labor market. Thus, the relentless flow of bad news from the industrial labor market is countered in small ways. In addition to the metalworking firms, which are strongly represented at these annual events, the chamber allows employers from outside its jurisdiction to compete for the attention of youth still seeking apprenticeships; the police, for example, use the event to recruit apprentices. Of the nearly eight hundred Leipzig youth who participated one year, some three hundred signed an apprenticeship contract. In short, local actors in Leipzig have sought to compensate for their own organizational weaknesses by coming together to share information, pool resources, and organize a series of initiatives aimed at fostering dual system training.

In Chemnitz, local actors' own descriptions of negotiations over training paint a very different picture, characterized at its nadir by one interviewee as a "war of all against all." Indeed, before the CDU mayor of Chemnitz was ousted in 1993, the city was notorious for its conflict-ridden local administration.[79] Partly in reaction to the blockage of municipal administration, the ICM (discussed in the preceding chapter) was founded to put political pressure directly on the state and the Treuhandanstalt. In light of the unusual constellation of trade unions and employer associations in one interest organization, however, a number of potentially conflictual issues had to be removed before the organization could pursue its primary goal of influencing privatization and industrial policy. Vocational training was thus *not* included in the ICM's mandate.

Although Chemnitz does have a Coordination Round, it meets only once a year, in February, as opposed to every two weeks in Leipzig. The local chambers' activities generally consist of somewhat isolated efforts to address issues of supply and demand. For example, when the chamber of industry and commerce invited 120 firms to an event on vocational training, only one company actually attended.[80] Thus, both the style and the outcomes of local group efforts in Chemnitz present a striking contrast to those in Leipzig, where efforts to promote coordination appear to have helped generate a sizable growth in firm-based training. The key point is not so much that the Leipzig chamber and local labor office are more capable or industrious than their counterparts in Chemnitz as that this process in Leipzig is better coordinated in the sense that the various local actors physically come together to do it, and their doing so correlates with better outcomes.

These findings, however, raise a further question: Why are local actors

---

79. The SPD official who replaced the old mayor was confirmed in office in 1994 with 73% of the vote.

80. Interview: Chemnitz, 1995.

more able or willing to cooperate in Leipzig than in Chemnitz? Interviews with key actors in both localities suggest that the differences in behavior are the product of the different patterns of intergroup relations manifest in the two cities. In Leipzig the key actors involved in training—chambers, schools, employer associations—are embedded in a network of secondary associations that are linked through many horizontal ties. Communication among the different groups is frequent and relatively open. As a result, these intermediary organizations are not only well informed but also have come to depend upon and sometimes even trust one another, which facilitates collective problem solving and the pooling of scarce resources. Like all of eastern Germany, Leipzig faces a range of serious problems, yet the networks just described have encouraged multiple actors to remain engaged with the problems rather than defecting (as do firms that free-ride and refuse to train) or resigning (because no one organization can hope to "solve" the problems).

In contrast, patterns of intergroup relations in Chemnitz are much more polarized. Although the city does not suffer any particular shortage of secondary associations or interest groups per se, they have clustered in opposing camps. Ties linking the groups within each camp are strong, but linkages across the two clusters are few and tenuous. As a result, the much more limited flow of information among the key intermediary organizations involved in training in Chemnitz reduces their ability to engage in collective efforts. In short, the same actors have behaved differently in Leipzig and Chemnitz not out of whim or ideological commitment, or even because they possess unequal resources, but rather because they are embedded in different settings that provide them with different levels (and quality) of information and different opportunities to collaborate in the resolution of common problems. The comparison thus illustrates the important role that local sociopolitical relations play in the process of institutional transfer in the East.

CONCLUSION: CIVIL SOCIETY AND STATE RESPONSIBILITY

This chapter has argued that shifting responsibility during institutional transfer may require building actors and institutions simultaneously. Ending central state control of schools and apprenticeships has spurred remarkable changes in education in the East. Yet despite massive government funding, the presence of various institutional supports, and the concerted efforts of western parties and interest groups, the process of institutional transfer remains fraught with difficulties. Demographic declines threaten to undermine the fragile new school systems at a time when parents are increasingly questioning their basic structures. And the training arrangements being established in the East are often weakly linked to firms, remain highly dependent upon state funding, and too often provide youth with training that will not translate into future employment.

This chapter also reinforces the proposition that a model (such as "the German model of vocational training") can mask variations. Training difficulties are the product not only of the paucity of private firms willing and able to participate but also of the weaknesses of the underlying sociopolitical infrastructure on which the institutions of the dual training system rest. In Leipzig, despite the variety of economic difficulties it shares with other localities in eastern Germany, a vibrant network of local interest groups and secondary associations played a major role in the development of the new training institutions. Again, effective institutional transfer depends in part upon local sociopolitical relations. Localities with rich patterns of associationalism and intergroup cooperation appear to provide more fertile soil for institutional transfer and development than do other settings with fewer secondary associations or more parochial ones.

Bringing such qualities of society back into analyses of institutions is necessary to an understanding of why the same structures operate differently in different places. Doing this, however, requires a more nuanced treatment of "civil society." One cannot simply regard it as a dichotomous variable, distinguishing a "good" civil society from a "bad" one on the basis of rough indicators such as numbers of associations. Instead, one must examine more carefully the qualitative features of that society (that is, the organizational attributes of the different groups and the patterns of interaction among them) in order to see how different patterns shape behavior in distinct ways. In addition, one must be careful not to treat civil society as if it exists in a vacuum or in a zero-sum relationship with the state.

Relations between institutions and groups in civil society are complicated and highly interdependent. Understanding these relations and how they change over time is already key to many analyses of institutional behavior, and it is clearly central to issues of institutional transfer. Yet traditionally, analyses of institutional arrangements such as the German dual vocational system, or the secondary schools, describe (in highly stylized terms) the way things are supposed to work as opposed to how they actually operate. As an academic convention, this parsimonious style of presentation lends itself easily to comparison. But as a way of enriching our knowledge and furthering a variety of policy-related debates concerning training, skill formation, and work reorganization, the approach has serious shortcomings. Often these highly stylized accounts take on an ahistorical and noncontextual quality by focusing primarily on the institutional design while frequently slighting the broader social, political, and economic contexts in which it was developed and embedded. Further, they do so by homogenizing a diverse set of structures and practices into a purported model without specifying whether that abstraction stands for the modal, mean, or outlying value or whether it is merely an ideal type.

Finally, this chapter has unpacked the process of legitimating transferred structures—a process that must take place on several levels—by exploring the wide swings in opinion toward the former GDR and FRG schools, as well as the acceptability for the western states of eastern experimentation. The same West-dominated political parties that enthusiastically "lent" their models in 1990–91 have since used the West-dominated KMK—the point of aggregation of structural differences—to limit eastern experimentation with those models.

Securing legitimation is also a challenge while employers' organizations push hard for extra-firm training, essentially demanding state funding for training while defending continued private control. But it is unclear whether public support can long endure for a system that is "dual" in name only.[81] Indeed, the chambers of commerce and industry are in a position actually to profit from the shortage of in-firm training slots by virtue of their importance as providers of extra-firm training (along with employer associations and trade unions that have also set up their own training centers). This circumstance may eventually contribute to a public perception that private actors live on state funding and provide little public good in return. The heavy reliance on extra-firm slots is emblematic of the way the dual system has been modified to address the challenges of reunification: what were once crutches of the system have been redefined as pillars.

Thus, the chapter ends where it began: with debates about the location of legitimate authority. Trade unions have responded to the situation by calling once again for the transfer of authority over training from the chambers to the Federal Labor Office. Some SPD officials in eastern Germany have echoed these calls for complementing the heavy state role in financing training with more authority over content. Their basic argument is that global competition has produced a movement for "lean production" all over Germany, making occupation-based skill acquisition obsolete. The social partners, it is held, are too slow to reform the curricula, and changes in the competitive environment may make such an effort suspect in any case. In the short term, so the thinking goes, the Federal Republic should try to reintegrate advantageous pieces of the GDR system—such as dual academic and vocational qualifications—into its own system and, in the longer term, aim to reintegrate much of the basic natural science and engineering curriculum into schools and tertiary education, leaving firms to concentrate on the further training of adult workers (and using the "French model" of mandated firm training budgets to ensure that adult training is paid for by the firms).[82]

81. Often, the state even pays the wages (through employment creation schemes) of the chambers' advisory personnel. Moreover, since municipal corporations for electricity generation and waste disposal are eligible for training subsidies, the state may pay promotional bonuses to other state actors to induce them to train.

82. Olaf Sund, "Das duale System der Berufsbildung" (Friedrich-Ebert Stiftung Conference paper, April 27, 1995, Wittenberg), 5.

Against the background of developments such as these at the *Land* level, and of the increasing state prerogatives in industrial policy at the national level, there is additional evidence that the "semisovereign" state is gaining responsibilities it is ill suited to bear. Given a very weak civil society in eastern Germany, exact institutional transfer has confronted unforeseen challenges. In response, the state has assumed tremendous new financial responsibilities, including some that push hard at the limits of constitutionality.

CHAPTER SEVEN

Imitation as a Lever for Political Change:
Findings, Lessons, Theory

> A form without history has no power to perpetuate itself.
> —CORMAC McCARTHY, *Cities of the Plain*

Transfer is effective when it is pulled in, but pulling in means much more than voluntaristic and short-term borrowing. The pulling-in concept rests upon two pillars: variations in the organization and preferences of civil society, and the flexible character of state policy. A well-organized society can benefit from transfer by obviating the need to build actors and institutions simultaneously. Existing actors can help state policymakers pull in institutional designs from outside and put their own information-gathering capacity, organizational resources, power, or good name at the disposal of the new arrangement. That these actors might benefit materially from such redesign may be an important motive, but ideas about more efficient or fairer institutions can be equally powerful.

State flexibility is the second pillar of "pulling in." Because key institutions affect a wide range of interests while confronting complex political problems, some modification is virtually always necessary either before, during, or after the transfer. Because institutions affect the distribution of material, symbolic, and power resources, it is impossible to anticipate all potential problems. Thus, there is a need to build flexibility into the process of transfer. In the cases studied here, three levels of formal processes—regulatory, statutory, and constitutional—each generated tough choices for policymakers about the degree of flexibility to allow. One can find examples of some flexibility in all the cases, but the functional equivalent approach provided much more room for adaptation than did the exact transfer strategy. Indeed, the very aim of functional equivalence recognizes the extraordinary difficulties involved in the exact reproduction of foreign designs.

Flexibility is crucial also because formal political authority is insufficient (though necessary) for effective transfer. Even during the occupation, when formal authority was unlimited, power mattered mostly in the ability to use regulation to press for institutional change, disallowing certain German organizations until they made structural or procedural modifications. General Clay even used military government authority to suspend democratically derived statutory and constitutional provisions on codetermination and the socialization of industry. But although power could be used to *restrict*, it was much less useful for *compelling* the Germans to do entirely new things. Even very significant formal authority was insufficient to compel effective transfer; flexibility was crucial.

Focusing on civil society and on policy flexibility helps specify the conditions under which transferred institutions are likely to "take" in their new setting. The search for conditions for effective transfer is a rejection of two other analytical styles. The first, "blueprint optimism," assumes that institutions are legitimated by success and success alone. At its extreme, this approach concludes that any institution can be transferred anywhere—without fear of offending the sense of justice of those affected—provided it yields efficient outcomes. The second, at the other end of the spectrum, is the equally implausible idea that culture is such a formidable and omnipresent obstacle that it will always block institutional transfer.

The two pillars of pulling in refine the central argument that accounts for variation *across* cases: formal authority is likely to be insufficient whenever the state depends upon non-state actors for some component of institutional performance. The influence of civil society, in turn, makes clearer the need for flexibility in adapting the foreign model. True, without social actors pushing alternative proposals, it is much easier for policymakers to argue that there is "one best" system. But although a weak civil society increases the chance that institutions will be transferred unmodified, it also increases the risk that institutions will become ineffective or counterproductive, since there are no powerful groups that can work through them.[1] Transfer usually occurs in established policy domains, however, and so the process must usually engage established actors. And it is in such domains that the pulling-in concept is most useful. A "demand side" approach to transfer is especially important in policy areas marked by a history of failure—precisely the ones where state policymakers are most inclined to imitate. Policymakers who have been failing may already be short on resources and authority. If they then attempt transfer, it is likely that some constituencies—often those most capable of facilitating institutional performance—may gain, relative to oth-

---

1. For such cases, see Richard Locke, *Remaking the Italian Economy* (Ithaca: Cornell University Press, 1995), 28–29.

ers. Such benefits accrued to German advocates of industrial unionism after 1945.

Since civil actors strong enough to sponsor transferred institutions may also be strong enough to colonize them, scholars must augment data about the density of society's organization with information about what those actors want and about their endowment of resources. The process of legitimation matters greatly: it is one thing to muster enough votes to pass a law, another to make that law a functioning and accepted institution that changes actual practice. Confronted with a foreign design, indigenous actors struggle not just to defend their own material ox from being gored but also to defend their society's sacred cows.

The process of pulling in can reduce vexing legitimacy problems where a top-down, state-driven diktat cannot. First, to the extent that institutional effectiveness builds its own legitimacy, organizations that can provide local information and resources offer obvious benefits over national elites (or occupation authorities) forced to bear costs without such assistance. Second, to the extent that legitimation requires conformity with local norms of justice, local advocates can boost the status of what might otherwise appear an uncomfortable foreign practice. Third, if legitimation occurs slowly through actual contact with the institution, then any organization that can move the import from the realm of abstract legality to that of political fact also increases that contact for ordinary people. Non-state actors can provide legitimacy to new structures, but they often exact a price for their partnership with state elites.

FOUR CASES BUT MANY FACES: IMITATION AS A COMPLEX PROCESS

The core German cases (along with the shorter cases in Chapter 2 used to generate questions) demonstrate that imitation is a diverse and complex phenomenon. Attempts to explain it by single variables ruin the concept by narrowing it to a concern with the mere formal setup of institutions. Seeing imitation as a longer-term political process, in which institution building and actor building are interrelated and in which adaptation is almost always necessary, entails dropping the hope of neat and exclusive lines of causality. A great deal remains to be done, but all four German cases contain valuable lessons for bringing imitation into theories of political change (my final task).

First, imitation has been excluded from most accounts of institutional development because it is methodologically difficult to isolate. Transfer is most effective where indigenous—usually minority—traditions already exist, and so scholars must first understand the demands and capacities of the borrowing society before analyzing the effect of foreign-inspired institutions. In the case of industrial relations after World War II, for example, the lessons learned by German trade unionists during the Nazi dictatorship resulted in calls for a unionism that could democratize capitalism. Capitalism had been widely discredited, and so Germans saw good reasons to believe that a new system was achievable. The Allies, however, using their own societies as guides, helped defeat these ambitions through regulatory, statutory, and constitutional intervention to build a much less politicized industrial relations system. To do so, they made coalitions with German union leaders who were already committed to or could be won over to certain aspects of Allied designs (especially decentralization and industrial branch structures). Without indigenous support, transfer usually degenerates into irrelevancy. Yet with strong support, it becomes hard to distinguish from indigenous change.

Second, the argument that transfer is blocked by "culture" often exaggerates the unanimity of resistance to foreign models. There simply was no "German position" on union form and function after World War II; the early postwar years saw a bewildering diversity of actual practices. For the policymaker, such diversity means finding actors who are willing to sponsor a particular design.[2] For the scholar who sees institutional transfer as a means of boosting indigenous ideas as well as importing totally new ones, such diversity makes plausible the use of foreign designs even from societies that are culturally quite distant. We may be astounded that Meiji Japan looked to France for ideas about the organization of police forces. Yet future research may find that imitation between societies typically held to be culturally "close" (British and American, German and Austrian, intra-Scandinavian)[3] is difficult precisely because established actors find it easier to capture or block imported designs that have a family resemblance to ones they already know. In short, cultural distance between model and imitator is likely to be a misleading and weak predictor of the effectiveness of transferred institutional designs.

The failure of transfer in U.S. zone school reforms shows that the mere *existence* of social actors committed to similar reform proposals does not guarantee that institutional transfer will be effective. The most likely allies for American reform plans were on the German left, but OMGUS refused to make common cause with them because of the mounting Cold War. When OMGUS chose instead to pressure state governments for institutional change, German officials modified the reforms until they were essentially meaningless. The thesis that civil society can promote effective transfer must, therefore, be posed as probabilistic rather than deterministic. It matters whether or not civil society exists, but what also matters is the politics of the indigenous actors: do they actively try to pull in an institution, or do they mobilize

2. Further, Allied trade union models functioned as both procedural and functional models of organization. Allied *procedural* models (such as the union certification process) generally ruled out organizational initiatives that could not muster victories in shop elections; *functional* models provided constant reminders of what the Allies desired.

3. Francis Castles, ed., *Families of Nations: Patterns of Public Policy in Western Democracies* (Brookfield, Vt.: Dartmouth, 1993).

against the foreign design and try to damn it as an inappropriate and un-workable intrusion? Answering this question requires attention to policy preferences. Since states that attempt transfer—such as Meiji Japan[4] or the French Third Republic[5]—often do so in several policy areas at once, it is important to be able to explain differences in outcomes. Foreign models of industrial relations had an important impact in postwar Germany, whereas school models had very little, and these results can be explained in large part as an outcome of coalitions between occupation forces and German groups. In the postwar union case, for example, at the start there were two possible bases of worker society that had survived Nazism: illegal worker organizations, many oriented toward local antifascist resistance; and the old Weimar-era trade union leadership, often returning from exile. These two elements of civil society became the basis for two competing visions of trade unionism. The latter, in coalition with occupation officials in the two zones, eventually won out.

Failed imitation can matter greatly for subsequent institutional change. German efforts at school reform essentially disappeared in the wake of failed U.S. efforts. Why? Common schooling became problematic for German reformers in part because states with SPD governments had to be wary of the charge that they were agents of the "Americanization" of Germany. The case thus points to the important symbolic dimension inevitably played by foreign institutions. Large numbers of teachers and administrators were in fact willing to consider some U.S.-inspired institutional changes once these changes were disconnected from the politically sensitive subject of Americanization. But where the taint of association with foreign practices is strong, one apparent precondition for effectively rooting a transferred institution in a new society—namely, advocacy by indigenous social actors—may actually serve to block the transfer.

Many formal structures transferred to eastern Germany since reunification have yet to become effective. The indicators of problems were different in the different cases: in industrial relations, the weakness of both social partners and the widespread undermining of official bargains; in vocational training, the dependence on heavy state subsidies; in education, the growing disaffection of the eastern German population. Performance often has been poor: the wage-bargaining system de jure covers fewer and fewer firms and de facto allows most of the firms it does cover to undercut its provisions; the dual training system is paid for largely by the state. The open question is what effects the attempts at institutional homogenization will have on subsequent in-

4. Eleanor Westney, *Imitation and Innovation: The Transfer of Western Organizational Patterns to Meiji Japan* (Cambridge: Harvard University Press, 1987).
5. Allan Mitchell, *The German Influence in France after 1870* (Chapel Hill: University of North Carolina Press, 1979).

stitutional development. Indeed, it is not yet clear whether these basic structures will persist or will ultimately be displaced by more firm-level bargaining and state-run vocational training.

The industrial relations case shows that institutions reflect underlying (and sometimes unseen) political compromises. Relationships based on power and persuasion generally have to sustain institutions in the face of competing demands or incentives to defect. It is much easier to transfer institutional images than to transfer the political relations that sustain them. The latter difficulty is apparent in industrial relations because the *same* actors responsible for the West German system have controlled developments in the East. In the unions—unlike, say, public administration, where GDR structures were reformed but personnel largely retained—western Germans controlled not only policies but also organizational routines, so that there was much less chance of communication breakdowns. Many serious difficulties in eastern Germany result from the effect that a harsh wage environment has had on weak firms. Incentives diminish for firms and workers to join employer associations and unions. These weaknesses, in turn, result in interorganizational processes that often look more like shells than "institutionalized" patterns of industrial relations.

The eastern German case also implies that the organization-set concept, in which the outputs of one organization serve as the inputs of another, may exaggerate barriers to transfer. Comparative political economy commonly laments that effective institutions are so embedded as to be utterly unportable to other societies. But this case suggests that even when an institutional package is assembled as completely and with actors as well informed as is ever likely to happen in the real world, the precise problems identified by the organization-set thesis can still occur. One response is to assert that imitation can never work, but this claim does not square with evidence that imitation is commonly attempted and can be profoundly effective. The organization-set concept surely exaggerates the smoothness of interorganizational connections. Societies can be put together in ramshackle ways, and talk of institutional systems and subsystems often overplays the strength of the connections. In modified form, however, the organization-set concept can help analysts ask *what* the outputs are and *why* they are not being put out. These questions shift attention toward actors and somewhat away from organizational design.

Finally, the cases of school and vocational training reform focused explicitly on shifts in jurisdiction in the course of institutional transfer. Institutional redesign in eastern Germany shifted formal authority from the central state to the *Länder* (for schools) and to para-public authorities in the chambers and trade unions (for vocational training). German federalism gives a very different character to such decentralized imitation than does U.S. federalism. The key difference is that under German federalism the individual states are often more obliged than are their U.S. counterparts to negotiate the implications of their institutional variation. A constitutional provision mandates "equivalence" of living conditions throughout Germany, and cases are often brought before the German Supreme Court on the basis of this provision. The result has been the development of elaborate mechanisms for negotiating acceptable interstate differences.[6]

The egalitarian ideal requires aggregation mechanisms through which the amount and the effects of decentralization are authorized or countered to ensure that Germany does not grow apart. Thus, German states borrow from each other in a political context requiring that the mutual recognition of their standards be hammered out in institutions such as the Standing Conference of State Ministers of Culture (KMK). Germany's governing coalition has also, in recent years, sought to structure European federalism along similar lines. As East European policymakers look to imitate EU-approved structures, it is important to note that institutional transfer has a different character where a universal standard has been established.[7] Understanding the dynamics of aggregation in Germany permits insight into processes of imitation in eastern Europe—greater insight than can be gained from the diffusion literature on American federalism, where no analogous pressure exists. When analyzing processes of transfer, one needs to recognize that policymakers respond not only to demands from society but also to larger statutory and constitutional constraints on what can be imitated.

At bottom, effective transfer changes a society by adding an institutional tradition or by adding to an existing tradition. Either way, the transferred structure enters a politicized environment and competes with other institutions for preeminence. In Germany, comprehensive schooling still competes with track-based education, and industrial unionism with unitary and political unionism. But these alternative configurations do more than compete with each other. Each also functions within a tacit or formal division of labor: industrial unions enroll the vast majority of German workers, but white-collar and Christian unions siphon off tens of thousands more. Neither private schools nor the public *Gesamtschulen* seriously threaten the dominance of the track-based public system, but each still serves a significant clientele. The availability of private religious schools reduces ideological demands on public schools, and so this plurality of options actually promotes "purer" forms and drives more competition between institutional designs. The functional division of labor that results, however, is generally full of gaps and overlaps and is constantly contested.

---

6. The relevant provision is in article 72 of the Basic Law.

7. East European governments have had virtually no say about what those standards should be, whereas eastern German states have at least had some influence over common standards (as in the discussion of the twelve- versus thirteen-year *Abitur*).

LINKING IMITATION TO THEORIES OF CHANGE

Whereas imitation is intensely political, most conceptual approaches to imitation have been apolitical (diffusion) or only superficially interested in broad political struggles (policy borrowing). These theories of imitation turned inward because they were not closely linked to larger theories of political change. Within the usual understanding of political change, imitation is an orphan; theories of political change are blind to it. The three dominant research traditions in comparative politics—rationality, culture, and structure—all have active programs to investigate political change, but each could be pushed forward by taking seriously the problem of imitation.[8]

In rational choice theory, institutional change is usually theorized as a departure from prevailing equilibria. In the words of one leading proponent, Margaret Levi, such theory explains "the microfoundations of macroprocesses and events. It does this by means of an equilibrium analysis in which actors respond to each other's decisions until each is at a position from which no improvement is possible."[9] This view of institutions as unplanned equilibria can help explain why institutions may remain stable even when "best practices" beckon.[10] But a consideration of imitation might make rational choice theory richer and reduce its implicit reliance on "path dependence" or highly stylized "external shocks." It is questionable whether most actors involved in imitation have enough information about alternatives to make the kind of calculations that rational choice theory presumes. How might dispersed actors overcome the calculation difficulties that occur around the sometimes epic distortions in a politicized environment far removed from the actual foreign model? Thomas Schelling posits that certain ideas serve as "focal points" around which various interests can make informed calculations, and a widely admired foreign model clearly might serve as just such a focal point.[11] Yet, the *instrumental* use of ideas as mere crystallization points for institutional design often fails to do justice to the way that minority tradi-

---

8. My discussion of these traditions refers to the literatures reviewed in Margaret Levi, "A Model, a Method, and a Map: Rational Choice in Comparative and Historical Analysis"; Marc Howard Ross, "Culture and Identity in Comparative Political Analysis"; and Ira Katznelson, "Structure and Configuration in Comparative Politics"—all three in *Comparative Politics: Rationality, Culture, and Structure*, ed. Mark Irving Lichbach and Alan Zuckerman (New York: Cambridge University Press, 1997).

9. Levi, "A Model, a Method, and a Map," 23.

10. For fuller discussion, see Randall Calvert, "The Rational Choice Theory of Social Institutions," in *Modern Political Economy* ed. Jeffrey Banks and Eric Hanushek (New York: Cambridge University Press, 1995).

11. Thomas Schelling, *Micromotives and Macrobehavior* (New York: Norton, 1978). Judith Goldstein and Robert Keohane, eds., *Ideas and Foreign Policy: Beliefs, Justifications, and Political Change* (Ithaca: Cornell University Press, 1993), argue that ideas can "provide road maps that increase the actors' clarity about goals or ends-means relationships" and become "focal points that define cooperative solutions or act as coalitional glue."

tions exploit systemic disruption to reconfigure institutions. In short, attention to imitation might help rational choice refine limits to assumptions about stable actors and stable preferences.[12]

Recent cultural theorists have also sought to demonstrate the power of ideas in politics. Usually, they have done so by taking the institutional background as fixed, although there is no inherent reason why scholars who emphasize cultural practices ought to focus on continuity rather than on change.[13] The blanket proposition that cultural differences between nations will invariably block the introduction of foreign institutional models is false. The key source of confusion is the assumption that transferred institutions must "fit" the borrowing society. In fact, such a fit must be limited if the new institution is actually to change and improve prevailing practices. At minimum, attention to the politics of imitation will require a better specification of the concept of fit.[14] More ambitiously, however, cultural theories of change might elaborate how the abstract characters of "models" allow different constituencies to see models in different ways—and so make advocacy coalitions possible. The association with the rational choice concept of focal points is clear. The additional challenge to scholars interested in culture is to document how different constituencies actually see the model and how they project upon it their own desires and fears.

One of the costs of the argument that culture always blocks transfer has been a lack of focus on how shared systems of meaning might help promote transfer. Minority traditions sometimes use these break points to reconfigure the larger system, providing cultural theorists a chance to evaluate culture in the service of institutional *change*. Cultural organizations (including religious ones) can be powerful vehicles for groups that have been excluded from mainstream politics.[15] These minorities often try to make strategic use of foreign models. But to succeed, they generally need to make particularly effective use of culturally based notions of justice and to use idioms of communication that resonate effectively if they are to make the leap to mainstream politics.[16] A direct look at imitation might also help comparativists better understand how the pressures for institutional change exerted by common ex-

12. One example where ongoing game plays are conceptualized as targeting the shaping of rules of *future* games is Roger Noll and Barry Weingast, "Rational Actor Theory, Social Norms, and Policy Implementation," in *The Economic Approach to Politics: A Critical Assessment of the Theory of Rational Action*, ed. Kristen Monroe (New York: HarperCollins, 1991).

13. For elaboration and criticism of this tendency, see John Kurt Jacobsen, "Much Ado about Ideas: The Cognitive Factor in Economic Policy," *World Politics* 47 (1995): esp. 308–9.

14. One effort is Kathryn Sikkink, *Ideas and Institutions: Developmentalism in Brazil and Argentina* (Ithaca: Cornell University Press, 1991).

15. Abner Cohen, *Custom and Politics in Urban Africa* (Berkeley: University of California Press, 1969), esp. 201–11.

16. The large social movement literature on "framing" is relevant here. See, e.g., David Snow et al., "Frame Alignment Processes, Micromobilization, and Movement Participation," *American Sociological Review* 51 (1986): 464–81.

ternal processes (such as demands for further democratization or economic globalization) are refracted by different cognitive and cultural contexts (and not just by fixed differences in national institutions). The implication is clear: nominally similar structures actually have different functions and meanings in different settings, even when imitation has manifestly occurred. Lineage, it turns out, hardly determines function.

Finally, attention to imitation will challenge structural theorists to leave more room for contingency. In Ira Katznelson's terms, a social science that aims to "construct situations so that individuals can ascertain the possible" requires the use of different cases not as ideal-typical exemplars of particular variable outcomes but rather as contingent and contradictory sites of contestation and tensions—tensions that could push outcomes in a range of different ways.[17] Some of those tensions are political (for example, the incentives to defect from compromise institutional patterns: Chapter 5); others are geographical (such as mastering the wide variety of educational practices contained in "the German model": Chapter 6). But further tensions are imaginable, and the typological sketch in Chapter 2 of geopolitical competition, military occupation, regime integration, and multilateral conditionality can surely be extended.[18]

Such work should also heed Katznelson's skepticism about the ability of strongly variable-driven case studies to provide historically grounded generalizations and follow his advice to specify "configurative" relationships between cases and larger processes. The key, of course, is not to set up an idealized model and then say that transfer has failed to live up to that model but, instead, to begin with the proposition that the original model has both geographic variation and political tension—and that both lead to potential for deviation or defection from the stylized model. Deviation and defection can be driven by structural factors or by values or by the interests of local actors, but in any case the tensions emerge clearly in periods of institutional flux. The chance of surprises not only presents an unexpected challenge to policy elites but also helps students of institutions go beyond the statics of most comparative institutional theory (where institutions are held to be constants that cause different outcomes in different places).

In short, the analytical problem is tough, but the empirical phenomenon is not going to go away. International travel, epistemic communities, social communication, and modern technologies all make imitation increasingly common.[19] The mosaic of cases presented in this book shows that imitation

17. Katznelson, "Structure and Configuration," 94–102.
18. For a recent effort in this direction (focused on "benchmarking"), see Michael Dorf and Charles Sabel, "A Constitution of Democratic Experimentalism," *Columbia Law Review* 98 (March 1998): 267–472.
19. For evidence, see, respectively, Westney, *Imitation and Innovation*; Peter Haas, ed., *Knowledge, Power, and International Policy Coordination* (Columbia: University of South Carolina Press,

can shape and change political and economic structures. Where structures change, hearts and minds may change as well. So when elites attempt to change formal institutions, they also set in motion a process that challenges attitudes and beliefs. Such challenges will provoke political responses that reverberate across other institutions. And this is where the fun begins. A nation's institutional landscape contains both a hierarchy of competing solutions and a division of labor between loosely interdependent structures. Within that landscape, individual institutions must both compete and cooperate. Institutional transfer, by upsetting both of these always provisional balances, generates an important kind of politics—a politics rich in surprise and symbolism. Widely and increasingly attempted as a tool of reform, transfer deserves a central place in contemporary theorizing about political change. The research agenda is challenging, but it is also exciting. It presupposes an interest in what institutions mean to people as well as what they do for them.

1997); Karl Deutsch, *Nationalism and Social Communication: An Inquiry into the Foundations of Nationality* (Cambridge: MIT Press, 1953); Everett Rogers, *A History of Communication Study* (New York: Free Press, 1997).

Index